THE BLITZ
ON BRITAIN

DAY BY DAY – THE HEADLINES AS THEY WERE MADE

Daily Mail

THE BLITZ ON BRITAIN

DAY BY DAY – THE HEADLINES AS THEY WERE MADE

Maureen Hill and James Alexander

Research Alice Hill

Trans
Atlantic
Press

This edition published by Transatlantic Press in 2010

Transatlantic Press
38 Copthorne Road
Croxley Green
WD3 4 AQ
United Kingdom

A catalogue record for this book is available
from the British Library.

ISBN: 978-1-907176-71-5
Printed in China

ACKNOWLEDGEMENTS
Thanks to Alan Pinnock for his knowledge and painstaking
research that made this book possible.

Thanks also to Steve Torrington, Dave Sheppard, Cliff Salter,
John Dunne and Alison Pickering

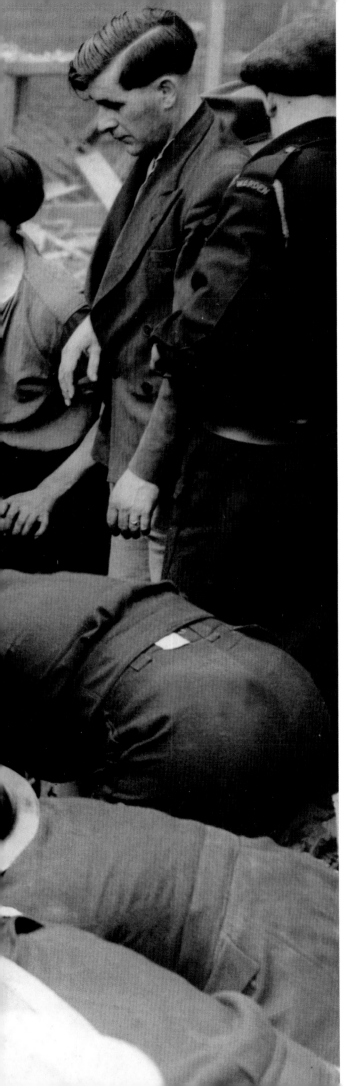

Contents

Introduction

The Blitz on Britain was one of the most significant events of the Second World War. From early September 1939 until the end of March 1945 the civilian population across the length and breadth of the country endured five and a half years of fear of aerial bombardment. From daylight raids in the early period, to massed bombers raining down high explosive and incendiaries, to the stealthy attacks of the V1 and V2 bombs, (the latter falling faster than the speed of sound so that their detonation was heard before the sonic boom of their descent), the experience of the Blitz brought a new form of terror to the Western world. The photographs in this book, supported by an informative text, help bring that experience vividly to life.

During the 1930s, Britain had been expecting war and London had experienced bombing raids during the First World War, but, nevertheless, the scale and the extent of the Blitz was unimagined and unprecedented. The Luftwaffe had established a benchmark for bombing with their pilots' support for Franco's Fascist regime in the Spanish Civil War; Guernica became the byword for destruction from the air until Coventry replaced it. Learning from the Spanish experience, Britain prepared for conflict; the government planned worst-case scenarios that included hundreds of thousands killed in the opening attacks, gas attacks, widespread panic with civilian revolt and general chaos. Plans were put in place for evacuation of the cities, gas masks were issued, the Anderson Air Raid Shelter was pre-fabricated for distribution and the Civil Defence network, starting with the Air Raid Precautions infrastructure, was put in place. At the same time, the RAF worked to build up its aerial defence with squadrons of its new fighter aircraft, the sleek Supermarine Spitfire and the enduring Hawker Hurricane.

The War, against all expectations, started quietly for Britain's civilians, though it was a busy time for the country's service personnel, especially the British Expeditionary Force sent to support the defence of France. For several months there was an uneasy lull, the Phoney War, during which civilians returned from their evacuation billets and people settled back to a life not too dissimilar from that pre-war, albeit with blackout and a gas mask over the shoulder at all times. With the German blitzkrieg in the spring of 1940 and the British retreat from Dunkirk, Hitler believed that the time was ready for the invasion of the British mainland. The Battle of Britain erupted in July 1940 as Britain fought for its existence with ëThe Fewí of RAF Fighter Command battling against the massed might of the Luftwaffe, which aimed to destroy it as a precursor to invasion.

With German invasion plans thwarted by the RAF's success in the Battle of Britain, on 4th September 1940 Hitler threatened to raze British cities to the ground and reduce London to rubble. Three days later, London was burning. ëI personally have assumed the leadership of this attack,í Göring announced, ëand today I have heard above me the victorious German squadrons.í This was just the start of an intensive nine-month bombardment that concentrated on London and Britain's major industrial cities and ports from September 1940 through to May 1941. While attacks eased after this period as the Luftwaffe engaged on the Russian Front, British civilians were never free from the fear of attack. And raids did come, singly sometimes and at other periods more intensively, such as the Baedeker raids in 1942 or the pilotless V1 and V2 raids late in the war.

In order to give scope to the remarkable visual record presented here, there are a number of abbreviations and references deployed in the text to save space: time annotation is in the form of the 24-hour clock; bombs are classified as HE or IB being High Explosive and Incendiary Bombs respectively; weights of German bombs are in metric tonnes or kilogrammes while Allied bombs are weighed in Imperial tons or pounds; Anti-Aircraft defence is abbreviated to AA. Within the narrative any night raid is designated to the day's date, thus an attack that took place at 0100, 2nd January would be in the entry relating to the night of 1st January. The Night Blitz which took place between September 1940 and May 1941 is narrated day by day; other episodes of the Blitz are described in dated entries but are not continuous, instead recording, chronicle style, the days on which specific events took place.

The Blitz on Britain brings together photographs and newspaper headlines of the most important events of the Luftwaffe bombing campaigns on Britain. The 560 photographs are selected from the archive of Associated Newspapers and they show just how extensive and sustained the bombing was: from Land's End in Cornwall to the Shetlands and Orkneys in the North, Germany's bombers left their mark. The wonderful images in this book are supported by a timeline of the events and captions to the photographs, which often quote verbatim from the original picture editor's notes recorded on the backs of the photographs, although often the locations shown in the photos were ordered by the Censor to be removed before publication. The information from these photographs as well as the stories published in regular daily editions of the *Daily Mail* and the *London Evening News* provided an invaluable source for the detailed narrative. Additionally, the author and editors are greatly indebted to the records quoted in the definitive trilogy, *The Blitz Then and Now*, published by After the Battle, which proved an excellent source for much of the detailed statistical information in the book regarding numbers of aircraft, bombs and casualty figures.

This inspiring collection of photographs, supported with a meticulous timeline and series of comprehensive captions give an unparalleled visual history of the Blitz on Britain.

FRONT PAGE advertisements appear to-day in Page 3.

Daily Mail

FOR KING AND EMPIRE

NO. 13,529   MONDAY, SEPTEMBER 4, 1939   ONE PENNY

IN BRITAIN'S WAR CABINET

BRITAIN & FRANCE AT WAR WITH GERMANY

We meet a challenge which would be fatal to civilised order—THE KING

OUR NEW WAR CABINET

GREAT BRITAIN AND FRANCE ARE AT WAR WITH GERMANY.

At nine o'clock yesterday morning Germany was informed that unless Britain received satisfactory assurance by 11 a.m. that Germany had stopped aggressive action in Poland "a state of war would exist as from that hour."

At 11.15 Mr. Chamberlain announced to the nation that "no such undertaking has been received and this country is at war with Germany."

France delivered a similar ultimatum to Germany at noon, to expire at 5 p.m. At that hour she considered herself at war. No formal declaration of war was made.

Churchill as First Lord

BRITAIN'S War Cabinet, set up by the Premier yesterday, includes Mr. Winston Churchill as First Lord of the Admiralty. These appointments have been made:—

WAR CABINET

EMPIRE WITH US

As soon as Britain's position was known the Empire began to line up behind her. First to declare herself at war was Australia. New Zealand quickly followed. The Canadian Cabinet meets to-day.

The King in a noble message to the Empire last night declared—

"We have been forced into a conflict. For we are called, with our Allies, to meet the challenge of a principle which, if it were to prevail, would be fatal to any civilised order in the world.

The King's Message

BROADCASTING to the Empire last night, the King said: "In this grave hour, perhaps the most fateful in our history, I send to every household of my people both at home and overseas this message, spoken with the same depth of feeling for each one of you as if I were able to cross your threshold and speak to you myself.

"For the second time in the lives of most of us we are at war.

"Over and over again we have tried to find a peaceful way out of the differences between ourselves and those who are now our enemies. But it has been in vain.

"We have been forced into a conflict. For we are called with our allies to meet the challenge of a principle which, if it were to prevail, would be fatal to any civilised order in the world.

Pursuit of Power

"It is the principle which permits a State in the selfish pursuit of power to disregard its treaties and its solemn pledges; which sanctions the use of force or threat of force against the sovereignty and independence of other States.

"Such a principle stripped of all disguise is surely the mere primitive doctrine that might is right, and if this principle were established throughout the world, the freedom of our own country and of the whole British Commonwealth of Nations would be in danger.

"But far more than this—the peoples of the world would be kept in the bondage of fear, and all hopes of settled peace and of the security of justice and liberty among nations would be ended.

"This is the ultimate issue which confronts us.

"For the sake of all that we ourselves hold dear and of the world's order and peace it is unthinkable that we should refuse to meet the challenge.

"Stand Firm"

"It is to this high purpose that I now call my people at home and my peoples across the seas who will make our cause their own. I ask them to stand calm and firm and united in this time of trial.

Poles Launch Counter-attack

POLAND yesterday launched her counter-attack. She struck at East Prussia in the Deutsch Eglan sector. After violent fighting the town of Zbaszyn, taken by the Germans on Saturday, was recaptured.

The Polish attack suggests that a German claim on Saturday that their forces driving east and west across the neck of the Corridor had made contact was unfounded.

In the south violent fighting was reported around Czestochowa, the Lourdes of Poland. The Germans claimed that the town had fallen, and the Poles admitted that it was in flames.

North of Czestochowa, the Germans claimed to have captured the town of Wielun, after crossing the River Warthe. Polish sources state that the town's municipal hospital was bombed during the attack. Wielun is about 10 miles from the German frontier on the Eastern front.

Polish radio stations announced last night that Westerplatte, the Polish camp in Danzig Harbour, was still resisting German attacks from land and sea.

The camp, already attacked four times, was under fire from a German cruiser.

GERMAN TOWN SHELLED

According to the German news agency, German troops marched into Oderberg yesterday after constructing an emergency bridge across the Oder. The permanent bridge had been blown up. Oderberg was taken over by the Poles on the break-up of Czecho-Slovakia.

Another Berlin report states that the Poles have shelled the German town of Schomberg. A church and a school were hit, but the casualties were only one killed and one seriously wounded.

A communique issued by the Polish Embassy in Paris yesterday stated that during the night of September 1 the German Government proposed that air bombing be limited to military objectives.

24 TOWNS BOMBED

The Polish Government accepted this proposal, but on Friday and Saturday German aeroplanes raided 24 Polish towns.

They were Lublin, Radomsko, Brzesc, Grudziadz, Rowne, Rzeszow, Lublin, Biala-Podlaska, Tczew...

LORD GORT HEAD OF FIELD FORCE

THE King has appointed General Viscount Gort, Commander-in-Chief of the British Field Forces, General Sir Edmund Ironside, Chief of the Imperial General Staff, and General Sir Walter Kirke, Commander-in-Chief of the Home Forces.

POLES SMASH WAY INTO EAST PRUSSIA

Warsaw, Sunday.

Officials in Warsaw to-night state that the Polish Army has smashed a way across the northern border into East Prussia, after driving the Germans from several Polish towns in bitter fighting.

On the northern front the Poles are reported to have defeated the German effort to drive a barrier across the upper part of the Corridor by driving the Germans back across the border.

The Poles say they have broken through the German fortifications as far as the railway terminus of Deutsch Eylau. One of the most important towns recaptured is stated to be Zbaszyn.—British United Press.

CONVOYS AGAIN

The convoy system is to be introduced for merchant shipping. Many classes of railway wagons are to be requisitioned.

ROME REPORT OF "NEGOTIATIONS"

According to Reuter message Vatican paper "Osservatore Romane" says: "London and Paris are maintaining close diplomatic contact with Rome. Fresh negotiations to resolve European difficulties believed to be progressing.

GENERAL FRANCO'S APPEAL

Broadcasting last night, says Reuter, General Franco appealed to the "good will and responsibility of Governments and nations to employ all their efforts to localise the present conflict.

GERMAN LINERS TAKE REFUGE

Lisbon reports that five German liners—Pretoria, Windhuk, Adolph Woermann, Wameru, and Adolph Leonhardt—had taken refuge in Lobito Bay, Angola (Portuguese West Africa).

11.00, 3 September 1939, Sunday

British Prime Minister Neville Chamberlain broadcast to the nation:

'I am speaking to you from the Cabinet Room at 10 Downing Street. This morning, the British Ambassador in Berlin handed the German government a final note, stating that unless we heard from them by 11 o'clock that they were prepared at once to withdraw their troops from Poland, a state of war would exist between us. I have to tell you now that no such undertaking has been received, and that consequently this country is at war with Germany...'

Left: Many German and Czech refugees were among the crowds that gathered at Downing Street to hear the inevitable announcement as Prime Minister Neville Chamberlain declared, 'This country is at war with Germany'.

Opposite page: *St Paul's and the devastation to all the areas surrounding the cathedral.*

War Declared

THE DAILY MAIL, Wednesday, September 13, 1939.

Daily Mail

FOR KING AND EMPIRE

Roadmakers are imPRESSED by NUTTALL'S MINTOES

A letter a day while he's away
Waterman's
EMPIRE MADE

NO. 13,537 WEDNESDAY, SEPTEMBER 13, 1939 ONE PENNY

R.A.F. FLY PREMIER TO FRANCE FOR SUPREME WAR COUNCIL

Latest News

300-m.p.h. 'Plane Escorted By Squadron of Fighters

By WILSON BROADBENT, Daily Mail Diplomatic Correspondent

IN circumstances of the utmost secrecy, the Prime Minister, who is in his 71st year, flew to France yesterday to attend the first meeting of the Supreme War Council of the Allied Powers. He made the journey in one of the R.A.F.'s fastest machines, capable of a speed of 300 miles an hour.

Mr. Chamberlain took off from an aerodrome on the outskirts of London, and a flight of fighter machines escorted his aeroplane.

Lord Chatfield, Minister for the Co-ordination of Defence, accompanied the Prime Minister with two officials.

M. Daladier and General Gamelin, the French Commander-in-Chief, represented the French Government at the meeting, which took place "somewhere in France."

Only a handful of officials in Whitehall knew of Mr. Chamberlain's mission. They

PIRATE GETS HIS PREY —THE FIRST PICTURE

Here is the first actual picture of the sinking of a helpless merchant ship—the Cunard freighter Bosnia—by one of Hitler's U-boat pirates.

It was taken from a rescue ship at the moment the torpedo struck. Study this picture closely: it is the first of its kind, and you will see very few more, for the underwater menace is fast being strangled by the British Navy.

Already the U-boat victims grow fewer. In the past 48 hours only three sinkings—one of those a neutral—have been reported.

The Navy's chasers, helped by R.A.F. spotters in the air, and the convoy system, rapidly getting into its stride, are making their weight felt.

The U-boats have had their fling. They will strike a few more blows yet. But their doom is a certainty.

STOPPING OF U.S. SHIPS

Mr. Cordell Hull, U.S. Secretary of State, announced yesterday (says a Washington message) that a statement will be issued as soon as facts are assembled on United States attitude towards British blockade and German counter-blockade, and stopping of American vessels on the high seas. He had just been informed of stopping of American freighter Wacosta by a German submarine, which made a search for contraband.

GERMANS GET POLISH HARVEST

Germans have set to work on conquered Polish farms "to harvest the potatoes and beetroots from the fields the Poles have so kindly toiled on," German radio announced last night.

NEUTRAL STATES' ECONOMIC TALK

Permanent Committee of the Oslo group of Powers—Belgium, Holland, Norway, Sweden, Finland, Denmark, and Luxemburg—met in Brussels yesterday. Various economic problems arising out of the war were discussed, and

British

3rd September, Sunday

Britain and France declared war on Germany after Hitler launched his astonishing Blitzkrieg on Poland on 1st September. Having previously turned a blind eye to the Nazi annexation of Austria in March 1938, Britain and France were party to the Munich Agreement that led to Germany's seizing of the Sudetenland from Czechoslovakia in September that year. At the end of August 1939 Germany signed the Molotov-Ribbentrop Pact with Russia, which, as well as guaranteeing non-aggression between the two nations, set out a blueprint for the division of Poland and other European countries.

Hitler had no wish to commence war with Britain; it was still the major power of Europe and he had no particular quarrel with the ethnicity of most of the population., though by now Britain was hosting many Jewish refugees who had fled from Nazism. Hitler was determined to force Britain into a treaty that would prevent a direct conflict. While the fanatical German leader made many tactical mistakes, his greatest strategic error was misjudging the conduct of the War against Britain. Some of Hitler's decisions are interpreted as his having some sympathy and respect for Britons and things British, however, there seems no reason to doubt the general malevolence that launched his ideological objectives with such brutality and oppression.

In the remaining days of September, the world watched Germany rip through a poorly defended Poland, to be joined by opportunistic Russia on the 17th who stepped in to take its share of the spoils accorded to it in the recent pact with the Third Reich.

Though the first air-raid siren went off on this day, it was a false alarm; but as the month progressed, Britain realised that this was not a rehearsal: conscription had been enacted in April and during this month 1,500,000 Anderson Shelters were distributed to the nation, the evacuation of the young and vulnerable from cities threatened by air attack was stepped up, with 1.5m people relocating during September. The Government had prepared plans to relocate as many as 4.5m civilians.

Opposite left: *'Watching The Raid. These people forgot their ARP but had a good view from their East Coast town yesterday when anti-aircraft guns were firing at a Nazi raider over the Thames Estuary. They heard the drone of engines, the guns blazing away - and stopped to watch the battle'.*

Opposite right: Carrying their gas masks in cases and wearing luggage labels to identify them, this group of children from the Hugh Myddleton School in Clerkenwell were in the first wave of evacuees to leave London on the day Hitler invaded Poland, 1st September, 1939.

Top: '*27's' Sign On Today: Long Queue At London Labour Exchange. The long queue of men waiting to sign on today, May 25th, at a London labour exchange, when those in the '27' class were called upon to register.*'

Above: *'A damaged house in the South of England.'*

The Phoney War

The violent attacks expected by Britain at the beginning of the War failed to happen. The full might of the Blitzkrieg strategy of Germany's Wehrmacht concentrated on the rapid subjugation of France, the Low Countries and Scandinavia. Britain sent an Expeditionary Force to support France against the German invasion which led to ignominious defeat and the evacuation from Dunkirk, in May 1940, of hundreds of thousands of troops, minus their weapons and transport.

The period from September 1939 to May 1940 became known as the Phoney War: Britain waited, relatively untouched as the sound of distant battle steadily approached.

17th October, Tuesday

The first Luftwaffe aircraft to be shot down was a Heinkel HeIII brought down by AA fire in the Orkneys. From the early days of the War, the Luftwaffe engaged heavily in reconnaissance – particularly of Britain's shipping routes and the Naval Fleet based in Scapa Flow. At the same time, the latest German tactical weapon, the magnetic mine, took a heavy toll on British shipping until counter-measures were devised. As Nazi technology developed, the mines became more resistant to countermeasures.

30th April, Tuesday

The minelaying Heinkel HeIII that crashed at Clacton-on-Sea, on the Essex coast, just before midnight, caused the first major civilian tragedy of the War on British soil. The bomber came down on Victoria Road, damaging several houses and completely destroying the home of Mr & Mrs Gill, who were killed. Many civilians who had rushed out to see what had happened were badly injured when one of the two mines the bomber was carrying exploded; flying splinters of glass were a major cause of injury and the event drove home to the civilian population that the warnings of Home Security should be observed. This was the first major test for ARP and rescue services: the national newspapers praised the local services for their effective handling of the crisis. However, there was much still to be learned: an object identified as a hot water tank was, as the site was being investigated, eventually identified as the second mine which had not exploded; thanks to this, the latest developments were revealed and British countermeasures adapted accordingly.

Main picture: 'Mine Plane Blows Up in English Town. Four members of the crew and three civilians were killed and over 160 people have been treated for injuries as the result of explosions which followed the crash of a big German mine-laying plane at Clacton-on-Sea. The scene of the crash.'

Right: 'After the Bomber Explosion. Boys search debris at a Clacton preparatory school for lesson books and trophies.'
Damage caused by the exploding mine was extensive over the surrounding area.

Far left: *'Rescue workers clear the rubble – all that remains of the Gills' home.'*

Left: *'The bed in which Miss Muddle was asleep. The wrecked dressing table is on the right and the wing of the plane can be seen in the garden through the window. Miss Muddle was take to hospital with head and chest injuries.'*
Miss Muddle had a lucky escape in the Clacton explosion.

'We Shall Defend our Island'

Above left: *'Bombs on SE England. These pictures taken after a raid on SE England in the early hours of this morning are an object lesson to the population of Britain, showing the benefit derived by people who had protected their windows with sticky tape as against the complete wreck of windows with no protection. Although the bombs fell only 25 yards away from this house, the windows remain almost intact.'*

Left: Gas masks in their shoulder bags or brown cartons were carried everywhere: 38 million were issued to civilians and service personnel in anticipation of the outbreak of war. As this picture shows, many were mislaid; here, they are being stored away in the London Underground lost property office at Baker Street station.

Top right: *'Picture taken yesterday at a south coast town which was raided during the night. The people were learning the facts about the raid from official statements posted up outside the police station.'*

Above right: *'A shop and home above wrecked as a result of a bomb-blast 'somewhere in the south of England''*

10th May, Friday

Winston Churchill became Prime Minister of Great Britain.

14th May, Tuesday

On this day came the formation of the Local Defence Volunteers – later to be christened Home Guard by Churchill in a July broadcast. This same day, the Netherlands capitulated to Germany.

26th May, Sunday

The first of nearly 400,000 Allied troops began their bedraggled journey home from the beaches and harbour of Dunkirk; the evacuation continued from other French ports after Dunkirk was overrun.

4th June, Tuesday

'We shall defend our island, whatever the cost may be. We shall fight on the beaches, we shall fight on the landing grounds, we shall fight in the fields and in the streets, we shall fight in the hills; we shall never surrender.' Winston Churchill, addressed the House of Commons after the Dunkirk evacuation. His speeches would continue to inspire the nation with their timely rhetoric. On the 18th he called upon Britons to meet their greatest challenge: *'Let us therefore brace ourselves to our duties, and so bear ourselves, that if the British Empire and its Commonwealth last for a thousand years, men will still say, 'This was their finest hour.''*

22nd June, Saturday

France surrendered and the new Vichy government was set up to rule occupied France, under Marshal Pétain. The collaboration of the Vichy government with the Nazi regime was regarded by the British Government as a grievous betrayal by their French allies.

No. 13,798

FOUR DIVE BOMBERS DOWN IN BATTLE

Spitfires Beat Off Heavy Attack on Convoy

GERMAN dive bombers which attacked a convoy in the Straits of Dover last evening met with a heavy barrage from the convoy itself. Then Spitfires roared into action, and in a terrific battle broke up the attack, shot down four of the bombers and a fighter, and drove the rest back across the Channel.

Another enemy bomber was shot down by A.-A. fire.

Enemy aircraft had been over England during the previous night but, after losing 12 machines on Saturday, the Germans seemed disinclined to face up to the British fighters of A.-A. defences.

It was not until late yesterday afternoon that the Nazi raiders again ventured to reach British shores. Once again they met a resolute, violent defence.

China: British Peace Bid

SINGAPORE, Sunday.

EFFORTS by the British Government to bring

Squadron Leader Douglas R. Bader.

Legless Pilot is R.A.F. Ace

"London in Ashes Before Slavery"

Premier Declares Britain's Faith

MR. Winston Churchill declared Britain's faith in the future in no uncertain terms last night.

Referring to the possibility of an invasion he said :—

"All I can say is that any plan for invading Britain which Hitler made two months ago must have had to be entirely recast in order to meet our new position."

Speaking with great conviction, he added : "We shall defend every town, every village, and every city. The vast mass of London, fought street by street, could easily devour an

Top: *'Air Battle Over SE Town. Picture shows: Barrage Balloons in flames after having been attacked by enemy aircraft.'* The 'SE Town' is Dover which had been crossed out on the photograph's caption.

Above: *'Householders in a South East of England town escaped death while sheltering in their Anderson shelters, when their homes were wrecked by bombs from raiding German aircraft. Picture shows A boy with his cage of budgerigars beside the Anderson shelter in which they found safety while their home was wrecked by bombs.'*

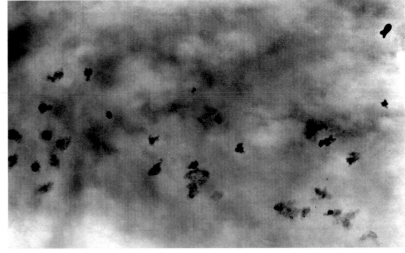

Left top: *'After the Raiders Have Passed. Photograph shows: damage caused to the houses after the raiders have passed on the SE Coast.'*– *Daily Mail* 16th August.

Left centre: *'Church Wrecked by Nazi Bombs. A view of the wrecked interior of a church at Portsmouth after Nazi bombers raided the town. No doubt the Germans claimed this was a factory or harbour building.'* Picture published in the *Daily Mail*, 15th August.

Left below: More than a hundred people were trapped in a public air-raid shelter underneath this furniture depository when three German planes attacked Southampton in August. Burning debris blocked their exit. All were safely rescued with help from fire-fighters, seen here damping down the remains.

Right top: *'Air Battle Over SE Coast Town. The Anti-Aircraft barrage of fire.'*

Dover is removed from the photograph's caption in the *Daily Mail* of 15th August.

Right above: Volunteers fill sandbags in the London suburb of Hampstead during the first days of the War.

Opposite top: Wherever blast damage could endanger human life, sand bags were used to absorb the explosive force: millions had to be filled.

Opposite left: *'Bomb-wrecked house in south west London. A house in south west suburb of London wrecked by a direct hit during the raid last evening.'*
More damage from raids on 15th August.

Opposite right: *'The home of Mrs Sears and next door that of Mrs Webb of Mitcham after a bomb had exploded today. Both were out at the time. Demolition squad at work.'*

10th July, Wednesday

Luftwaffe attacks on British shipping had been steadily escalating, with increased aerial minelaying. Alongside this, raids on coastal towns – especially in the South East – had also increased. This day is generally regarded as the start of the first phase of the Battle of Britain, the campaign called by Germany *Kanalkampf*, (the Channel battles). Direct bombing of towns by either side had been avoided and any civilian targets destroyed were assumed to be in error. However, as the Battle of Britain unfolded, there was no doubt that the gloves were off and the Luftwaffe, probing and reconnoitring Britain's defences, were definitely attacking towns and homes. The main target of *Kanalkampf* was shipping: daylight incursions past the coast brought heavy German losses as Britain's embryonic coastal radar – the RDF chain – alerted Fighter Command's squadrons of Hurricanes and Spitfires.

17th July, Wednesday

Hitler ordered the final planning and implementation of Operation Sealion – the invasion of Great Britain – to take place in the early autumn.

Daily Mail

FOR KING AND EMPIRE

No. 13,824   WEDNESDAY, AUGUST 14, 1940   ONE PENNY

2D.

R.A.F. WIN AGAIN—6 TO 1

57 Nazis Down In Mass Raids

Raising 'Exempt' Age

One More for the R.A.F. 'Bag'

WE LOSE 9 'PLANES: TWO PILOTS SAFE

THE R.A.F. won another great victory in the non-stop Channel air battle yesterday, when they shot down German raiders at the rate of six to one. Fifty-seven enemy 'planes were definitely destroyed, it was officially stated, but the total was expected to rise when full reports were received.

Nine British fighters were lost during the day-long battle, but two of the pilots are known to be safe.

Mass enemy attacks on aerodromes and shipping all along the coast from Sussex to the Thames Estuary began soon after dawn, and in the afternoon the battle spread to the South-West Coast.

Here four blazing German 'planes crashed between two towns. Others fell into the sea, and one lifeboat made six trips to pick up survivors.

Last night the air battle was resumed over the South-East Coast, but the raiders were driven out to sea before they could drop any bombs.

Bombs were dropped on Southampton last night. Several fires broke out, but were soon extinguished. There were few casualties, though they included fatal injuries.

Bombs were also dropped in the Isle of Wight and Berkshire and Wiltshire country districts. No casualties were reported. Several R.A.F. aerodromes in South-East England were attacked, and at one a number of casualties were caused, including some fatal.

They Soon Scored

By noon it was clear that for the third day in succession the British pilots were exacting a heavy toll.

Reports from the British pilots poured into Fighter Command headquarters minute by minute telling brief but dramatic stories.

One squadron of Spitfires chased a large formation of Dornier bombers right across the Channel and damaged at

The Little Ships Get A Chance

Enemy Rammed

BRITISH motor torpedo boats early yesterday caught out two German light naval vessels and attacked them, set a 'plane ablaze and had a running battle with an E-boat.

The two enemy naval vessels when sighted were only about 100 yards from our torpedo-boats, which were travelling at about 30 knots, stated the Admiralty last night.

One of our motor-torpedo boats, thinking that the enemy ahead was an E-boat and being too close to take other action, rammed the enemy.

The enemy ships were, however, larger than E-boats, and the motor torpedo boat itself suffered some damage to her bows.

Point-blank Fire

Another of our motor torpedo

An R.A.F. man with fixed bayonet standing guard over the wrecked tail of a Junkers 88, which was shot down over the South Coast during yesterday's air battle.

New Increase in Railway Fares

By Daily Mail Reporter

ANOTHER increase in railway fares is planned to take effect on October 1. It will be just over 6¼ per cent. on existing fares—or 17½ per cent. above pre-war fares. Charges for goods will be similarly raised.

London omnibus, trolley bus, tram, and underground railway fares will also be affected.

Surprise will be caused to the general public by this further unexpected increase, as fares rose 10 per cent. on May 1.

"The increase in wages and the higher cost of coal, timber, oil, and other essentials for railway operations have made an increase in fares and charges unavoidable," it was stated in authoritative circles yesterday.

Public Inquiry

"The Government has announced

31 SEAMEN OWE LIVES TO HIM

WHEN the steamship Earlspark (Denholm Line steamers, Ltd., Glasgow) was sunk by enemy action with her master and six of the crew missing, First Officer Alexander Brown took charge

Albania is at War

DUCE FAILS STEM REV

From TERENCE ATH
Daily Mail Special Cor

SALONIKA reports that heav tinuing between native reb Albania.

The rebel force, it is estimated men operating against Italians in th Kurvelesh mountain districts. Mati i district.

The tion wh the ou of brui attacks c of villag nevertheless put down their ow superiori

The against 120,000 forcemen from Ital

It is n contingen Prush, n has been the coun the past

ITALIANS' ATTACKS SMASHED

AN Italian attempt to storm positions held by our Forces in Somaliland has been repulsed.

Yesterday's communiqué from the British G.H.Q. reports a general attack on our positions covering the Jugargan Pass on Sunday.

"In spite of intensive support by low-flying aircraft, attacks were broken up and repulsed by our artillery and small arms fire" it states.

"In one place, the enemy obtained a small local advantage but were immediately counter-attacked. One large enemy bomber was brought down by infantry fire."

"Fierce Battle"—Rome

Italian Forces clashed with the main body of the British Forces on Sunday, says yesterday's Italian communiqué.

Fighting continued on Monday with a series of fierce engagements, the communiqué adds. The Italians claim to have captured Adaleh, a township which lies between Hargeisa, which they took recently

Atroci

These morning guards i which it smuggle Albania

On the last night Prefect o gendarm Italian the last causing tude arou who has

THURSDAY, The Daily Mail, AUGUS

'PLANE QUIZ

Spot them with the aid of these clues

THE Nazi bombing raids are responsible for the latest quiz—aircraft recognition—a game for everybody. The stakes are high—split seconds saved by prompt recognition may mean lives spared and another bomber in the "bag."

With few exceptions modern aircraft are of **MONOPLANE** construction. To some people all monoplanes look alike, but proficiency in distinguishing the principal types may be attained by training observant eyes upon these recognition "points":—

WING POSITION in relation to the body or fuselage, and distinguished as high, mid, and low wing. The sketches which follow show wing types:—

"SHOULDER" HIGH WING
Dornier 215 (Bomber).

"NORMAL" HIGH WING
D.H. Flamingo (Transport).

"PARASOL" HIGH WING
Henschel 126 (Observation).

"LOW" MID WING
Heinkel 116 (Troop Transport).

"NORMAL" MID WING
Wellington (Bomber).

"GULL" LOW WING
Junkers 87 (Dive Bomber).

"NORMAL" LOW WING
Junkers 52 (Parachute Troop Transport).

NUMBER OF ENGINES.—Note the single engine of the Henschel 126 and Junkers 87. Two engines, one on each wing, can be distinguished in the heavy bombers. The Junkers 52 is exceptional, having three engines, two in the usual wing position, and one mounted centrally on the nose. The four engines of the Heinkel 116, a heavy troop transport, assist recognition.

TAILS—SINGLE OR TWIN.—Aircraft tails, like car radiators, are most characteristic. Study the sketches carefully and remember that some British machines have twin tails; i.e., double fins and rudders.

Dornier 17.   Vickers Wellington.   D H Flamingo.

The Battle of Britain

12th August, Monday

The next phase of the Battle of Britain was initiated – Göring's campaign to destroy the RAF and Britain's aircraft production capability – *Adlerangriff* (Eagle Attack) finally launched on Eagle Day, 13th August, filling the skies with Luftwaffe planes destined to attack RAF airfields near the coast and to tempt RAF fighters into the air where the Luftwaffe had a numerical advantage. The Ju87 dive bomber known as the Stuka failed to have the impact it had achieved in the European Blitzkrieg and was shot down in great numbers by Fighter Command. This latest phase of the Battle crescendoed and moved steadily inland to the core of Fighter Command's bases. On this day, long-range guns on the French coast opened up for the first time on Dover: over 3,500 high explosive shells would follow until the batteries were taken out in 1944.

24th August, Saturday

The Luftwaffe now made a series of no-holds barred attacks on RAF airfields, attempting to destroy the planes of Fighter Command on the ground. 500 German aircraft flew over Britain on this day, arriving over London's docks to drop their bombs. Stray HE fell on Central London in a night raid – an accident, possibly, but one that would change the course of the War, provoking a retaliatory raid by Bomber Command on Berlin the very next night. This was the most exhausting period of the Battle for Fighter Command, with its pilots flying continuous sorties by day and being subject to bombing raids in the hours of darkness.

30th August, Friday

On this day, under ceaseless pressure from the Luftwaffe, Fighter Command flew 1,054 sorties and with a high percentage of their key airfields damaged or out of action, Britain's fighter crews were almost spent. 300 RAF fighter pilots were lost in August and only 260 could be replaced. Around 300 RAF fighter aircraft were lost in a two-week period while almost 200 were seriously damaged. In Berlin, Hitler, incensed by the temerity of Bomber Command's raid on the 25th, now exercised a decision forbidden to his commanders: he was about to instruct bombing be directed away from RAF airfields and towards Britain's cities. The fourth phase of the Battle of Britain was about to begin: The Blitz.

Main picture: *'Croydon After the Air Raid. A big bomb crater. Five people were unhurt in the shelter in the right foreground.'*
Evening News 17th August, reporting after a major raid on Croydon aerodrome – at that time London's main airport and nucleus for aircraft production. After the outbreak of War it was closed to civil aviation and designated for military use only.

Right centre: *'Mrs Williams who, with her baby, sheltered in a cupboard under the stairs was unhurt, she is seen in the wreckage of her home with a money box undamaged after the Surrey raid.'* Daily Mail 19th August.

Right: *'Air Raids on London. Damage at St. Giles Church, Cripplegate EC.'* Daily Mail, 27th August.

No. 13,834   MONDAY, AUGUST 26, 1940

ANOTHER 25 GERMAN 'PLANES SHOT DOWN

THE London skyline silhouetted against the glare of fires started by the German bombers during their night attack on the city, and (below)—

400 Miles Under a Rail Coach

Boys' Free Ride

TWO lads arrived in London yesterday after travelling 400 miles from Glasgow on a battery beneath a railway coach.

They were William O'Donnell, aged 16, and David Steven, aged 13, both of Kilbowie, Clydebank, who had stealthily climbed on to the train before it left Glasgow at 9.30 on Saturday night.

When the train was approaching London it pulled up in a tunnel at Camden Town.

There the boys jumped from their hiding place beneath one of the coaches. O'Donnell was found unconscious near a live electric rail, which he had apparently touched. He was taken to St. Pancras Hospital with burns and shock.

The younger boy was found uninjured wandering near the tunnel. He was taken to Albany-street Police Station and later removed to St. Marylebone Public Assistance Institution.

There he waited for the arrival of his father from Scotland.

RAF Fire Big Nazi Works

Bases Bombed

WIDESPREAD raids were made by the R.A.F. on Saturday night, the targets including aerodromes in Germany and military objectives in Italy.

An Air Ministry communiqué states: "R.A.F. attacked military objectives in towns in South-West Germany, including Frankfurt, Ludwigshaven, and Stuttgart.

"Many aerodromes in France, Belgium, Holland, and Germany were attacked, among them being those at Flushing, Haarle, &c.

"Wonderful Cockneys"

"THE spirit of everybody was magnificent. You cannot beat the Cockney in his reaction." That is what a London vicar said about his parishioners.

"When the raiders were detected," he added, "the whole of my parishioners, including some old people of over 90, went to an air-raid shelter.

"I prayed with them while the bombs were falling."

LONDON RAIDERS MISS WAR POINTS

THE German Air Force renewed their attacks on Britain yesterday afternoon, and there was one big aerial battle over the South-West. Twenty-five enemy 'planes were destroyed. Four British fighters were lost, but three of the pilots are safe.

The Air Ministry also announced that the final figure of German aircraft shot down on Saturday was 50. Nineteen British fighters were lost, and 12 of the pilots saved.

Not a single point that could in any way effect London's war effort was damaged when German raiders bombed the London area from a great height early yesterday morning. If the raiders had any real war objective in view their effort was a dismal failure.

A church, some commercial buildings, and suburbs were damaged—that was all. There were some casualties, but only a few deaths.

The courage of the London people, many of whom spent the night in shelters, was praised by A.R.P. workers. Screaming bombs, a spectacular fire and explosions failed to arouse any panic.

TOWNS ARE PROUD OF TRAWLER

THE feat of H.M. trawler Arctic Trapper in bringing down two enemy bombers and probably damaging two more with three anti-aircraft shells on Saturday has given particular pride to Grimsby and Cleethorpes

Above: 'More Air Raids Today. German Bombers today raided several parts of the suburbs of London and dropped several bombs. Picture shows: View of one of the damaged shop fronts in one of the streets. Scenes near Coulsdon.'
The location is crossed out in the caption of this *Daily Mail* picture dated 19th August.

17

Blitz Comes to Britain

Left: *'Last Night's Bombing: London Area. Photograph shows: Wrecked house in the London area. A demolition party was at work early this morning.'*

Below: At night inside an ARP post in Essex: the dimmed light casts shadows; the outdoor lamp on the table has a special deflector and the conventional torch next to it could only be used in locations where light could not spill out. The ARP, or Air Raid Precautions, began as early as 1924 to meet the threat of possible bombing – already experienced in the Great War. ARP wardens were all volunteers from varying walks of life, who by day continued their civilian jobs then, in addition, took on responsibility for the safety of their local community, from issuing gas masks to checking the blackout. It was their detailed knowledge that could keep track of the local population and during the War, the warden numbers built up to 1.5m. The wardens pictured here are photographed early in the War, not yet sporting their characteristic uniform of black denim overalls.

Bottom: One of the Ministry of Information Regional Bulletins posted in a London suburb. Newspaper publication of this notice was denied by the censor.

DEAF FREE OFFER!

Picture "Log" of Convoy's Ordeal

THROUGH THE DOVER STRAITS UNDER SHELL FIRE

R.A.F. Sink 4 Italian Ships

THE Italian Navy has suffered a severe blow from the R.A.F. Four warships, including two submarines, were destroyed by our bombers in one of the most brilliant exploits yet carried out by the R.A.F. in Africa.

The story was told in an official communiqué issued in Cairo yesterday, which stated:—

Italians Ask for More

THE Italians reoccupied what is left of Fort Capuzzo after the naval bombardment, says last night's Cairo communiqué.

GORING'S PLANS UPSET

By *NOEL MONKS, Daily Mail Air Correspondent*

THE opinion is gaining ground in R.A.F. circles that Göring has been made to realise that the surest way for him to lose his air force was to keep on carrying out massed daylight attacks on Britain.

So for five days running he has kept his squadrons at home and has sent only "tip-and-run" raiders, not with the idea of destroying military objectives, but purely as "morale-breakers."

"Our aircraft made a low-flying attack on enemy warships anchored in Bomba roadstead (Libya), obtaining direct hits and destroying two submarines, one destroyer, and a submarine depot ship.

"All our aircraft returned safely.

"The attacking aircraft were fired on by heavy anti-aircraft pom-poms and multiple machine-guns.

South Africans' Part

"Our bombers also attacked the landing ground at Derna, as well as motorised transport concentrations, a repair depot, and shipping.

"Many bombs exploded among aircraft and motor vehicles, causing considerable damage. We suffered no casualties.

"In Italian Somaliland Mogadiscio aerodrome was subjected to a series of raids by bombers of the South African Air Force. Direct hits were scored on transport concentrations in the vicinity of the administrative buildings, which subsequently were seen burning.

"Direct hits were also scored on buildings, hangars, a wireless transmitting station, and barracks.

"Three enemy aircraft are believed to have been badly damaged. All our aircraft returned safely.

"Numerous reconnaissances were carried out on the Kenya-Italian Somaliland frontier. In a raid Assab naval barracks were bombed.

Alexandria Alarms

Alexandria had three air-raid alarms early yesterday. The first lasted 55 minutes, the second 70 minutes, and the third 10 minutes.

Only a few bombs were dropped.

These pictures taken by "Daily Mail" cameraman H. A. Wallace, who was aboard one of the ships in the convoy that was shelled in the Dover Straits, tell their own story of the convoy's hazardous trip under shell-fire from German guns on the French coast. From top to bottom they are:

Shells bursting in the sea as the convoy approach the straits. More shells that failed to find their mark. One of the escorting warships laying a smoke screen round the ships. And safe at last as the convoy had sailed through the straits and well out of range of the German guns.

OUR GUNS REPLY —ON CALAIS "Ports Still Open"—U.S.

IT was revealed in London yesterday that British guns

MINISTRY of INFORMATION BULLETIN

MESSAGE from London Civil Defence Headquarters as follows:—

Air Raid Casualties in the Metropolitan Police District in the raids on Thursday, Friday and Sunday last were as follows:—

Midnight 14th. August to Midnight 15th. August.
Killed 89.
Injured and taken to hospital 91.

Midnight 15th. August to Midnight 16th. August.
Killed 73.
Injured and taken to hospital 109.

Midnight 17th. August to Midnight 18th. August.
Killed 15.
Injured and taken to hospital 45.

WYNDHAM DEEDES.
Regional Information Officer,
London Region.

22nd July, 1940.

DEAF 30 DAYS' FREE TRIAL

1st September, Sunday

After August's ferocious daylight raids on Fighter Command airfields in the South and East, September began with something of a lull; nonetheless on the 1st three waves, each of over 50 aircraft, crossed the coast during the day heading for inland targets that included the key sector airfields of 11 Group, among them Biggin Hill and Kenley. The cost to the Luftwaffe was around 30 aircraft. Night raids concentrated on Kent, the Bristol Channel and South Wales with bombers operating singly, attacking airfields and industrial targets according to opportunity.

2nd September, Monday

Five daylight attacks with bombs falling on Maidstone and Rochester; in almost 1,000 sorties there were civilian deaths and damage to property as well as airfield attacks. Over 41 enemy aircraft were brought down. During the night bombers made solo raids across Britain.

Bombs fall on houses in Maidstone, Rochester and other targets around the Thames Estuary.

Above: After a direct hit this house is beyond repair.

Left: A demolition squad gets straight to work on this damaged house to stabilise the structure prior to making repairs if possible.

'Why Don't You Take Shelter?
Here are two pictures which I took in Central London today during an air raid alarm at
1.35pm. And here are some of the answers given to me by passers by when I asked them
the question 'Why don't you take shelter?'
Lady 'I've got an appointment.'
Man 'It's too hot to take shelter today anyhow.'
Lady 'We always drive them off before they get here.'
Lady 'Nothing ever happens.'
Man 'I don't like being Stived up.'
Girl 'It's our lunch hour break.'
The last answer was too disconcerting to ask any further because a flapper replied 'Why
don't you. **** off?'
A Policeman's comment is worth noting. He said 'It would be sticky if something happened.
They'd grouse if they didn't get a warning, English people are funny anyway.'
                                                                    - W R Turner 4 September'

Hitler Turns on the Cities of Britain

3rd September, Tuesday
600 Luftwaffe aircraft were active during the day, mainly targeting the South East with North Weald Sector airfield getting the worst punishment. Night raids by 150 aircraft bombed Merseyside, Bristol Channel, Kent and Tyneside.

4th September, Wednesday
While two major daylight raids attacked airfields in the South East, the Short Brothers factory in Rochester and the Vickers Armstrong works at Brooklands, Hitler announced retaliatory raids on Britain in revenge for Bomber Command's attacks on Berlin on the night of 25th August. He accused Churchill of ordering indiscriminate bombing of the civilian population, for which the Nazi leader promised the erasing of British cities. The words spoken by Hitler on this day were a defining statement affecting how the war would progress.

5th September, Thursday
From 09.30 the Luftwaffe resumed their attacks on 11 Group airfields in two waves totalling over 150 aircraft. During the afternoon another attack by over 50 planes was directed at Thameshaven's oil storage tanks. In response to the attacks the day before, Fighter Command instructed tighter defence of these vital installations leading to fierce aerial battles during the day. 25 German aircraft were lost and the civilian death toll was 44 with 87 seriously injured.

6th September, Friday
In three major daylight raids targeting airfields the Luftwaffe lost as many as 50 aircraft. During the night, numerous reconnaissance missions flew over London and the Royal Victoria Docks were the target for bombs that killed 18 people. Widespread raids put most of the country on alert. Near Northampton a German spy who parachuted in was captured and like others before him became a double agent, code name 'Summer'.

Right top: *'Though the bungalow occupied by the Griggs family in South East England was wrecked by a German bomb, the family, including two young children, were safe in their Anderson shelter. The raiders, who were attempting to pierce London's defences, met a tremendous barrage of anti-aircraft fire and at least six of them are reported to have been shot down. The picture shows Mr. and Mrs. W. Griggs, Mrs. J. Griggs, a sister-in-law, Morris Griggs, aged three, and Janet Griggs, aged two, amid the debris in the bungalow.'*

Right: *'Bombs damaged houses, shops and other civilian buildings during all night raids on the London area. One attack lasted nearly eight hours. With most people in their shelters, however, the number of casualties was small. This picture shows cats and kittens in amid the debris in a damaged street in the London area.'*

Daily Mail

FOR KING AND EMPIRE

No. 13,845   SATURDAY, SEPTEMBER 7, 1940   ONE PENNY

R.A.F. 'KILL' FIVE IN TEN SECONDS

TARGET OF A NAZI RAIDER

Prison Ship Rescue

Navy Again

A BRITISH submarine has rescued the captain and crew of a British merchant ship who were being taken under guard to Germany for internment, says an official Admiralty communiqué.

H.M. Submarine Truant (Lieutenant-Commander H. A. V. Haggard, R.N.) was on patrol off Cape Finisterre when a strange ship was sighted.

The submarine came to the surface and closed to investigate, ordering the ship to stop.

The ship proved to be the 5,781-tons Norwegian ship Tropic Sea. This ship had been captured by an enemy raider some time before.

Scuttled Her

She was being sailed for Germany with a German prize crew in charge.

She had on board the captain and crew of 23 of the British s.s. Haxby (5,207 tons) which had been sunk by the enemy raider, her own Norwegian crew, and a cargo of wheat.

When H.M.S. Truant ordered the Tropic Sea to stop the ship was scuttled by the German prize crew by means of explosive charges which were kept ready in position. The German prize crew and the British and Norwegian prisoners took to the boats.

H.M.S. Truant took on board the 24 British seamen and the Norwegian captain of the Tropic Sea and his wife, being unable to accommodate more survivors.

The submarine left the remainder of the Norwegian crew and the German prize crew in the boats. These were not then overcrowded and the sea was a flat calm.

H.M.S. ...ported that ... left in boats ... Flying-b... Force we... rescue th... have bro...

London Smashes Up Three Attacks

232 IN A WEEK

THE figures are incomplete, but they show the power of the R.A.F. During the past week 232 enemy aircraft were shot down. We lost 96 fighters but 56 of the pilots were saved.

Since war began Germany has lost 1,667 'planes over and around Britain; of these 1,593 have been destroyed since the first mass raid on June 18.

Göring's battalions made another determined assault yesterday. London had three warnings, and alarms were also sounded in towns in the North-West, South-East, and the North-West of Scotland.

THE Nazi air hordes still try to reach London — and fail. Yesterday British fighters in one battle accounted for five of the enemy in 10 seconds.

The Capital had three warnings, but the cost to the Germans was THIRTY-FOUR 'planes. Nine of our fighters were lost, but six pilots are safe.

German 'planes were also reported over North-East Scotland and North-West and South-West England.

The fighting which occurred over the Thames Estuary when London had its third warning was said to be the fiercest ever seen in the area.

From the Thames Estuary area, scene of many dogfights, came news of a German bomber exploding in mid-air. Another observer reports seeing a parachutist descend from a stricken 'plane.

Earlier there had been a dawn raid on the London area, and bombs were dropped in one district, crashing on two houses. Two people lost their lives.

During the night bombs damaged two women's wards in a hospital in Kent. A few patients and two nurses were killed.

There were heroic scenes as the hospital staff worked to release the patients.

A large force of enemy aircraft crossed the Kent coast in the morning, and splitting up into a number of sections attempted to launch simultaneous attacks on several R.A.F. aerodromes.

Waves of 200

The enemy force came over...

R.A.F. Smash Enemy Targets Again

WHEN the R.A.F. "start something" over enemy territory they see it through. Those "hidden targets," for instance, have had another hammering. So...

WRECKAGE of a station and a damaged train, hit by Nazi bombs during the latest "tip and run" raids by a lone German raider in the South-East of England.

Michael Resumes as King

CAROL EXILE AGAIN AFTER NIGHT OF CLASHES

From CEDRIC SALTER, Daily Mail Correspondent
BUCAREST, Friday.

AT 6.30 this morning, after his third consecutive sleepless night, King Carol signed his abdication in favour of his 18-years-old son, Prince Michael.

Half an hour later he and a small group of loyal friends left the capital for an unknown destination.

At 8 a.m. Prince Michael was sworn in as King. At 9.30 King Carol's farewell proclamation, in which he begged the country to rally round his young son, was published in special editions of the newspapers.

At 10 a.m. King Michael spoke a few words into the radio, promising to uphold all that he had just undertaken in his oath.

City Rejoices

Immediately a vast crowd gathered round the palace, cheering and singing a patriotic song that for the last four years would have meant arrest and possibly death.

Flowers were showered upon them from the skyscraper building that runs the length of the Avenue Bratianu. Flags are flying, and everywhere are signs of national rejoicing.

This dramatic surge of events succeeded 24 hours of acute tension. Throughout yesterday, General Antonescu, the Iron Guard Dictator-Premier, sought in vain to form his new Cabinet only to find that all leaders of the country capable of inspiring confidence would not serve with him so long as King Carol remained.

Last night, shortly after 11 o'clock, a large crowd of youths formed outside the National Theatre and marched along the Calea Victoria.

Shots were fired over their heads by huge detachments of soldiers and armed police that guarded every approach to the palace. The demonstrators dispersed before they reached the great square, though not before a fusillade of...

AXIS PLAN DANUBE CONTROL

Daily Mail Correspondent
BELGRADE, Friday.

AXIS plans to take over control before winter of the Danube, Europe's most vital waterway for oil and foodstuffs, have reached their final stage.

Nadamlenski, the Italian secretary of the International Danube Commission, of which Britain is a member, hurriedly left here to-day in a Lufthansa 'plane for Vienna to attend the conference recently called by Hitler.

The aim of the conference is to liquidate the International Danube Commission and set up a new control under the influence of the Axis.

Germany may even demand the right to police the entire river.

Mr. D. W. Keane, Britain's permanent delegate to the International Commission, was not...

Japanese to Invade Indo-China

SHANGHAI, Friday.

ACCORDING to reports reaching Shanghai, the Japanese have already entered or are on the point of entering Indo-China in secret.

Their wish to forestall a counter-invasion by the Chinese.

It had been previously reported that the authorities in Indo-China had agreed to permit this transgression.

Reports from Chungking state that the Chinese Government has been informed that an agreement has been signed at Hanoi between the French and Japanese authorities permitting Japanese forces to land in Indo-China.

The reports state that Japan is entitled to land 12,000 marines at three points.—British United Press.

LATEST

D.S.O. FOR HERO OF DAKAR EXPLOIT

Lieutenant-Commander Bristowe, the London stockbroker who crippled France's new 35,000 tons battleship Richelieu at Dakar in July, has been awarded the D.S.O. for his bravery and skill in the operations.

Lieutenant-Commander Bristowe returned to the Navy on the outbreak of war, and became "Fighting Bristowe."

NAZIS LOSE 38

Late last night it was announced that 38 German ... R.A.F. machines ... pilots safe.

First Raid of the Blitz

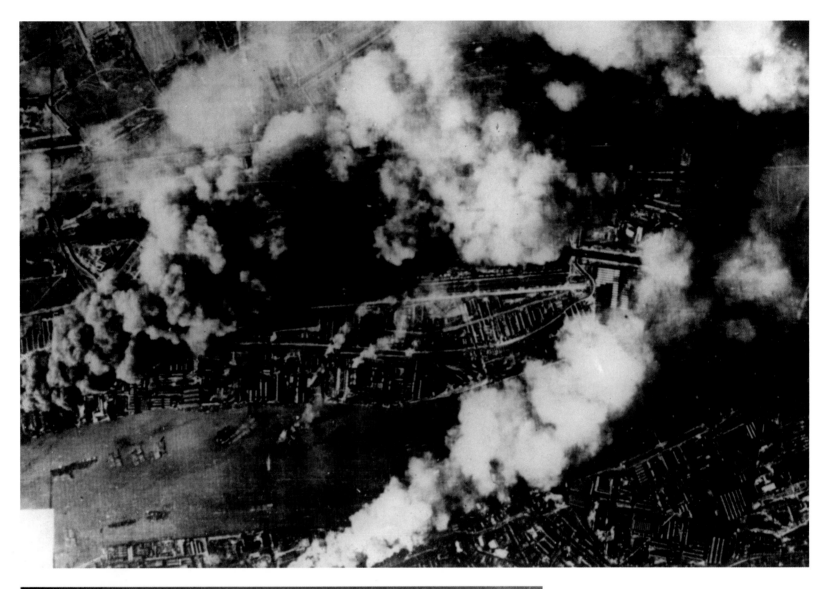

Above: *'An aerial view of London's docks after they had been fired by the first Nazi raid and lit up the skies so dramatically on the night of Sept 7 and 8. It would seem, though, there was more smoke than fire.'*

Note to Art Editor: *With reference to the aerial picture of the fire in London's dockland – registration no. 230014 – circulated to you today, September 27th, the original caption did not make it plain that this picture was one received from official German sources and it is an aerial view taken from a German plane during the first big attack of the Nazi raiders on Sept. 7th.*
The text of this caption appears on the back of the photo and shows that the picture, published on 28th September was not released until almost three weeks after the event. It was, of course, a daylight raid but during the raid the residents of the rest of London didn't realise its enormity until at night they saw the skies bright with the fires burning in the East End.

Left: A silhouette of the East End skyline ablaze.

Opposite: *'Raiders Damage Hospital and Houses in the East End of London. Wrecked houses.'*

Above: 'Furniture and belongings of residents in the London area which was bombed last night, assembled in the roadway early this morning.'

Right: 'Military Objective. This is the Kent hospital in which women patients were killed during the night raid. The picture shows you one of the two smashed wards. Among this debris Sister Gantry crawled, giving morphine injections to the injured women while rescue work went on.'

Opposite: Two pictures of St Thomas's Hospital, damaged in an air raid on 8th September. Germany claimed to be bombing only 'Military Objectives': these pictures proved otherwise.

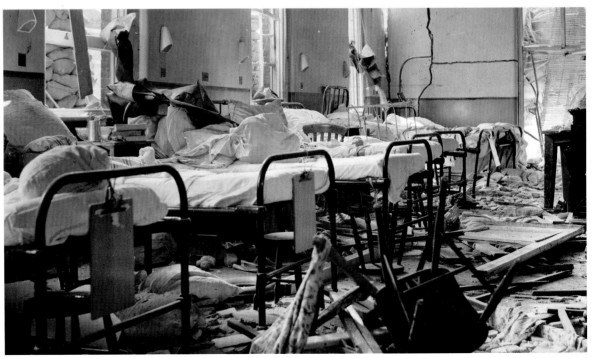

Waking up to Destruction

7th September, Saturday

The first bombs in what was to become known as the Blitz fell during daylight hours on a beautiful, sunny September day.

300 bombers escorted by over 600 fighter planes crossed the coast of England en route for London and started bombing the East End at around 16.35 before they carried on to attack the City and Central London. In this raid 430 people were killed and 1,600 badly injured. Damage was caused to two major power stations, homes and factories along the Thames and three major London railway stations.

20 Squadrons of RAF Fighter Command rose to meet the incoming raiders and succeeded in shooting down over 40 aircraft.

Thousands of incendiary bombs were dropped around London's docks and the huge fires they started provided a guide and target for the night-time raiders. All night, until 04.30 next day, the Luftwaffe bombed the East End. Throughout the day and night fire-fighters battled to control 19 major, 40 serious and nearly 1,000 small fires. Doctors, nurses, ARP wardens, policemen, rescue workers and a host of others fought to save lives, maintain order and offer comfort. As well as the huge number of casualties thousands were made homeless on this one night.

The Anglo-American Oil Works at Purfleet was set alight and was still burning on 13th September. Countless horrors were experienced by Londoners as the bombs rained down; an ARP station in West Ham suffered a direct hit which wiped out 13 key members of the local Civil Defence organisation; the widespread conflagrations threatened to cut off many people who were panic-stricken and disorientated – the entire civil population of North Woolwich was evacuated to safety by ferrying them across the Thames in small boats.

When the All Clear sounded, dazed Londoners tried to grasp the new reality they would have to deal with for the next 57 nights in a row, waking up to destruction and the absence of the basic necessities of water and drainage, gas, electricity as well as a much damaged transport system. 7th September was christened 'Black Saturday' by the people of London.

Those responsible for conducting the war realised that things were even blacker than they appeared to London's hard-pressed citizens. Intercepts from Enigma on 7th September indicated that Luftwaffe aircraft had moved from Norway to France; conditions of tide and moon between the 8th and the 10th would be favourable for invasion. The chiefs of staff met at 17.30 in the underground war room in Whitehall. Ominously they began their conference to the repercussions of the bombing. The defence forces of Britain received the codeword 'Cromwell', bringing them to full readiness.

Fires Still Burning in the East End

8th September, Sunday

Between 11.00 and 13.00 around 100 daylight raiders attacked Kent.

Winston Churchill toured the East End in the afternoon and found the population in good spirits, despite the severity of the previous night's raid. In the early evening thousands of East Enders trekked towards the West End to seek shelter in the basements of the larger stores or the Tube, although the Luftwaffe were soon to include these areas in their targets.

Guided by the still-burning fires from Saturday's raids, the bombers returned at about 20.00. on Sunday night; the attack continued until 05.00 the following morning. Again many fires were started and damage was severe, particularly to roads and railways where all main lines to the south were blocked.

9th September, Monday

The King toured many of the damaged sites in the East End during the day. Minor raids in daylight were followed by another night of heavy attack that left 370 people dead. The casualty rate would have been considerably more had not the RAF successfully challenged and broken up the daytime raiding formations and those of the early evening. 400 German aircraft crossed the coast at about 20.00 hours to be met by around 200 British fighters from Groups 11, 12 and 13.

St Thomas's Hospital was the latest hospital to be damaged when it took a direct hit on block 1. Photographs of hospitals and schools in ruins were fed to the reading public to raise their ire and indignation: the Government was deeply concerned about public morale under the devastating bombardments – anger and hatred were preferred to terror and despair. The bombing of hospitals also affected RAF Bomber Command's standing orders and pilots were now instructed not to return with their bombs if they couldn't find their designated target but could release them at their discretion on targets of opportunity even if it might harm civilians.

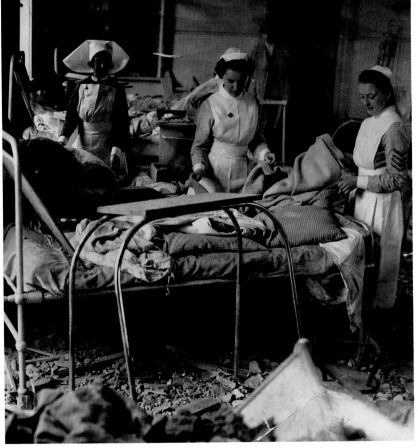

Left top: **The King talking to women whose homes were bombed in the very first raids of the Blitz.**

Left bottom: *'And this was the scene inside a bombed South London hospital – one of three hit during the night. In spite of their nerve-racking night, the nurses were there on duty, cleaning up in damaged wards.'*

Above: 'His Majesty met and talked with residents in the districts which have sustained damage and was cheered wherever he went. Here, the King is viewing damaged houses in East London.'

Left: 'A wooden extension to a school which was damaged in last night's raid.'

Chaos on London's Roads

10th September, Tuesday

Bombing was less severe than on the previous nights and there were fewer casualties. Nevertheless, there were isolated raids across the country and prolonged attacks on London caused fires in the capital's docks area and some damage to railways. The northern outfall sewer which discharged into the River Lea was breached.

London's worst incident was in the early hours when a heavy bomb hit South Hallsville School in Canning Town which was sheltering hundreds of bombed out East Enders who had fled from Silvertown and the Tidal Basin area of West Ham. The buses supposed to be carrying them to safety failed to arrive. The official figure of 73 dead was contested later, suggesting it was several hundred, and the episode highlighted the need for improved communication. It also built resentment in the East Enders who felt their safety was unimportant to the authorities.

To the west, a delayed action bomb fell on Buckingham Palace where the King and Queen were in residence.

Left top: *'This omnibus in South London was blown to pieces when it was hit by a bomb during a recent raid over London.'*

Left centre: *'The London scene today after Saturday's raids – following Hitler's revenge threat – on the capital. Bombs were showered indiscriminately, anywhere. The car was one target.'*

Left bottom: *'How public road transport suffered in the third night of Germany's terror raids. The tram was flung over by a blast in South East London. You can see the edge of the deep bomb crater, and the debris flung over the street.'*

Opposite: *'One bomb did this to a police station in the London area. A wall was blown down; a dormitory bed rested perilously near the edge. But the police were making the best of things there yesterday.'*

Churchill inspects the damage.

Above left: 'Mr. Churchill's cheering smile as he was inspecting raid damage in the City yesterday – his second tour of bombed areas. Behind him in this Daily Mail picture you can see the fire towers still reared against burning buildings. Thousands of City workers gave the Premier a rousing cheer. To one man's 'Are we downhearted?' they roared 'No!'. A few yards farther on a shout of 'Are we going to win?' produced an immediate 'Yes!'.'

Above right: 'The night before, the Premier toured the East End while an air raid was on. Here he is amid the wreckage of buildings bombed and gutted on Saturday night. He was given a tumultuous reception: 'Good old Winston,' and 'We can stick it all right,' yelled people who had lost their homes. 'Cheer up, we're winning,' were the Premier's words to one old lady.'

Left: 'A South West London Hospital. One of the damaged wards of a London hospital after the raid. Nobody was seriously injured.'

Churchill's Rallying Call

11th September, Wednesday

Winston Churchill broadcast to the nation in the evening as bombs were falling. His speech rejected the idea that the bombing would demoralise the 'British Nation, or the tough fibre of the Londoners...'. Instead, Hitler's incendiary and explosive bombs had 'lighted a fire which will burn with a steady and consuming flame until the last vestiges of Nazi tyranny have been burnt out of Europe.' He also warned of Hitler's plans for an imminent invasion. For that reason, the same night, Bomber Command attacked the Channel Ports of France where large numbers of invasion barges were gathering.

Mid-afternoon around 250 bombers attacked England's south coast and 30 bombers penetrated inland to attack London causing considerable damage. At night, in moonlit conditions, raiding continued across the country with concentrated attacks on London from around 20.00 until 05.30 the following morning; a massive anti-aircraft barrage boosted civilian morale and scored a few successes.

Right above: **Fire-fighters attack one of the many dockside fires.** *'London's Front Line Civilians Carry On. The world has been thrilled by London's ARP workers, who have had little or no rest since Saturday evening. Fire-fighting has become one of the most important duties of the front-line civilian.'* – Daily Mail, 12th September 1940.

Right below: *Regent Street, bombed when the Luftwaffe spread their target areas from the East End and docks to include the West End with its shops, cinemas, theatres and restaurants.*

Daily Mail

FOR KING AND EMPIRE

No. 13,849   THURSDAY, SEPTEMBER 12, 1940   ONE PENNY

CHURCHILL WARNS BRITAIN AGAINST INVASION

"Next Two Weeks Are Crucial"

Bomb on the King's Home

"EVERY MAN WILL DO HIS DUTY"

MR. WINSTON CHURCHILL last night warned the people of Britain that though Hitler has failed to master the R.A.F. his plans to invade this country on a great scale are steadily going forward.

"We must regard the next week or so," declared the Prime Minister, "as a very important week even in our history."

"It ranks with the day when the Spanish Armada was approaching the Channel . . . or when Nelson stood between us and Napoleon's army at Boulogne."

The Premier sounded a call to duty— "Every man and woman will therefore prepare to do his duty."

Hitler's effort to gain mastery of the air over the Channel by day had failed conspicuously, and we were daily stronger.

Mr. Churchill said:—

"When I said in the House of Commons the other day that I thought it improbable that the enemy's air attacks in September could not be more than three times as great as it was in August I was not, of course, referring to barbarous attacks upon the civilian population, but to the great air battles which had been fought out between our fighers and the German Air Force.

Air Mastery Key

"You will understand that when the weather is favour-

Berlin Howls at the R.A.F.

'Did Not Want War'

WHILE London stands undaunted under the hail of Nazi bombs, Berlin yesterday sent up a bitter wail about the tremendous battering of the German capital by R.A.F. bombers during Tuesday night.

"Germany did not want this war," raved the official news agency. "Again and again the Führer tried to settle the conflict by other means. It was always relying on high accord brought these efforts.

Then the inevitable

"England has now got what she wanted. She is the German sword might."

"Despairing"

Berlin—a city which has been little sleep for where 500 people have so far by British described yesterday traveller who arrived from the German cap

He and another in traveller from Bru declared that Germ army officers, and a already begun to des

The traveller from that he had talked officers there, and "extremely depressed

One officer declared later we are done kaput."

Hitler's 'Peace'

ISTANBUL, Wedne may make another offer" in the course few weeks, accordin mation received he

The information documents seized from every week from.

THE King and Queen inspecting the damage caused by the time bomb which exploded at Buckingham Palace. Other pictures in BACK PAGE.

Canteen Tea for the Queen

Fierce Dog Fights Over the Thames

WAVES of German 'planes made determined efforts to reach London yesterday afternoon, and Hurricanes and Spitfires engaged them in a series of tremendous dog fights at various points over the Thames Estuary

R.A.F. SHOWER BOMBS ON NAZI BARGE FLEET

ANOTHER series of raids on the concentrations of German barges and other ships lurking in harbours and docks along the French, Belgian, and Dutch coasts was delivered in bad weather by the R.A.F. on Tuesday night.

Calais docks bore the brunt of one of the heaviest attacks. The first salvos were released over the harbour at dusk, and for the next three hours the dock basins and shipping were heavily pounded.

The first crew to arrive saw their bombs bursting along the east side of the main basin and a fire at the edge of the tidal harbour.

A few minutes later another pilot made a shallow dive attack. The bomb-aimer let go a heavy salvo and there was a brilliant white flash, followed by a very big fire.

The weather grew steadily worse and later raiders which approached the French coast through thick cloud were met by violent anti-aircraft fire from heavy batteries and many light guns round Calais. Tracer shells made splashes of light yellow about the raiders and were active.

Fires and Explosions

One aircraft crew saw a long line of fires, three of them blazing around the Basin Carnot.

A clear interval enabled another crew to drop their bombs right along the barges massed in the Basin Carnot. As the high-explosives poured into the packed vessels which lined the whole east side of the basin and extended three-quarters of the way across it chunks of debris were flung into the air.

Ostend harbour was bombed for nearly eight hours.

German ships in Boulogne Harbour were also bombed. Other squadrons flew further north to raid Flushing.

Meanwhile the enemy's gun emplacements on Cap Gris Nez, which had bombarded Dover, were attacked again.

R.A.F. Blow to Berlin—BACK PAGE.

Mystery Explosions on Coast

HEAVY explosions shook the South-East Coast yesterday morning.

It was not known whether they were caused by bombs or by shells from German long-range guns on the French Coast.

Anti-aircraft guns opened fire on a lone German 'plane flying at great height which might have been a bomber or a reconnaissance 'plane "spotting" for German artillery.

LATEST

R.A.F. PILOTS SAVED

Crew of R.A.F. bomber, reported missing on Tuesday after raid on Berlin, picked up off South Scottish Coast by Coastal Command launch. Bomber had run out of petrol.

Captain reported he found his target—the gasworks in Berlin—on fire and he improved on a lot."

& THE WAR

RECTORS
A QUESTION

petrol pooled
dering just how
milability
ling brand of

Buckingham Palace Bombed

The bombing of Buckingham Palace on 11th September held much significance for the nation in general and the people of London in particular. From the earliest raids on the Docks and the East End, it was felt by the inhabitants that they were taking the brunt of Nazi attack. Relatively unscathed, people of Westminster watched the East End conflagrations as a great glow in the night sky while thousands of East Enders fled towards Westminster in the hope of safety. The fortitude of the King and Queen in remaining in residence was magnified by this first bomb. There would be six further bombing incidents threatening the Royal Residence.

Opposite: *'Buckingham Palace has been damaged by a time bomb which exploded with terrific force at 1:30 am Tuesday. The bomb, believed to be a 250-pounder, fell near the Belgian Suite, burying itself 10 feet deep, and forcing up some of the terrace. Their Majesties, accompanied by Mr. Churchill, inspected the damage done. They are shown here walking among the debris.'*

Left top: The King and Queen amid the rubble of the terrace at Buckingham Palace.

Left below: King George and Queen Elizabeth continue their inspection of the bomb damage.

Right below: *'The King and Queen and Mr. Churchill see the damage done to Buckingham Palace by a time bomb. This was the swimming pool which had been converted specially for Princess Elizabeth and Princess Margaret Rose, who got fond of swimming two years ago.'*

Above & left: 'King and Queen's Tour of Air Raid Damage in South London. The Queen chatting to women and children during their Majesties' tour of inspection of air raid damage in South London today.'

Delayed Action Bomb

12th September, Thursday

At 02.25 a raiding German aircraft dropped a delayed action SC 1,000 bomb in the vicinity of St Paul's Cathedral. It penetrated deeply into the ground at an angle, lodging near the Cathedral's clock tower foundations. The news of this peril was not released until Sunday 15th, after it had been bodily removed, put on a lorry and driven at high speed to Hackney Marshes where it was exploded.

Unexploded bombs, or UXBs, created uncertainty and great danger to the civilian population. Bomb disposal units were formed in May 1940 and by September there were 220 of them but they were overwhelmed by the volume of UXBs which had a backlog of nearly 4,000. A categorisation which prioritised disposal was issued on 8th September. The prominent incident at St Paul's drew a great deal of attention both to the threat of UXBs and to the Bomb Disposal Squads that had to contend with them. The increasing heroism of his servicemen led the King to introduce the George Cross medal at this point and Lieutenant Robert Davies, who personally drove the St Paul's UXB to Hackney Marshes, was among the first recipients of the award on 30th September.

Daylight and night raids were lighter than those of recent days, consisting mainly of single aircraft instead of formations of bombers. This change in tactics was probably in response to the losses the Luftwaffe had suffered from the AA guns the previous night.

Above right 'Churches, hospitals, and blocks of flats were among the 'military objectives' hit by German bombs on Tuesday night. A woman in her homely apron looks at the damage to a London flat caused by a wanton bomb. But Londoners carried on.'

Below right: *'London Church Bombed by Nazis. The crucifix stands alone, surrounded by shattered masonry and debris – all that remained of a London church after a Nazi bomb struck it.'*

Below left: Nurses clearing up and salvaging in a wrecked ward.

This page: '*A bomb which fell in the roadway outside Buckingham Palace during the second attempt by German raiders to bomb the Palace exploded and made a crater in the roadway, tearing down some of the railings. There were no casualties. The pictures show workmen at work repairing the damage to the roadway and railings after the bomb had exploded.*'

The King and Queen Bombed Again

13th September, Friday

Apart from an isolated incendiary raid on Belfast, daylight operations focused on London and the South East. In the morning the sirens sounded at 09.45 and the All Clear did not come until nearly 14.00; during this long daylight attack, once more six bombs fell on Buckingham Palace causing significant damage to the roadway at the front, the quadrangle at the back and to the chapel. Having recently returned from Windsor, through his sitting room window the King actually saw the two bombs fall on the quadrangle. The bombing proved a boost to Londoners' and the nation's morale: there had been rumours that the King had been booed on his tour of the bombed areas on Monday 9th. The Queen now remarked, 'I'm glad we've been bombed. It makes me feel I can look the East End in the face.' Indeed, the bombing of Buckingham Palace helped to encourage a feeling of solidarity between all Londoners.

That night German bombers braved poor weather, returning in singles and without fighter escort. The damage and casualties in London were much lighter than on the first few nights of the Blitz.

14th September, Saturday

The Luftwaffe flew extensive daylight operations that included bombing raids on Warrington, Clacton and Brighton where a direct hit on a cinema killed 35.

Two significant raids were launched on London with over 100 aircraft involved in each; they were fairly successfully contained by RAF fighter squadrons but caused considerable damage to residential property in Fulham and Chelsea with a number of casualties. Despite favourable weather, the night-time raids were less intense over London and more widespread across the country, lasting only about two and a half hours in total. Again, the Luftwaffe bombers were unaccompanied by a fighter escort, giving rise to speculation that they were being rested for a more massive onslaught. In the Nazi camp Hitler postponed his invasion plans for another three days, still confident that the reports given by his staff meant that Britain was on its knees and the conditions for Operation Sealion, the codename for the Nazi invasion, would soon be achieved.

Above: 'When a famous London Catholic church was destroyed by a German bomb the crucifix remained upright amid the ruins.'

FOR KING AND EMPIRE

Still the Best

No. 13,851   SATURDAY, SEPTEMBER 14, 1940   ONE PENNY

MORE BOMBS ON PALACE

The King and Queen Escape Unharmed

FIGHTER'S VICTORY SWOOP

GERMAN C.-IN-C. "IN THE FIELD"

THE King and Queen escaped injury yesterday when enemy 'planes deliberately bombed Buckingham Palace.

This outrage occurred during London's longest day raid of the war—it lasted 4hr. 10min. Incendiary bombs also fell in Downing-street, but did no damage.

German Bomb Did This

Meanwhile, a Berlin message to Bâle stated that Field Marshal von Brauchitsch, Commander-in-Chief of the German Army, had joined Göring "in the field" somewhere on the French coast.

This is generally accepted in Berlin as meaning that operations against Britain will be

15th September, Sunday

The reason for the Luftwaffe's 'resting' of fighter aircraft and pilots on the previous few nights became apparent in two massed attacks by around 600 aircraft during the day. Each wave was met by a massed defending force of RAF fighters: 22 squadrons scrambled to meet the first while, opposing the second, 31 RAF squadrons – over 300 planes – harried the enemy formations. The numbers of British fighters opposing them astonished the attacking bombers who had been told by their leaders that the RAF was a spent force. The BBC announced in the evening that 185 German aircraft had been destroyed by the pilots of RAF Fighter Command and the gunners of the AA batteries. Although in reality the number of German planes lost was nearer 60, nevertheless it was a crucially important victory for Britain's defending forces.

British success in fending off these daylight raids was seen as part of the reason for Hitler deciding, on 17th September, the indefinite postponement of Operation Sealion. The 15th September became known as 'Battle of Britain Day'.

Despite their losses in the massed daylight raids, the Luftwaffe mounted a series of further raids throughout the late afternoon and night that lasted until 05.00 the following morning. Outside of London, Portland was bombed and Me Bf110s of the elite bombing unit ErproGr210 attempted to attack the Supermarine works at Woolston but were thwarted by Southampton's strong AA defences. In London a number of the 180 bombers that flew across the country that night created a great deal of damage across the capital.

Bombed Out of Their Homes

Opposite top: **Carrying what they can, Londoners leave their wrecked homes behind them.**

Opposite below left: **People salvaging their furniture and belongings from their wrecked homes.**

Opposite below right: **Despite the almost total destruction of this home, the living room remains almost undisturbed – even the vases remain unbroken on the mantelshelf.**

Below: **Salvaging belongings the day after a raid.**

Crater in the Strand

16th September, Monday

As the clear-up from Sunday's severe bombing continued there were a number of minor raids during the day throughout the London area. One large-scale attack in the early morning was successfully repelled by RAF fighters. At night, bombing was widespread across most Metropolitan districts but damage and casualties were not heavy.

Opposite & above: Two views of a huge bomb crater in the Strand, left after the incredible air battle over London. on Sunday 15th September.

Right: *'Leopold Harris, who was released from Camp Hill Prison, Isle of Wight, a month ago after serving a sentence of penal servitude in connection with the fire conspiracy case, was at home in a London suburb last night with his wife and daughter when the house was destroyed by a bomb. All three were taken to hospital, where it was found that Leopold Harris had injuries to the scalp, a fractured jaw and multiple bruises, and was suffering from severe shock. He was detained. His wife and daughter were also injured. This picture shows a view of the damaged house in which Mr. Harris and his wife and daughter were injured.'*

(Harris was sentenced at the Old Bailey to 14 years in prison for leading a gang of arsonists that made fraudulent insurance claims in the thirties.)

Blast Effects

17th September, Tuesday

Mid-afternoon, 300 raiders crossed the Kent coast but were intercepted and failed to get to their London targets. During the night, the Luftwaffe had greater success, concentrating their efforts on London and the South East but ranging across the country from Glasgow to Cardiff. In the early hours of Wednesday 18th, a number of bombs landed in Central London. The Oxford Street stores of John Lewis, Bourne and Hollingsworth and D.H. Evans were among the casualties. One of London's worst incidents that night took place when a small bomb penetrated the ceiling of Marble Arch subway: although only the nose of the bomb came through, the force of the blast killed 20 of those sheltering there, ripped the clothes from the occupants and tiles from the walls causing terrible injury to another 20. Still only 10 days into the Blitz, ARP personnel were being confronted with scenes they could never have dreamt of in their worst nightmares.

A further development noted by Home Security on this day was the beginning of the use of deadly parachute mines by the Luftwaffe. These huge bombs were developed for use at sea but then were configured for dropping on land; their fuses could be set to detonate while in the air or for delayed action after coming to earth. Exploding over the target area the parachute mines could create a devastating blast zone as much as 2 miles in radius. In the first recorded deployment over Britain 12 were logged for the night of 16/17 September – all dropped in the London area.

Right above: 'In this remarkable photograph a turntable ladder lies twisted over the roof of William Beardmore's Great Portland Street office and showroom. Firemen perched 80ft high on the fully extended ladder were dealing with an incendiary blaze when a high-explosive bomb burst in the street, blowing the ladder bodily into the air. The top, with the hose and operators attached to it, crashed to the ground. Two firemen were killed and two others reported missing. Beardmore manufactured the 'Rolls-Royce of taxis' and gave up its Hendon factory to the war effort. In the post war slump the business collapsed.'

Right below: Firemen busy after a bomb had caused a gas main fire. Gas explosions could occur hours, even days, after the original bomb damage was sustained – even small leaks could build up deadly pockets of gas that could poison people in their homes or explode without warning.

Above: This shattered street in Stepney shows the impact of a High Explosive blast achieved by the heaviest German bombs – in particular the parachute mines becoming more widely used by the Luftwaffe. Bricks bonded with soft lime mortar were simply pulled apart by the blast and vortex effect of the detonation, laying bare the inner lathe and plaster structures which would normally be tinder dry, ready to be ignited by the accompanying incendiary bombs that were dropped in great profusion by the Nazi planes.

Right: *'Rescue parties working among wrecked Anderson shelters in the East End.'*

Parachute Mines

18th September, Wednesday

Fire-fighters spent the day hosing down the smouldering remains of Oxford Street, while as many as 800 Luftwaffe aircraft were involved in daylight raids targetting London, sometimes singly, sometimes in formation. The first of three attacks comprised fighters only – with the clear intent of taking on and defeating the RAF defenders. Amazingly, no real damage was caused in London although frustrated bombers found targets of opportunity in the Thames Estuary area.

By night, around 230 German aircraft bombed London while outside the capital smaller numbers of aircraft operated over the country with the only substantial attack being on Merseyside.

The Intensive raids that took place on London from 21.00 until 05.00 the following morning caused great damage and a significant death toll of more than 200 people and 550 injured. The high death toll on this and the previous night was no doubt boosted by the increasing use of parachute mines, with 36 dropped during the night of 18/19 September. The use of landmines incensed Churchill as their deployment over a large city like London could not be controlled and it was inevitable that their destruction zone would have a dreadful and terrorising effect on civilians. Since they dropped by parachute the casing of these weapons did not need to be as heavy as a conventional bomb and the thin material fragmented in the blast. As they were originally naval weapons the responsibility for disarming them lay with the Royal Navy – often presenting unenviable tasks when parachutes became entangled in obstacles such as trees. Ascertaining their state in such locations was extremely difficult, made worse by anti-tamper devices.

The British Government zealously guarded public information about the use and effectiveness of what the Nazis called the Luftmine and it wasn't until Autumn 1944 that statistics were released.

Bombs wrought havoc on London's prestigious shopping streets.

Left top: Burlington Arcade, viewed from Burlington Gardens; the home of prestigious boutiques is little more than a wreck after bombs hit during the night of Friday 13th.

Left centre: Bond Street looking south towards Piccadilly.

Left bottom: *'Damage was done when Oxford Street again became a 'primary objective', but rescue work was so efficient that even display dummies were taken to places of safety. The hat and costume go on.'*

Opposite top & bottom right: Two views of Oxford Street on the morning of Wednesday 18th. Fire-fighters are still hosing down the smouldering buildings. John Lewis's flagship store with its awning blinds down was gutted – just a smoking shell remained.

Opposite bottom left: *'Today's Raid Damage. The scene in the famous Lambeth Walk with wreckage from the demolished stalls.'*

19th September, Thursday

Poor weather during the day kept German raiders away barring reconnaissance sorties and a few isolated bombings. In the evening six raids over London caused little material damage but numerous casualties. Elsewhere raids took place over the Isle of Wight, Suffolk and Liverpool.

20th September, Friday

During the day a large formation of about 100 German aircraft was turned back by RAF fighter planes. The German aircraft were mainly fighters, consistent with the Luftwaffe's tactics of attrition; a few bombers succeeded in reaching South East London and dropped their loads but damage and casualties were light. A raid on Brighton killed 12.

Night raids caused more extensive damage to power and communications – principal targets for the bombers. Stepney Gas Works and the railway bridge at Southwark were hit, as were other rail links, causing serious disruption. Outside London the Luftwaffe concentrated on Suffolk and Essex; parachute mines fell in both Essex and Kent as well as on London.

Right top: Rescue workers passing food through a tube to Jack Reeves, who spent 17 hours trapped before he could be released. The picture shows how basic were the tools used by the rescue workers in many situations. Heavy rescue squads were formed in 1939 in anticipation of such damage but they comprised normal tradesmen. They were little prepared for the carnage they had to deal with but worked heroically, often in great personal danger.

Right below: *'Today's raid damage pictures in Berkeley Square.'* This picture shows the stark contrast between modern steel construction compared to the traditional built town houses of London's mainly Georgian West End: here all that remains standing of a large building is the lift shaft.'

Opposite top & bottom left: *'Damage to County Hall – fallen masonry on the terrace.'*

Opposite right: Rescue workers look for survivors in a damaged building on Lambeth Walk.

Pegasus Flies

Above left: Pegasus, which topped the Tower of the Temple Library, is captured on camera as it flies off as demolition work progresses after the Library was bombed on 19th September.

Above right: This shows how serious the damage was to the tower. With the unstable spire removed the old stonework was able to remain standing until repaired.

Left: 'Here is a typical London street raid shelter. No pretensions to beauty about it, but it does its job, as thousands of Londoners who would otherwise be casualties know. Bombs were showered on this little South London street. Wreckage from the houses was scattered on the roofs of the two public shelters in the middle of the road, but those inside were unhurt.'

Opposite top: Peter Robinson's at Oxford Circus, hit when the Luftwaffe returned to the West End again.

Opposite bottom left: Wreckage of buildings in Bruton Street.

Opposite bottom right: Damage to the back of the Selfridges store on Oxford Street.

21st September, Saturday

A day and night of much reduced German activity. After an evening sweep of mainly fighter planes attempting to reach London, the rest of the night was given over to a stream of single bombers and small formations attacking targets from Scotland to East Anglia.

22nd September, Sunday

RAF Fighter Command's quietest night since the beginning of the Blitz, with little activity by the Luftwaffe, though in London 72 were killed and 224 injured. A raid on Luton – a suspected parachute mine – wrecked a transport depot and numerous houses.

23rd September, Monday

During daylight hours 200 German aircraft, mainly fighter planes, converged on London but were driven back before reaching London's outer defences. Single aircraft attacked coastal towns and one made it through to drop bombs on London.

Night-time saw much more activity than over the previous weekend. Raids were widespread across London, causing considerable damage to road and rail links and many more deaths than in recent days owing to direct hits on two shelters. Outside London over 60 incidents were spread around the country.

On this night, at Churchill's insistence, Bomber Command diverted its attention from attacking the barges massed on the French channel ports to send over 100 bombers to Berlin, their target the gas and power utilities. It may have eased Churchill's anger over parachute mines but the raid was not very successful: the bomb that might have made a difference, falling in Hitler's Chancellery garden, failed to explode.

Above: 'London Carries On. A shop in Regent Street.'

Right: East Enders queuing up to enter public air raid shelters.

Opposite top: *'I think it is wonderful that they should carry on doing their job after losing their homes and spending nights in the shelters,'* said the Queen yesterday, when she paid a visit to the London Hospital. She was referring to two women over 70 who are cleaners at the bombed hospital and were bombed at home as well.' – *Daily Mail*, 24th September 1940. The picture shows the Queen standing with a hospital nurse. Debris of part of the hospital is in the foreground.

Opposite bottom left: Business as usual on Lambeth Walk.

Opposite bottom right: *'The telephone worked but the conversation is not as private as it would be in peacetime. A minor inconvenience of air raids on London.'* Daily Mail, 28th September 1940.

The George Cross

24th September, Tuesday

No large-scale attack was able to penetrate RAF and AA battery defences during the daylight hours. Dive bombers attacked the Supermarine works at Woolston, Southampton, in two waves separated by three hours: a direct hit on the works shelter killed 24 and injured 75.

At night there was a large number of raids throughout the London area, the most intensive centrally, north of the river; many incendiaries were dropped with ensuing fires.

Outside London scattered raids were carried out across Britain; Liverpool suffered from fire damage.

In response to the bravery being shown facing horrific air attacks upon London and Britain generally, the King announced in a broadcast to the Nation and the Commonwealth that a new medal– 'The George Cross'– was to be awarded 'for valour and outstanding gallantry' on the home front: this would rank next to the Victoria Cross while The George Medal would be more widely conferred.

25th September, Wednesday

Notable daylight action took place when around 60 German aircraft attacked the Bristol Aeroplane Co's factory at Filton. Bombs dropped from 11,000 feet hit the target and delayed action fuses interfered with clearance which began immediately with 300 navvies and 30 lorries. Damage to the plant was severe; 82 were killed and 170 injured. Subsequent attacks hit Portland and Plymouth.

A day of minor German sorties across London was followed by a night of widespread raids until the early hours of Thursday. The continuous raiding set out to confuse the controllers of Fighter Command: the courses taken by aircraft taking off from Holland or France might appear to be heading for London but then divert to other targets, while other raiders might appear to be heading to provincial targets then turn for London. During the night 70 people died in London and 74 outside.

26th September, Thursday

Although London escaped any daylight attack there was a large number of raids across the country, from Whitby in the north to Southampton in the south. During the afternoon the heavy attack on the Southampton area targeted the Supermarine Works at Woolston and the nearby Vickers Armstrong Factory; production at both was halted. Further east, Dover was shelled and 50 homes destroyed.

At night, raids on London began at about 20.30 and continued until about 05.00 on Friday. The night's raids caused a greater amount of damage than of late – the Houses of Parliament, the docks and some rail links all suffered to various degrees, while Liverpool and Merseyside experienced an attack that caused severe damage and many fires in the docks area.

27th September, Friday

A very busy day for the Luftwaffe: during daylight hours around 800 aircraft invaded the skies across Britain coming in waves of fighters and mixed fighters and bombers: most were broken up by RAF fighters. In one attack, only 20 of a formation of 300 aircraft reached Inner London. German losses of 56 aircraft approached those of 15th September. Despite these daytime losses, the Luftwaffe were able to mount night attacks by 200 bombers across the country, with 120 penetrating London's defences during the night until 06.00 Saturday. St Pancras was just one area of many that experienced heavy casualties.

During the day, Government officials set about a pilot scheme for distributing ear-plugs to Londoners tormented by the noise and lack of sleep from the bombing, sirens and guns of the AA batteries. They were to prove unsuccessful, as most people felt they would rather hear the noise and know what was coming than remain in peaceful ignorance.

Below: *'Men clearing debris in front of houses damaged by a bomb in North West London during the night raids.'*

Opposite top: *'Firemen playing their hoses on the smouldering ruins of premises destroyed by a heavy bomb in Tottenham Court Road, a famous London thoroughfare.'*

TEMPLE OF THE LAW HIT BY BOMBS

Sleep Coaches (1940)

A SERVICE of sleep coaches is now in operation to take Londoners to quiet country spots for the night. These *Daily Mail* pictures show how it is worked. Above, the coaches are ready to start.

The queues line up and their tickets are checked.

A drink at the "local" before closing and bedtime.

Lord Hewart Still Looks Down

By GRAHAM STANFORD, Daily Mail Reporter

THE Lord Chief Justice—in oils—gazes down on the wreckage of the Inner Temple Hall, E.C., where benchers, barristers, and students have met to dine, wine, and talk for years past.

Lord Hewart's was the only portrait undamaged when a high explosive bomb tore through the oak ceiling in a recent raid. That bomb blew the ancient bronze statues of the Knights Hospitallers and Templars to pieces; wrenched the fine carved door off its hinges, blasted the Lord Chancellor's coat-of-arms from the wall.

But when I visited the Hall yesterday and climbed over the débris of the Law's tradition, the portrait of the Lord Chief Justice—untouched and unsmiling—still stared down on the wrecked benches where the Bar foregathered.

A white-haired barrister's clerk stood by my side. He shook his head sadly when he saw what the German bombers had done.

But his eyes lit up when they fixed on the Lord Chief Justice. "It's like a symbol," he said. "The Law—unshakable."

Eminent K.C.s, young barristers and old clerks gathered round the Hall like mourners, recalling the great occasions it has known.

They talked of the art treasures now hidden under masses of stone; of the oak benches where the King has dined, which are now just matchwood.

Only the rare wine in the cellars below was saved.

Briefs Buried

In all, four German bombs fell in the quiet Temple courts, which are the heart of English law.

I left the Hall, and saw barristers searching among the débris for wigs, gowns, and scarlet brief bags.

Some were actually looking for legal documents necessary for current cases. They found parts of them, charred and dirty, blowing about the paving stones.

Many windows in the courts were broken by the blast from a bomb which burst in St. Clement Danes, in the Strand. The famous church of St. Bride's, off Fleet-street, was also hit.

Police Injured by Bomb: 1 Dies

Divisional Detective-Inspector Arthur Thorp and other West End police officers were injured by a bomb explosion early yesterday. They belong to a squad who have done good work during the bombing in Central London.

Sergeant Collins, who was promoted recently from the Flying Squad, died later from his injuries.

Duke Works On in Raid

The Duke of Kent chatted with dock labourers during two air raids when he visited the dock areas of a north-west port yesterday. Many of the men recognised him as he passed and accompanied a cheery greeting with the "thumbs-up" sign.

Later the Duke, who was dressed in Air Force blue, inspected contingents of A.F.S. volunteers and Home Guards.

MAJOR IS PRISONER

By Daily Mail Reporter

NEWS has been received in London from Major J. B. (Johnnie) Dodge, D.S.O., D.S.C., who is a prisoner in Germany.

Major Dodge, who is a close friend of Mr. Winston Churchill, was recently adopted as Conservative candidate for Gillingham in Kent. He tells a thrilling story of how he was captured.

He got his men down to the beach at Ste. Valery-en-Caux, near Dieppe. Then, seeing a British ship about three miles out to sea, he decided to swim to it to tell those on board where our troops were.

He had almost reached the ship when it turned and sailed away.

He tried to make his way along the shore, but the tide was low. He was eventually captured.

On his way to a German prison camp he attempted to escape by jumping overboard from a small steamer. He was in the water for two hours, but was recaptured when he landed.

Above: A view of the Tate Gallery after it had been hit by a bomb – the empty frame once housed John S. Copley's *Death of Major Pierson at St. Helier* but it, together with all the other works of art, had been evacuated to safe storage at the beginning of the war.

Fire Watchers Save Big Business

It's Your Opinion

POSTBAG ANALYSIS: Demands for unlimited reprisals on German cities rose to 80 per cent. of all the hundreds of letters received yesterday. But there was also an increase in the number who oppose the policy, mainly on the ground that we should not descend to the German level of barbarity. About one in eight oppose. Here are some more typical letters for and against.

SIR,—"Now go and smite Amalek, and utterly destroy all that they have, and spare them not, but slay both man and woman, infant and suckling, ox and sheep, camel and ass" (I. Samuel, Chap. xv.; verse 3). This was God's command to Saul as retribution for wickedness, and Saul's disobedience brought him down.

No sophistry can evade the Divine authority. If Saul was God's instrument for reprisals and vengeance, is it not presumable that this country is His instrument for the infinitely greater wickedness of Hitler and Mussolini?—**Chris. A. Thompson, York.**

SIR,—Would it not be possible for our Government to notify the German Government through diplomatic channels that unless the indiscriminate bombing of civilians is stopped within so many days six towns in Germany will be thoroughly bombed as a reprisal?—**J. Bevan Cousins, Plymouth.**

SIR,—Send your investigators among the rank and file of the people, and you will find that demand for reprisals is blowing up to explosion point.—**T. E. Williams, Bedford.**

SIR,—The bombing of military objectives may hasten the war, but the voice of the people might finish it. Let us hear what Berlin has to say after 48 hours' bombing. Humanitarian reasons are simply blue-pencil nonsense. — **W. Ellis, South Molton.**

SIR,—For God's sake put women in charge of the R.A.F. policy before it is too late.—**Molly Roche, Welwyn, Hertfordshire.**

What Would You Do?

SIR,—Will those who urge the indiscriminate bombing of Berlin ask themselves this question: If I were given one bomb to drop, should I drop it on a house, thereby demolishing it and killing perhaps a dozen people; or should I drop it on an aerodrome with the prospect of demolishing a dozen Nazi 'planes which would otherwise be used to invade London?—**Colin Robertson, Finsbury Park, London, N. 4.**

SIR,—The fact that the Nazis are so inhuman as to bomb defenceless civilian population

LONDON'S fire-fighters, regular and auxiliary, have been the admiration of the country and the world during the past three weeks of an air attack which has spared neither hospital, church, nor school. They sleep when they are not working, which means that they get very little sleep. Here they are, vigilant and alert, fighting a blaze at a bombed furniture depository in North London.

By Daily Mail Reporter

A LONDON business chief surveyed his slightly scorched office walls yesterday and said to me: "My fire watcher saved the building. I thought rather unnecessary when the Government made me

Daily Mail

FOR KING AND EMPIRE

Culmak

No. 13,863   SATURDAY, SEPTEMBER 28, 1940   ONE PENNY

FIVE DAY RAIDS ON LONDON

Terrific Dog-fights Over Suburbs

Roosevelt Silent on Axis Pact

V.C. at 18 'Did Some Quick Thinking'

Daily Mail Correspondent

GLASGOW, Friday.

MR. James Hannah, foreman craneman employed by the Clyde Navigation Trust, was on duty beside his crane to-night when I gave him the shock of his life.

"Your airman son," I said, "has been awarded the Victoria Cross."

Mr. Hannah looked at me for a second, stepped back, and then grasped one of the great steel girders at his side.

"The V.C.," he gasped. "Surely not. I thought he might get the D.F.M., for after all he is only a sergeant. But the V.C. . . ."

And so the father of the first Scots V.C. of this war learned the news while he was "going to it" on Clydeside.

His hero is an 18-years-old Sergeant John Hannah, until 13 months ago a shoe salesman in Glasgow. He is at present in an R.A.F. hospital.

His mother heard the news while she was sitting at tea in a neighbour's house. The neighbour heard it in a wireless bulletin and ran to tell Mrs. Hannah.

Mother's Tears

SKIES FULL OF FALLING NAZIS

Saved 'Plane

LARGE forces of enemy bombers tried several times yesterday to shatter London's defences. Instead, they were shattered themselves. Only a few of the successive waves crept through.

Anti-aircraft gunfire on the coast was the first obstacle for the daylight raiders. Those who penetrated inland were pounced on by Spitfires waiting for them.

Machine-gunned off their courses, seeing their colleagues whirling down in flames, the Nazis zig-zagged desperately towards London—to meet the devastating A.A. barrage of the capital.

This made them sheer off across the suburbs and run full tilt again into the arms of the fighters.

Meanwhile in the West enemy aircraft crossed the Dorset coast and reached the outskirts of Bristol. They were driven off by our fighters and damage and casualties were not heavy.

A few bombs fell in Central London during the long air battle and several in South and South-Western districts. Some damage to houses was caused.

In South London an industrial building was hit, and there were several casualties, some fatal. Bombs were also dropped in several places in Kent and Essex, but reports show that damage and casualties were slight.

122 DOWN

One hundred and twenty-two German aircraft were shot down yesterday. Thirty - one of our fighters were lost, but the pilots of 14 are safe.

'O.C.' for Bombed People

New Home-finder

LONDON is to have two "air raid dictators" —one to look after people bombed out of their homes, the other to speed up the clearance of débris and the restoration of damaged public services.

Mr. Henry Willink, K.C., M.P., aged 46, is to be special commissioner for the care and rehousing of the homeless.

Sir Warren Fisher, aged 61, until recently North-West Regional Commissioner, becomes special commissioner...

CONFERENCE WITH THE BRITISH ENVOY

President Roosevelt conferred with Lord Lothian, the British Ambassador to the United States, yesterday afternoon on the new Axis pact. Earlier at his Press conference the President had refused to comment on the pact.

By Daily Mail Diplomatic Correspondent

JAPAN'S signature of a ten-years pact with Germany and Italy is obviously intended to impress the world as a dramatic stroke of Nazi diplomacy.

It certainly has not impressed either London or Washington. In both capitals such an agreement has been expected for some time, in view of the close relations which have been fostered by extreme elements in both countries.

The signature of the agreement does not appear to add anything to the understanding which previously existed. It can be taken for granted, however, that in the talks between the United States and the Australian Government which have been taking place in Washington Japan's friendship with Germany has been fully taken into account.

Surprise was expressed in London yesterday, however, that Japan appears to get very little out of the agreement.

It is considered hardly likely that Germany and Italy, both of whom are engaged in the

AXIS MOVE IN SYRIA FEARED

ISTANBUL, Friday.

ACTION may soon be taken to determine the future of Syria, in which Turkey has the most vital interests, and in well-informed circles in Istanbul it is believed that action may be only a matter of days.

After the débâcle of Dakar it is believed that the Axis Powers may attempt an early diversion there in order to occupy the attention of part of the British Forces which are now held in readiness to stem the Italian drive on Egypt.

Turkey is believed to have

Woolton The Whaler

Lord Woolton, Food Minister, is sending a whaling expedition to the Antarctic to make sure of sufficient whale oil for margarine the year after next.

He told the North Staffordshire Chamber of Commerce at Stoke-on-Trent yesterday that the country could be assured that there were adequate stocks of food for some time to come.

There might be a little less butter and bacon every now and then, but compared with the background of war such things were trifles in the eyes of the housewife.

Lord Woolton made a special appeal to local authorities to ensure that people should continue to be fed in towns and cities singled out for intensive air attacks, and he asked local authorities to provide mobile feeding units and communal kitchens.

LATEST

H.M. TRAWLER LOCH INVER IS LOST

H.M. Trawler Loch Inver (temporary Skipper T. Hardcastle, R.N.R.) is overdue and must be considered lost, states Admiralty. Next-of-kin have been informed.

SUNER MEETS CIANO

Berlin, Friday.—Señor Suñer...

Stand to Your Jobs

Morrison's Call to Workers

Defences Ready

Throughout the day came reports of falling raiders during a series of warnings in the London area. A.A. shell bursts pock-marked...

IN an "Order of the Day" to arms workers, issued...

28th September, Saturday

Sustained daylight raids by the Luftwaffe managed to land a few bombs in East London and along the south east coast but the enemy was unable to cause heavy damage. The intense German activity was met with fierce defence by RAF fighters.

    Night raids were more successful and until the early hours of Sunday, bombs were dropped London-wide. Many incendiaries fell, starting a large number of fires. London's death toll was 72, 24 of them at Friern Hospital.

29th September, Sunday

During daylight hours the Luftwaffe only attempted small-scale attacks. At night, raiding was by single aircraft. The total number of aircraft raiding London fell far short of the average 163 per day and damage and casualties were slight compared to other days of the Blitz.

Left: 'The King and Queen stay with their people in bombed London. For the past three weeks they have been visiting damaged areas, encouraging the victims of indiscriminate bombing by their calm courage. This picture was taken while the King and Queen were on a visit to North West London. They are seen looking at debris after Nazi bombers had passed.'

Houses of Parliament Under Attack

Left: Road blocks scattered over the roadway after a bomb had exploded at Westminster near the Houses of Parliament.

Below: Damage to the Houses of Parliament – Richard the Lionheart's sword is bent by the blast from a German bomb.

LONDON PASSENGER TRANSPORT BOARD

TO ALL ABLE-BODIED MEN

The trains must run to get people to their work and to their homes.

The space at the tube stations is limited.

Women, children and the infirm need it most.

Be a man and leave it to them.

30th September, Monday

The Luftwaffe attacked Kent and Portland in six substantial attacks some of which were ultimately targeting London while others raided the key airfields of 11 Group: a day of major attrition after the relative peace of the previous day. German losses were heavy – 46 aircraft shot down and a number damaged, to say nothing of the deaths and injuries inflicted on skilled pilots and air crew.

Night-time raids were more successful – a total of 275 German aircraft operating across the country of which around 175 converged on London's Inner Zone from all directions. The death toll in London was relatively light at 35.

Above: Londoners asleep in an Underground station – the steps of the escalator becoming their pillows.

Left: Despite official rejection of using the Tube for shelter, the public overrode them and by the end of September official announcements like this one showed that the authorities had decided to accept the Tube as shelters and make them as organised and functional as possible.

Opposite above: Damage caused by a bomb in Aldersgate Street is surveyed by a fireman.

Opposite below: Looking south across London Bridge after an air raid.

Brown & Polson *Cornflour*

No. 13,864

FOR KING AND EMPIRE

MONDAY, SEPTEMBER 30, 1940

R.A.F. ROB GORING OF HIS BIG CHANCE

September 'Knock-out' Plan Defeated

By NOEL MONKS, Daily Mail Air Correspondent

WITHOUT counting yesterday's total the R.A.F. in September destroyed 1,008 Nazi aircraft. The month regarded by many experts as most likely for invasion closes with the R.A.F. definitely on top.

The Germans in the month have lost in air personnel nearly 3,000 men, 1,000 of whom have been made prisoners of war.

The R.A.F. in the Battle of Britain have lost 286 fighter 'planes—and the pilots of 135 of these are safe.

It can be definitely stated that the German Air Force have lost their chance to knock out the R.A.F.

With their numerical superiority there was a good chance of at least a partial success. That chance goes by the board with the passing of September.

In the month when the Nazis were expected to make their supreme attack on the R.A.F. in a desperate attempt to secure even a temporary aerial superiority as a preliminary to the launching of an invasion the R.A.F. hit back harder than ever and maintained their steady monthly average of 1,000 enemy aircraft destroyed over Britain.

Four weeks ago yesterday, on September 1, a high official at the Air Ministry said to me: "As far as the R.A.F. are concerned this is the critical month of the war."

No 'Knock-out'

The Nazis, in September—the last month of good weather—made several large-scale daylight attacks in which as many as 800 enemy 'planes were engaged, but they failed like all others in their two main objects :—

(1) To dislodge the R.A.F. from their Southern bases, and

(2) To force the R.A.F. to "pack" the London and Southern areas with fighters at the expense of important industrial centres in other parts of Britain.

On three days in the month—September 7, 15, and 27—the R.A.F. bag of Nazis passed the 100 mark, the record being 185 on September 15.

The simultaneous daylight raids on London and a South-West area last week showed the Nazis how wrong they were in imagining that because of the intense attacks on London that area was depleted of fighter squadrons.

Suner Off to Rome for Talks

SEÑOR Serrano Suner, Spanish Home Minister, after a fortnight's visit to Berlin, left yesterday for a short stay in Munich before going on to Rome.

Count Ciano, Italian Foreign Minister, fresh from signing the Axis-Japanese alliance, also left Berlin yesterday direct for home.

So far nothing has been revealed officially as to what Señor Suner will discuss with Mussolini and Ciano in Rome.

But the Rome radio yesterday declared: "The visit will not rest

MOSCOW GIVES U.S. "ANGLE"

Moscow, Sunday.

SOVIET newspapers to-day give great prominence to extracts from the United States Press emphasising Anglo-American collaboration, and the enhanced chances of a British victory.

They also display Mr. Cordell Hull's statement.

There is still no comment in Soviet newspapers on the Japanese Axis alliances.—B.U.P.

Able-bodied Should Not

Commanded the Shark, Lieut.-Commander Peter Buckley.

'Lost' Men of Shark are Safe

COMMANDER, officers, and a number of the crew of the submarine Shark, presumed lost in July, are believed to be safe.

Two letters from Lieutenant-Commander Peter Noel Buckley, in command of the submarine, reached his parents' home in Cheshire on Saturday and stated that he was safe in hospital in Norway.

Although wounded in the head and knee, he wrote he was "getting on well and being well looked after."

The four other officers of the Shark were Sub-Lieutenant Robert Douglas James Barnes, R.N.R., Lieutenant Denis Hugh Bryan Barrett, R.N., Warrant Engineer Cyril Coltman Loder, R.N., and Lieutenant David Ewart Wheeler, R.N.

It is believed that all are prisoners of war, together with a number of the 39 ratings.

Fighting Brothers

The 670-tons Shark, described as Britain's latest "pocket submarine," was the tenth British submarine to be lost since the start of the war.

Her commander comes from a family which has devoted itself to the Services. One of his brothers, the eldest, was a lieutenant in the submarine service and died at Malta eight years ago.

Another, aged 23, is a lieutenant in the R.N.V.R., a third is an artillery lieutenant.

Lieutenant-Commander P. N. Buckley is 30 and unmarried. He was educated at Holmwood School, Freshfield, Lancashire, went on to the Royal Naval College at Dartmouth, and volunteered for the submarine service some years ago.

Berlin Gun Posts Pounded

Power Plants Crippled

BERLIN suffered another pounding by R.A.F. bombers during Saturday night.

This time electric power stations and anti-aircraft positions in and around the capital were the targets. They were heavily bombed.

The naval base at Wilhelmshaven was also strongly attacked and fires and explosions caused.

The new enemy invasion base at Lorient, in the Bay of Biscay, was again raided.

Weather Defied

An Air Ministry communiqué states. "Operations were carried out last night by bomber forces of the R.A.F. over Germany and the occupied Channel ports.

"Weather conditions generally over North Germany were unfavourable, but numbers of our aircraft reached their objectives in Berlin and district. Electric power stations and anti-aircraft gun positions were bombed.

"Elsewhere in North Germany the targets included important railway centres and aerodromes. The naval base at Wilhelmshaven was strongly attacked and fires and explosions caused.

"Munition works at Hanau, near Frankfort, suffered severe damage.

"Along the Channel coast Havre, Fécamp, Boulogne, Calais, and Dunkirk were heavily bombed, as well as the line of big-gun emplacements near Cap Gris Nez. The enemy base at Lorient was again attacked.

"Two of our aircraft are missing from these operations."

Nazis Say—

Germany's communiqué yesterday said :—

"A few R.A.F. bombers during Saturday pushed forward to Berlin, but the British 'planes turned back before reaching the barrage without dropping any bombs.

"One 'plane was shot down by anti-aircraft fire."

One of the recent R.A.F. raids on Berlin "would have done credit to the New York Fair," says the writer of what is described as an uncensored letter from the German capital published in yesterday's New York Post, quoted by Reuter.

"I have just been through a genuine, unadulterated air raid on Berlin," says the writer.

"The Tommies have been here before, but never on such a persistent and big-time scale.

"Although it is just about noon on the day after the raid no newspapers have yet carried a report of it."

The last major daylight battle between the Luftwaffe and the RAF had been fought on Monday, 30th September. German casualties had proved too great to maintain the same level of daylight attacks for the rest of the Blitz. While daylight attacks would continue through October and half of November, they would be on a much reduced scale and after November even lighter still.

Meanwhile for civilians in London, life had taken on a new routine. After work at home, office or factory, people would head in the evening for shelters whether or not the alert sounded. There, they were growing accustomed to sleeping amid the din of the night raids, ready to emerge next day for work. Absenteeism, even during these early days, was remarkably light it was almost a matter of pride to carry on as normal a life as possible.

Manchester and Merseyside Raided

1st October, Tuesday

Raids were launched throughout the day by the Luftwaffe: 16 of them involved single aircraft but 4 others were formations of 30-70 aircraft, all of which focused on coastal areas, including Southampton and Portsmouth, and RAF airfields; highflying 109s bombed south London while a single raider bombed and machine-gunned Croydon.

Widespread night raids across the country were heavier than by day and resulted in some damage in Manchester and Merseyside as well as London but fewer deaths than on recent nights.

2nd October, Wednesday

Daylight raids were again only minor but German aircraft – among them bomb-carrying Bf109s – managed to penetrate the defences and drop bombs around Woolwich, Camberwell and Lewisham. Coastal towns in Kent and Sussex were also raided. The night was the quietest since the first day of the Blitz, 7th September, but there were still raids across London almost continually from dusk until dawn the next day while raiders also attacked the Manchester area.

Left above: **The ruins of this church bombed during Tuesday night** *'somewhere in the south east of England'* still smoulder as firemen play their hoses on the embers.

Left below: **A family group looks over this astonishing sight demonstrating the arbitrariness of the Blitz. A falling bomb could devastate parts of a building while leaving others relatively unscathed; some occupants would survive by some chance, while others died.**

Right: **Many children had been evacuated in September 1939 but had drifted back home when no bombing had come. More were evacuated at the beginning of the Blitz but many families decided that they would rather face the bombing together and children were often to be seen playing in the damaged, rubble-strewn streets and bomb sites.**

Opposite: *'She Saved The X-Ray Apparatus: Yesterday's* Daily Mail *picture in Central London after the night raids. The girl, a doctor's assistant, was carrying off part of an x-ray apparatus salvaged from the ruins in a famous street* [Harley Street] *which received a direct hit.'* Daily Mail, 2nd October 1940.

CHAMBERLAIN TO RESIGN

Continued Ill Health Forces Retirement

ANDERSON MAKES WAY FOR MORRISON

By WILSON BROADBENT, Daily Mail Diplomatic Correspondent

MR. NEVILLE CHAMBERLAIN, Prime Minister when war broke out, has decided to resign from the War Cabinet. An official announcement will be made almost immediately.

I understand that Sir John Anderson has offered his resignation and that his post as Minister of Home Security will be taken by Mr. Herbert Morrison, the present Minister of Supply. Sir Andrew Duncan, President of the Board of Trade, will probably become Minister of Supply.

Mr. Chamberlain's resignation from the office of Lord President of the Council, which he accepted when he handed over the Premiership to Mr. Churchill, will lead to other important changes in the Government.

Mr. Ernest Bevin, Minister of Labour, may now enter the War Cabinet, although not as Lord President. That post may be reserved for Mr. Lloyd George, about whom there are persistent reports that sooner or later he will join the Government.

Mr. Chamberlain is 71 years old. His decision follows his continued bad health.

Although he rapidly recovered from the abdominal operation he underwent six weeks ago the improve-

Science 'Brains-Trust'

They Will Help to Fight the War

By Daily Mail Reporter

SCIENCE, represented by half a dozen of the most brilliant scientific brains in the country, has declared "total" war on Germany.

These six men, it was announced yesterday, have been entrusted with the task of bringing to the notice of the War Cabinet the war uses

Premier when War Broke Out

MR. Neville Chamberlain, Prime Minister when war broke out, is to resign. His ill health continues and makes it impossible for him to carry out his work as Lord President of the Council. A recent picture.

CABINET STOP MERCY SHIPS

Danger of Gales and U-Boats

THE Government have decided to send no more children overseas under the official evacuation scheme until further notice.

This decision follows recent sinkings of evacuee ships, in one case with heavy loss of life among the children. "Reluctantly," it is stated, "the Government have come to the conclusion that during the winter season of gales and heavy seas they cannot take the responsibility of sending children overseas."

The parents of more than 10,000 children still awaiting evacuation will be disappointed.

The decision comes at a time when U-boats are waging an intensive and merciless campaign. It is emphasised that the scheme is suspended—not abandoned.

A British steamer arrived at an eastern Canadian port yesterday with a number of children on board, says an Exchange Ottawa message. Some of the children are going to the United States and others to Ontario.

"JUST as every new move by the German Air Force in the day time has been successfully countered and mastered, so at night our forces, scientists and technicians have been adapting their knowledge and their machines to the new attack . . . Hitler's attack on this country has been foiled."—Mr. Ernest Brown, Secretary for Scotland, speaking at Oban last night.

Night Attackers Meet Check

FEW GET THROUGH: TWO DOWN

LONDON'S reinforced defences were again in action last night. And in 4 hours only one of Göring's night raiders got through to the central area. The rest battered at the defences on the outskirts but were checked and turned away.

Up to midnight at least two bombers had been brought down—one shot to pieces by A.A. fire over Edgware, the other felled by night fighters.

Two separate waves were sent against the capital before midnight and the first sheered off very quickly, giving London its earliest night "All clear" since the blitzkrieg began.

A considerable time elapsed before the next "Alert" heralded the second wave of raiders.

This wave consisted of larger formations than the first, and from the roofs in Central London they could be seen vainly trying to break through the outer ring of defence marked by gun flashes and star shells.

Only odd raiders, at long intervals, managed to get past the new secret defence weapon.

Wall of Light

LATEST

NIGHT FIGHTERS 'KILL' HEINKEL

A Heinkel bomber was shot down by a British fighter patrol over the North Sea off the N.E. coast of Scotland late last night.

'CHASED

Sir John Makes Shelter Tour

3rd October, Thursday

Poor weather conditions meant there were no formation raids during the day, but the Luftwaffe flew sorties in singles and pairs dropping scattered bombs across London and beyond – notably on the De Havilland works at Hatfield where significant damage resulted. The pattern of raids by single aircraft continued through the night but in no great numbers. Casualties and damage were both slight.

4th October, Friday

Again, overcast weather conditions limited the scale of the Luftwaffe's attack. By day and night, raiding was carried out mainly by single aircraft. During the day attacks were launched at Shellhaven and Corringham refineries without damage. At night the single aircraft followed one another in rapid succession – on average about one every two minutes; it was calculated that around 270 aircraft were involved, 175 reaching London to carry out widespread bombing.

Direct Hit on the Tower of London

5th October, Saturday

RAF and AA defences were again kept busy by six daylight attacks mounted by the Luftwaffe in improved weather conditions: four targeted the South East with two successfully penetrating the Inner Artillery Zone (*IAZ*); the other two attacked Southampton and the Isle of Wight.

The weather also brought many more night-time attacks over the capital where the Tower of London received a direct hit. Raids also targeted the Eastern Counties and the Midlands, with the Germans employing both formation and single aircraft raids until the early hours of Sunday.

6th October, Sunday

Very poor weather conditions made this one of the quietest days and nights of the early Blitz. No significant daytime attacks took place on London but east and south coast towns suffered raids.

During the night raids no casualties were reported and damage in and around London was slight, although Northolt Aerodrome suffered some damage when a single aircraft bombed it during the day.

Opposite above & below left: *A section of the Tower of London was damaged and a Yeoman Warder killed when the North Bastion received a direct hit by a bomb on 5th October. Pedestrians stop to view the damage to the Tower.* [Note from the censor says the photo below must not be published.]

Opposite below right: '*When an enemy bomb fell near an Anderson shelter in the South West London area the lives of three people inside were miraculously saved – thanks to the shelter. The picture shows a member of the Home Guard and a rescue squad by the side of the Anderson shelter in which the three people were saved.*'

Top & above: Staff of John Lewis in Oxford Street sorting goods salvaged from the store after September's bombing.

Right: '*Just another hospital hit by a Nazi bomb. This one was in North-West London, and the children's ward was damaged. Here are two nurses removing their tiny charges to safety.*'

Deadly Rush Hour Raids

Above & Opposite below left: Rescue squads tear away the debris from the bomb damaage to reach the trapped victims.

Right: Street damage after raids during London's rush-hour on the 8th.

Below: *Clearing up debris after a bomb had dropped outside a well-known London station this morning.'* The station was Charing Cross which was hit at 08.50 on the 8th: the stick of three bombs fell on the line, on the main platform and through the roof of the District Line onto the Underground track. There was widespread damage to Charing Cross, where there were 50 casualties, and to nearby government offices in Whitehall. This photograph was not released by the censor until March 1944.

7th October, Monday

An improvement in the weather led to a stream of raids throughout the day by the Luftwaffe testing RAF defences while on course for London. This intensive activity led to high German losses with 19 aircraft shot down.

Night raids were again heavy over London, causing great damage and high casualties. Sustained raids took place on Manchester and Liverpool while 80 aircraft swooped on Scotland.

8th October, Tuesday

The pattern of large-scale day and night attacks caused significant damage and casualties – mainly in London where approximately 200 people were killed and 400 injured, many during the rush hour. However the Luftwaffe's operations were widespread across the country.

Churchill addressed the House of Commons summing up the month of the Blitz. He pointed out that improved shelter facilities and accurate air raid warnings had cut the death toll to one tenth of the pre-war estimates, but 'the destruction of property has, however, been very considerable. Most painful is the number of small houses inhabited by working folk which have been destroyed, but the loss has also fallen heavily upon the West End, and all classes have suffered evenly, as they would desire to do.'

Left top & above: ARP workers on the scene of one of last night's bombing attacks – a hospital in the London area.'
The hospital was St Matthews on City Road, a former workhouse built in the previous century. At the beginning of the war it had over 600 beds. The direct hit on the 8th killed many patients and a number of staff. Immediately after the hit the surviving patients were relocated and the hospital closed until autumn 1942.

The Evening News

LATE EXTRA

RHINO-SOLE
SYNTHETIC PLASTIC LEATHER
Just spread it on - Thats all!

Rhino-Sole repairs LEATHER AND RUBBER EQUAL TO NEW. Invaluable for Uskids, Crepe WELLINGTONS etc.
Obtainable from W H SMITH AND SON, TIMOTHY WHITE'S, Branches, and Dealers Everywhere.

ITS PIQUANT ITS DELICIOUS -H.P SAUCE

LARGEST EVENING NET SALE IN THE WORLD

NO. 18,322   SIXTIETH YEAR   LONDON: THURSDAY, OCTOBER 10, 1940

TO-NIGHT'S BLACK OUT
6.46 p.m. to 6.48 a.m.

ONE PENNY   6D per tube

WOOLWORTHS

ST. PAUL'S CATHEDRAL BOMBED
High Altar Destroyed: Main Fabric Undamaged

CITY CLOSING PRICES
On Page 5

BOMB PIERCED ROOF

MARBLE SMASHED AND WINDOWS DAMAGED

EXPLOSION ON THE ALTAR

It was officially revealed this afternoon that St. Paul's Cathedral has been bombed.

THE following communiqué was issued by the Air Ministry and the Ministry of Home Security:

"During a recent air raid on London an enemy aircraft dropped a bomb on St. Paul's Cathedral, piercing the roof at the east end of the Cathedral and destroying the High Altar.

"The main fabric of the Cathedral was not affected, nor was the Choir damaged, and no one was injured."

R.A.F. STOP ANOTHER RUSH HOUR ATTACK

200 RAIDERS: NOT ONE GETS TO LONDON

Strong formations of German bombers made attempts to attack London during the rush hour to-day. The R.A.F. stopped them.

FIVE waves of planes, some 200 in all, were engaged in the unsuccessful attack.

The formations crossed the coast of Essex and Kent and flew up the Thames Estuary, using various points on the coastline as crossing places.

Single Bombers

Each wave appeared to be heading for London, but British fighters and the anti-aircraft defences were not caught napping.

Every wave was beaten off—and not one of the raiders succeeded in reaching the London

The King and Queen talking to one of the mobile canteen workers.

The King Gives Canteens and Ambulances To London

The King has made a gift to London of four motor ambulances and eight mobile canteens.

To-day at Buckingham Palace he formally handed over the four ambulances and two of the canteens to Mr. Emil Davies, chairman of the L.C.C.

The remaining six canteens will be delivered during the next three weeks.

Each of the grey-painted vehicles bears the inscription "Presented by His Majesty the King to London County Council for the civil defence of London, October 1940." The inscription is surmounted by the Royal cipher.

"People Like Hot Tea"

Fleet Planes Busy
DESTROYERS BOMBED

HITS ON GERMAN SHIPS AT BREST

German destroyers at Brest, the former French Atlantic naval base, have been bombed by Fleet Air Arm planes, operating with the Coastal Command, it was revealed to-day.

Hits on the destroyers were observed.

Widespread raids on railways and industrial and oil plants in Germany and German-occupied countries took place during yesterday and last night. See Back Page.

R.A.F. RAID TOBRUK

JAPAN'S OIL: BRITAIN IN TOUCH WITH U.S.A.

Asked in Commons to-day to consider representations to U.S.A. to prevent export of oil to Japan, Mr. Butler (Foreign Office) said U.S. prohibition related only to certain grades. Government in touch with U.S. Government.

When asked "Cannot we have assurance that Government are not going to supply warlike material to Japan?" Mr. Butler replied:— "Importance of the matter fully realised."

MORE ANDERSON SHELTERS

In statement in House of Commons to-day Mr. Morrison, Home Secretary, said he would seek adequate steel supplies for additional Anderson shelters.

Steps would be taken to establish official control of cement, bricks and possibly other things so that supplies and prices should be controlled.

Dispersal of families in surface shelters should not be discouraged.

There was tendency to forsake Anderson shelters for sake of company, and street shelters because one or two had direct hits. Don't let us consider there is safety in great numbers.

People must have reasonable quiet in shelters. Night visits too frequent. Powers given to local authorities to take over basements as shelters. He hoped to get more accommodation in Stepney and Finsbury.

He was considering power for himself, through regional commissioners to say to local authorities: Either you take over basements or I do and you manage them.

BUNKS FOR 750,000

Contracts for timber bunks for 750,000 people placed. First deliveries expected at end

---

Another Narrow Escape for St Paul's

9th October, Wednesday

Churchill's speech to Parliament, the day before, noting an easing in the intensity of the Blitz in the first days of October, seemed to give a cue to the Luftwaffe, who stepped up the vigour of their day and night raids across the country and on London in particular. After its lucky escape in September, St Paul's now fell victim to one of the last raiders of the night whose bomb exploded in the roof above the High Altar, which was then completely destroyed by falling masonry.

Right: *'A hotel in London damaged by a bomb last night. Nobody in the hotel was injured, as they were all in the shelter.'*

10th October, Thursday

During the day and night there was an almost constant succession of raids by substantial formations and single aircraft. The focus, as usual, was on London but during the night operations spread wider without reducing the impact on the capital. The Luftwaffe lost 12 aircraft.

From the middle of September it became clear to the Luftwaffe that RAF Fighter Command remained a powerful threat to their medium and light bombers, especially when deployed in massed raids. Goering's orders regarding fighter escorts just made German losses worse but during September and into October the Luftwaffe changed its tactics to evade RAF and AA defences. Using Messerschmitt Bf109 fighter aircraft adapted to carry a single 250kg bomb, the pilots would fly at high altitudes of around 25,000 feet.

These aircraft could be over South London within 17 minutes of the first radar warnings. Spitfires took 22 minutes and Hurricanes 25 minutes to reach 25,000 feet from 'scramble' orders. The only way to counter these high-flying Messerschmitts was for RAF Fighter Command to mount a round-the-clock airborne patrol over Southern England – putting great strain on both manpower and equipment. These attacks combined with strong fighter sweeps, intermingled with Heinkel, Dornier and Junker bombers, kept the controllers of Fighter Command guessing and contained German losses while maintaining their attacking effectiveness.

11th October, Friday

By day the Luftwaffe flew seven major raids, with increasing use of high-flying bomb-carrying Messerschmitt 109s but few managed to reach Central London. Other parts of the country suffered little attention.

At night, although fog probably reduced the number of raiders, nearly 300 people were killed or injured by the bombing in London. Liverpool was repeatedly attacked and across the country 55 enemy raids were plotted during the night.

Left: Damage to St Paul's High Altar. A new High Altar was consecrated in 1958.

Damage to Westminster Abbey

Below left: *'First picture of raid damage to Westminster Abbey. The leaded windows were broken when a high explosive bomb fell between the Abbey and the House of Lords. Walls were chipped and pitted by flying debris.'*

Right: *'Bomb Crater Near St. Clement Danes Church.*
A.R.P. workers inspecting the crater made in a London street by a bomb dropped by German night raiders. The famous church behind received some damage from blast and flying debris. Nearby trees were uprooted.'

Below right: *'Tin Hats Will Speed Up Your Post.*
Postmen are being provided with steel helmets and are encouraged to make special efforts to achieve deliveries in bombed areas as part of the plan of the GPO to reduce postal delays. The picture shows a tin-hatted postman making his rounds in a bombed London area. Letters addressed to wrecked houses are marked accordingly and returned.'

12th October, Saturday

Attacks during the day and night followed a similar pattern to Friday 11th, raiding ending around 02.30 in the early hours of the following day on both occasions. Similar casualty figures were reported, but this night the Midlands received more attention with the bulk of provincial casualties in Coventry. It was a costly day for the Luftwaffe which lost 13 aircraft.

13th October, Sunday

Pressure from the Luftwaffe was very heavy in this 24-hour period: repeated attacks by German fighters came in waves over the country, some carrying bombs. Around 250 planes flew missions during the afternoon with successful penetration to the IAZ by three out of four attacks despite determined opposition from RAF fighters.

A night followed of intensive raids across the country with Liverpool and Bristol bombed as well as London. But it was a bad night for the capital when bombs hit several communal shelters, including a Tube shelter. In the worst incident a block of flats in Stoke Newington collapsed, immolating over 200 people sheltering in the basement – more than 150 died here alone, bringing the death toll to nearly 400.

During the evening of Sunday 13th October, Princess Elizabeth, with her sister Princess Margaret beside her, gave her first broadcast when she spoke to British children everywhere. Throughout the war the Royal Family, including the two princesses, remained based in London and refused to evacuate to what were considered 'safer' areas.

Right top: A concert in a Tube shelter. The pattern of daily life in London was now, for most people, to head in the early evening straight from work or home to the shelters before even waiting for the siren to sound, so used were they to the constant air attacks.

Right centre: A bombed house in Hackney. This picture was earmarked to be used for an appeal in the overseas *Daily Mail*.

Right bottom: *'Some of the 5,000 'Cleaner-Uppers' Begin Work Today. Tomorrow (Monday) 5,000 men of the Pioneer Corps will march into the most heavily bombed areas of East and South-East London, shouldering their weapons – picks and shovels. They are the great army of 'cleaner-uppers' who will tackle the big job of clearing up bomb damage. Today, the advance guard of the 5,000 started work 'somewhere in London'. This photo shows pneumatic drillers doing a spot of demolition themselves. A great slab of concrete is being broken up to be carted away by lorries.'*

Shelter Tragedy

14th October, Monday

A quieter daylight period for both sides but a busy night across the country with enemy attention focused on London and Coventry.

London reeled under another shelter tragedy – this time 68 died when a bomb hit Balham High Street Underground Station where about 600 people were sheltering at around 20.00. The bomb breached the Northern Line tunnel and in the aftermath water from damaged sewers and mains flooded in along with sand and soil. The station was pitch black as power went off and under the circumstances the death toll could have been much worse. Above ground an iconic scene was on view as a London routemaster bus had virtually disappeared – swallowed by the gaping bomb crater. Across the country the casualties total approached 1,000, nearly 200 of them fatal.

Keen to maintain calm in the civilian population, Home Security played down the severity of Monday night's raids This tactic angered and upset people who had survived a terrible night; as a result a list was published of 21 London areas where there had been heavy damage. The dilemma of balancing public information with the need for censorship would continue throughout the war.

Left: The Monument to the Great Fire of London in 1666 photographed on 14th October 1940 amid the debris of the Luftwaffe bombing.

Opposite above: Fire-fighters damping down the smouldering ruins of St James's Church in Piccadilly, hit during a night raid on 14th October.

Opposite left below: A trolley bus wrecked by a bomb.

Opposite right below: Damage to *The Times* newspaper building.

A Close Call for Winston

Right: On the night of the 14th, Winston Churchill, seen here inspecting bomb damage early in the Blitz, escaped injury while dining in the basement of 10 Downing Street when several bombs landed close by in Whitehall.

Below:'*It has been revealed that Mr. Churchill narrowly escaped being killed by a bomb during the blitz on October 14th 1940. The photograph shows damage caused by the raid at the Treasury.*'

15th October, Tuesday

A recurring pattern during the Blitz was the concentration of massed aerial attacks in the middle of the month, often assisted by a full or 'bombers' moon (There was also a reasonably regular pattern of heavy attacks at the end of the month.) 15th October was no exception and aided by a full moon, the capital was visited by 410 German aircraft that dropped a total of 538 tons of high explosive (HE) bombs along with numerous parachute mines and a new type of incendiary bomb that seemed to be more effective.

Again, the death toll was high at over 400 and nearly 900 people were seriously injured. Nine hundred fires were started and thousands of people, especially in East London, were made homeless. All rail traffic into and out of London was stopped. The Fleet sewer was breached and its waters poured into a railway tunnel at King's Cross. Three large water mains were also breached, depriving many areas of water – a not unusual occurrence, but in this case a larger area than usual was affected and it took longer to restore supplies. Battersea Power Station, Beckton Gas Works and even the BBC at Portland Place were all damaged by bombs. It was London's worst bombardment to date.

Outside London, Birmingham suffered intermittent but persisent attacks over a six-hour period.

16th October, Wednesday

While the homeless and others cleared up after the previous night's raid, daytime attacks on the capital were slight – fog hampering German operations.

Night-time activity by raiders was much less than on recent nights but London still suffered death and destruction from the bombs that did fall. Outside London, raiders attacked Birmingham and Liverpool.

Right top: **Two bombs fell on this sports stadium – The Ring at Blackfriars – on Saturday 19th.**

Right centre: **The damaged Court Room in Stationers' Hall, bombed on 15th October.**

Right bottom: *'Inside the burnt out library of Holland House, where a number of valuable books were destroyed when it was fire-bombed by the Luftwaffe.'*

Daily ...

WITH H·P SAUCE

NO. 13,877

FOR KING AND EMPIRE

TUESDAY, OCTOBER 15, 1940

LONDON'S BOMBING IS FIERCEST YET

CLEAR UP

The Cold

Below: 'The Temple Damaged. The Temple, ancient and beautiful square, one of the remnants of Old London, has been damaged during a recent raid. This picture shows one of the wrecked buildings in the Temple.'

New Explosive-and-Fire Missiles Dropped

By Daily Mail Raid Reporters

THE bombing of London last night was declared by experienced observers to be the most intense yet. There were more raiders than before, approaching from all directions and converging on the city. Later they arrived in formations.

Watch On 'Gib' is Doubled

avy Sweep Sea

Daily Mail Radio Station

RITISH naval and air forces are sweeping Western Mediterra-, judging by reports that area quoted by German radio last

The Luftwaffe last night used a new type of bomb, which is both explosive and incendiary at once. Some of these bombs exploded in mid-air.

Early raiders were met by an even heavier barrage than before. British fighters were up in numbers.

A raider, caught in searchlight beams, was surrounded by a hail of bursting shells and shot down in flames. It crashed with a terrific explosion.

A great number of bombs of all types, including time bombs, were dropped in the first hours of the raid. There were many more incendiaries than ever before.

Early this morning 70 districts reported that bombs had fallen.

FLARES SHOT OUT

Below: 'Temple Bombs. Nazis have bombed the Middle Temple Hall, one of the loveliest and most famous buildings in London. Much damage was done, but the main body of the hall and the vaulted roof are still there. This special picture shows workmen removing ornamental figures which escaped the general damage. A Daily Mail picture in the back page gives an idea of the destruction done to this 'objective'.'

Shower of Incendiaries From Night Raiders

LONDON BOMBED TO-DAY IN RUSH HOURS

ONE GROUP GET THROUGH DEFENCES

4 Crippled Girls Killed By Night Bombers

FAMOUS CHURCH SET ON FIRE

About a dozen German planes, which had cloud-hopped their way across London during the first "Alert," dropped a number of bombs on the capital during the rush-hour to-day.

For a moment, immediately before the bombs fell, the raiders could be seen flying across a patch of blue sky.

Bursting A.A. shells chased them through the clouds as they raced away towards the South-East.

LARGE numbers of incendiary bombs were dropped on London during the night's raids. They were followed by H.E. bombs and time-bombs. Many fires were caused.

was bombed. Four crippled girls were killed. Other girls there tried to rescue them.

Suburbs Attacked

The official communique, issued to-day, state:
"London and a town in the Midlands were the principal objectives during last night's raids, which were on a somewhat smaller scale than those of the previous night.
"In both these areas a number of fires were started and houses and industrial buildings were damaged. All the fires were speedily brought under control.
"In London and the suburbs a number of people were killed and others were injured. Casualties in the Midlands were less numerous, but included a small number of persons killed.
"High explosive and incendiary bombs were also dropped in the Home Counties, in several other districts of England and at a few points in Wales, but reports show that they caused little damage and few casualties.
The early hours of the raid were the fiercest since the night attacks began.

Flares Gunned

Searchlights swept the skies and guns poured shells along the course of the planes, which were more numerous than usual. The Germans dropped their bombs as soon as possible to avoid the risk of thunderous gunfire.
A number of flares were dropped

BERLIN BOMBED AGAIN, SAY GERMANS

R.A.F. BATTER OIL-PLANTS AND PORTS

It was officially announced in London to-day that last night R.A.F. bombers carried out attacks on oil plants and other targets in Germany and on enemy-occupied Channel ports.

BOMBS were dropped on Berlin, according to German sources.

Two air raid alerts were given in the capital.
The all clear after the first alert went about half an hour before midnight, while the second period did not end until nearly 5 a.m.

Low-Flying Planes

The thunder of a heavy anti-aircraft barrage and the drone of low-flying planes filled the air during the second period.
The first alarm was very quiet, with no A.A. fire and no planes audible and little searchlight activity.
The official German communique on the raids said:
"British planes flew over North Germany. Some reached Berlin and dropped bombs, damaging several dwelling houses.
"Virchow Hospital was struck by bombs, but there were no casualties.

"Three Shot Down"

"Other raiders were driven off by anti-aircraft fire.
"Three enemy planes were shot down in flames on their way to Berlin by night fighters."—B.U.P.

"BARBARISM" TO MINORITIES

AXIS INQUIRY INTO RUMANIAN DISPUTE

Rumanian and Hungarian charges and counter-charges about the "barbaric" treatment of minorities following the transfer of Transylvania are to be "investigated" by the Axis.
It is announced in Budapest that a mixed Italo-German commission has been set up.
An Italian delegate, Count Ruggero de Villanova, has arrived in Budapest to take his place on the commission. The German delegates are expected there to-day.

Berlin "Impatient"

An inspired statement issued in Berlin plainly hints at German impatience over the dispute.

"SISTER KAY'S" SECRET IS OUT

HOSPITAL NURSE IS THE DUCHESS OF KENT

When the Duke of Kent visited University College Hospital, London, recently, among the nurses presented to him was "Sister Kay," who was in the final stages of her training as a V.A.D.
The Duke smiled as "Sister Kay" shook hands with him and circled. She was his wife, the Duchess.
For three months, it was revealed to-day, the Duchess has worked hard as an ordinary V.A.D. trainee at the hospital.

Nurses Not Told

TURKEY CHALLENGES AXIS IN BALKANS

'Come Any Further and We Fight' Definite Pledge to Greece

Turkey will resist any further adventures by the Axis Powers in S.E. Europe. That is the one point that seems certain amid the mass of reports from the uneasy Balkan capitals to-day.

IT is stated in Bucarest that the Turkish Ambassador has told the Soviet and U.S. diplomatic representatives that the Turkish Government "will respect all engagements towards Greece."
Any change in the Greek status quo will be considered in Ankara as a direct menace.
The Turkish Ambassador is quoted as having said that his Government think that the massing of Axis troops in the Balkans has the Dardanelles and Syria as an immediate objective.

United Resistance

Turkey, he stressed, will "except a fight to its last consequences," retiring before no obstacle.
Finally, it is said such an attack of the Axis would provoke the united resistance of the Three Moslem States—Turkey, Egypt, and Syria.
In Ankara, it is again emphasised that Turkey will resist any attack on her territory and independence with all her force.
Diplomatic circles anticipate that closer military co-operation between Britain and Turkey is certain.

Tightening the Grip

Here is a summary of to-day's reports from other capitals involved in the Balkans manoeuvres:
Bucarest: More German troops have arrived in Rumania, bringing the total up to 45,000. It is understood that ten German divisions have been assigned to the country.
German airmen attached to the new German garrisons fought fires which broke out in

STAND BY HOBBY: A member of a Streatham A.R.P. stretcher party knits while he waits.

BRIDE LOSES HE HOME

WAS TO HAVE MOVED IN THREE WEEKS

When a bomb fell in one London suburb for the first time last night 21-year-old Joan Wodger lost

Above: 'Elizabethan Dining Hall Damaged in Recent Air Raid. The building of the Middle Temple Hall was begun in 1562. The hall stood the test of centuries until – in the autumn of 1940 – the blast of a German bomb wrecked it. The demolished timber seen at the end of the hall was once the carved wooden screen supporting the minstrel's gallery.'

Increased attacks on Midlands and Merseyside

17th October, Thursday

Maintaining their strategy of using fighter aircraft carrying single bombs and flying at high altitude to evade defences, the Luftwaffe managed to bomb London both by day and by night, although with far less severity than the raids earlier in the week; nonetheless nearly 100 died in the capital.

London Transport put out a call to the regions for buses to replace the many familiar red double-decker London buses damaged in the Blitz. Reinforcements in a variety of colours came from across the whole of Britain.

In the rest of the country Birmingham and Liverpool were again singled out for bombing raids.

18th October, Friday

During the day, Luftwaffe activity was slight and night fog made flying difficult. Nevertheless, there were still some raids over London throughout the night, causing about 45 deaths and some damage.

Birmingham came under attack again – consecutive nights of raids targeted the important munitions industry of the Midlands capital.

19th October, Saturday

Only one daylight raid was launched against London, but isolated attacks took place in other parts of the country.

In the early hours of darkness a heavy attack was mounted on London; later raiding involved single aircraft flying from France or Belgium every 20 minutes; widespread bombing caused many casualties with 174 killed and 538 injured. Elsewhere, Coventry's factories were bombed and Merseyside was raided yet again.

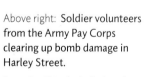

Above right: Soldier volunteers from the Army Pay Corps clearing up bomb damage in Harley Street.

Far right: This daylight bomb falling on 18th October was heard by a cameraman who was on the scene in less than a minute to find the police taking charge of events. Even on days when German activity was intermittent, the destruction continued.

Right: A policeman tests for gas leaks from this damaged lamp standard by the 'sense of smell' method.

20th October, Sunday

Formations of Messerschmitt 109s flying at high altitude attacked London during the day but little damage was done. Raiding continued during the night, fairly heavily until midnight and then with less intensity until 06.00 the following morning. Elswhere, the Midlands was again attacked, with a particular focus on Birmingham and Coventry, the latter of which suffered serious damage.

Leicester Square had been bombed on 15th October but the Press and Censorship Bureau did not allow publication of these pictures until later in October because the damage was caused by a parachute mine and although the pictures were released, no mention of the mine could be made. There was a great deal of debate in Government about how much information should be made public, for two reasons. First, accurate information about the extent of the destruction would give the Germans useful data when targeting their raids. Secondly, and what caused most debate, was the extent to which scenes of devastation, especially of landmark sites, would lower public morale, as against the damaging effects of rumours which circulated in place of no, or obviously inaccurate, information.

Left above: *'Leicester Square. Thurston's, home of billiards, was one of the chief sufferers from the Leicester Square bomb. But the building still stands, as do the headquarters of the Automobile Association next door. This picture shows damage in the square.'*

Left below: **With Thurston's to the right of the picture, a slightly different view of the devastation in Leicester Square – looking west along Panton Street towards Whitcomb Street.**

Clearing the Debris

Above: 'S.E. District Office, The Borough S.E. Bombed sorting office carries on although part of the building was demolished by an H.E. bomb. London postmen carry on sorting the salvaged mail with a very few letters missing. This picture shows the last of the mail being salvaged from the wrecked building.'

Right: Mid-October saw the start of a massive clear-up operation. The picture here shows some of the 5,000 men of the Auxiliary Military Pioneer Corps refreshing themselves with buns and tea provided by the Salvation Army before returning to the work of salvage and clearing the debris.

FRANCES PITT'S Nature Article is on Page 2

The Evening News

MONDAY, OCTOBER 14, 1940   Editorial Telephone: Central 6000

FIVE THOUSAND SOLDIERS BEGIN TO TIDY UP LONDON

IT'S "BACK HOME" FOR SOME

THEY'RE CLEARING UP THEIR OWN STREETS

FIVE thousand troops of the Pioneer Corps began to-day to tidy up London.

Detailed for the job of clearing raid wreckage, they set out from billets in lorries laden with picks, spades, tools, rope and other paraphernalia for the most severely bombed areas.

They were joined on the spot by unemployed men recruited at labour exchanges.

Salvage Task

These men will clear away the debris, pull down buildings which are dangerous, salvage materials such as bricks and wood, and generally make the stricken streets a better sight.

Some of the soldiers had travelled hundreds of miles, and many found themselves at work in their own districts.

"Personal Interest"

One of a squad who had had a road journey from Scotland to the capital, said:

"I wouldn't have missed this trip for worlds. My own home is only a twopenny tram ride away. I've got a personal interest in clearing up the mess."

Royal Engineers are taking part in the work as well as the Pioneers. Their task is to restore damaged roads and communications.

One of the first areas to come under the pick and shovel was a South-East London borough.

Houses First

Here working-class homes have suffered and it was noticeable that the troops, instead of starting on the wreckage of shops and business premises, were sent to a side street where poor people's homes on both sides of the thoroughfare had been smashed.

Thorough searches were carried out first for the tenants' property, which would be cared

Flashed a Torch With Planes Overhead

SPOTTERS ON SOCCER STANDS

KEEPING PLAY GOING DURING "ALERTS"

SPOTTERS may be posted on stands at football grounds so that matches can be carried on during air raid "alerts."

This has been suggested, though so far the idea has no official backing.

Vexed Question

The question of whether or not to continue matches after the "alert" is a vexed one.

It was learned to-day that the football authorities may shortly seek an amendment of the Government regulation which orders the suspension of games until the "raiders passed" signal.

Players Willing

Mr. Peter McWilliam, manager of Tottenham Hotspur, said to-day

A Jolt For Essex Soccer Clubs

EVERY amateur footballer in London has, I am sure, heard with profound regret that the South Essex Combination—which contained such leading clubs as Walthamstow Avenue, Leytonstone, Leyton, Clapton, Ilford and Romford—has had to close down, at any rate temporarily.

There is plenty of life in the old dog, however, and I am assured by the honorary secretary and treasurer, Mr. S. J. Buckley, that a resumption of league fixtures will take place directly conditions improve.

Crowds Fall Off

IT is not actually the air raids which have led to this momentous decision on the part of the council of the South Essex Combination, but the financial difficulties which most of the clubs have encountered.

One official said to me, "How can you run a club on gates of £2 when your overhead expenses are £10 a week?"

Although some London clubs have received fair support from their followers, those on the Essex side are drawing comparatively few spectators. This can be easily understood with the evenings drawing in.

Ground Closed

IN the upheaval the prospects of some famous amateur clubs seem just a little depressing. Ilford, for instance, have closed their ground and they will only be able to play away from home; Clapton

FORECAST FOR THE POOLS

LOCAL DERBY GAMES WHICH MAY BE DRAWN

By Foresight

The local Derby games, Brentford v. Fulham, Charlton v. Spurs, and Millwall v. West Ham, look to be the problem matches this week and they are well worth considering for the three draws in this week's Unity Pools.

The home sides with the best chances of winning are once again at the bottom of the coupon.

SOUTH REGIONAL

1 Arsenal	v Northampton
2 Birmingham	v Mansfield
3 Brentford	v Fulham
4 Cardiff	v Coventry
5 Charlton	v Spurs
6 Chelsea	v Q.P. Rangers
7 Leicester	v Luton
8 Millwall	v West Ham
9 Norwich	v Southend
10 Notts Co.	v Walsall
11 Palace	v Orient
12 Portsmouth	v Aldershot
13 Reading	v Bournemouth
14 Stoke	v West Brom
15 Swansea	v Bristol C
16 Watford	v Southampton

NORTH REGIONAL

1 Blackburn	v Rochdale
2 Brad City	v Leeds
3 Chester	v Everton
4 Chesterfield	v Sheffield Utd
5 Crewe	v N Brighton
6 Grimsby	v Doncaster
7 Huddersfield	v Barnsley
8 Hull	v Newcastle
9 Liverpool	v Man City
10 Man Utd	v Preston
11 Middlesbro	v Bradford
12 Oldham	v Burnley
13 Sheff Wed	v Halifax
14 Stockport	v Bury
15 Tranmere	v Southport
16 York	v Rotherham

SCOTTISH

1 Airdrie	v St. Mirren
2 Clyde	v Hearts
3 Falkirk	v Partick
4 Hibs	v Third Lanark
5 Morton	v Dumbarton
6 Motherwell	v Celtic
7 Queen's Park	v Hamilton
8 Rangers	v Albion

PONTOON GOALS

	Sept Oct		Sept Oct
	21 28 5 12		21 28 5 12
Airdrie	6 3 1 2	Mansfield	0 3 - 4
Albion	3 3 0 0	Middlesbro	3 3 3 3
Aldershot	2 3 3 3		

SPORTS GOSSIP BY THE TWELFTH MAN

3 POWERS MAY DEFY HITLER

BALKAN PACT TO STOP AGGRESSION

INCREASING resistance to the Axis drive in the Balkans is being shown in the few remaining free countries.

According to Bucarest reports, a three-power bloc—Yugoslavia, Greece and Turkey—may be formed as a barrier against any further thrust.

The report follows a speech by M. Svetkovitch, the Yugoslav Premier, in which he stressed Yugoslavia's determination to defend her frontiers, independence and freedom.

"With Our Blood"

The Premier said, "We warn everybody that we have founded this country with our blood.

"It is ours by our past, it is ours by history, it is ours by our sacrifices."

Obviously alluding to Albanian and Bulgarian aspirations to South Serbia, he said: "These regions are ours, there we fought. Here we have died. Only bloodshed can wrest them from us."

Another indication of Yugoslavia's firmer attitude is a report from New York that she has rejected a German demand for absolute control of her import supplies of wheat and other cereals and ores.

Turkey "Ready"

Trade talks between Germany and Yugoslavia are said to have reached a deadlock.

In Turkey feeling is strong that any Axis advance should be resisted.

The newspaper Tan said to-day: "The most important factor to prevent the Germans even dreaming of the Anatolian route is the presence of invincible Tur-

21st October, Monday

Early-morning fog and low cloud over Britain enabled the Luftwaffe to take advantage of the cover, making a number of attacks on London by day and night, but casualties in the capital were not as severe as other Blitz nights – around 50 deaths.

In the Midlands, Coventry again experienced heavy bombing during the night.

22nd October, Tuesday

A fairly quiet day and night for London as German operations were hampered by fog over the South of England. Coventry was not so lucky and again its factories were heavily bombed during the night, at the same time rendering 200 people homeless.

'More Leaves for London's Scrapbook. Three pictures, scenes from different bombed districts yesterday, that will take their place in the records of the Battle of London.'

Below left: ,This picture shows the Pioneer who saved the aspidistras in the great A.M.P.C. clear-up.'

Below centre: 'As part of the clear-up campaign, the Pioneer Corps salvages this piano from a wrecked home before the debris is cleared away.'

Below right: 'London Air Raid Damage. Some dummies from a damaged London tailors' shop, after a London air raid, being 'rescued' by members of the Pioneer Corps.'

Right above: 'Chancery Lane Safe Deposit, which was bombed and fired some weeks ago, and the vaults buried beneath the debris. Workmen are excavating through the debris to get at the vaults where many people have their treasure buried, most of which is in perfect condition.'

Right centre: The picture shows one depositor taking his goods away after they had been safely recovered from the buried vaults of the Chancery Lane Safe Deposit.

200th Raid on Merseyside

23rd October, Wednesday

Liverpool and Merseyside experienced their 200th raid of the war while, in the early hours of Thursday, bombers attacked factories in Scotland

In the capital, the poor weather conditions continued to work in London's favour, although the few night raids that were mounted still managed to evade British air defences to reach their targets.

On this day Churchill instructed the various ministries that information regarding German parachute mines should be carefully restricted when reporting enemy action and resulting damage. At the same time, Churchill maintained pressure on Bomber Command to plan escalated retaliation on German cities.

24th October, Thursday

Slightly better weather conditions brought more raiders over Britain and Birmingham was heavily bombed during the night with substantial damage to New Street railway station, factories and commercial property. In contrast, there was very little damage to London. Casualties, at less than 100, of which only 10 were fatal, were slight by comparison with other Blitz days.

25th October, Friday

Further improvements in weather conditions meant continuous daylight raiding across the country and much heavier attacks by night. Bombing was widespread throughout London resulting in greater casualties than over the preceding days of fog and low cloud – more than 100 deaths.

Large numbers of incendiaries dropped on Birmingham caused many fires while HE blasted factories and housing across the city.

At night, the RAF bombed Berlin and Hamburg in a 'reprisal' raid. It was Berlin's second major raid in four days. On the 21st, the RAF had attacked in a single raid lasting four hours.

 RUSH-HOUR TRAMS BOMBED

PILED wreckage of the five London trams that were hit during yesterday's rush-hour raid on London. The trams were drawn up close to traffic lights while a battle raged overhead. Two high-explosive bombs fell. One made a direct hit on the middle tram, crushing it like a concertina. The two trams on either side were completely wrecked ; the others badly damaged. "The raider jettisoned his bombs," said a passer-by. "Fortunately a lot of people had taken cover when they heard gunfire near." Three people were killed.

VELT IS G LEAD

tics Massing

ly Mail Correspondent

NEW YORK, Friday.
French crisis forced the campaign to a subsidiary apers to-day—an astonish preoccupation with Europe at election day (November

continued, however, with the lead and holding the Willkie hanging grimly to the President's coat tails. Mr Willkie has announced that he would

Above: 'Rush-Hour Trams Bombed. Piled wreckage of the five trams that were hit during yesterday's [25th] rush-hour raid on London. The trams were drawn up close to traffic lights while a battle raged overhead. Two high-explosive bombs fell. One made a direct hit on the middle tram, crushing it like a concertina. The two trams on either side were completely wrecked; the others badly damaged. 'The raider jettisoned his bombs,' said a passerby. 'Fortunately a lot of people had taken cover when they heard gunfire near.' Three people were killed.'

Left and opposite: 'Hit-and-Run Daylight Raid on London.' These pictures, all of the same incident, which occurred at 09.52 on Friday show the vulnerability of the lightly constructed trams. They probably were not the intended target, which was the railway and its bridge across Blackfriars Road: damage to the parapet and the track is clearly visible and, no doubt, the total of five trams destroyed in the attack would be considered a bonus by the Luftwaffe.

District Line Keeps Running

26th October, Saturday

RAF Fighter Command had some success in turning back small formations of Messerschmitt 109s during the day; the main attack around midday led to some German aircraft reaching London but with no significant success.

Night raids were spearheaded by 95 plotted incidents in the early evening and during the night many single aircraft managed to evade British air defences and reach their targets in London and Birmingham, the latter suffering its third heavy night of raiding in a row – resulting in great damage to factories and commercial property.

Below left: Salvaging goods in the silverware department of William Whiteley's in Bayswater. The department store was bombed and set on fire during the previous Tuesday night.

Above left: *Another London church has been hit in a recent raid on London. The picture shows damage to the entrance to the church.*

Below right: Bomb damage to the Regent Palace Hotel, near Piccadilly Circus.

Above left: The scene in Queen Victoria Street, Blackfriars, where the District Railway carried on operating despite the fact that a bomb had blown away the roof of the tunnel. The pictures were not allowed to be published until April 1941.

Above: 'London Carries on as Usual. The District Railway is still in operation, as this picture shows, despite the fact that during a recent air raid a bomb damaged the rest of the tunnel. A.R.P.s are helping the civilian contractors to clear up the debris.'

Below left: A bomb crater in Seymour Street by the side of Euston Station.

27th October, Sunday

Attacks in four main waves during the day followed the normal pattern but a bombing raid on Portsmouth and Southampton involved JU88s and had some success. In the early evening a concerted series of raids attacked many RAF airfields – some key to Bomber Command – destroying aircraft on the ground.

Successful night raids were carried out on London, Coventry and Liverpool but they were not as heavy as some earlier in the month.

28th October, Monday

Morning mist and fog inhibited flying before noon but during the afternoon the Luftwaffe teased Fighter Command again, only making one significant attack.

During the night, raids were mounted on London and Birmingham which were relatively light for London but the large numbers of incendiaries and many HE bombs caused widespread damage in Birmingham.

Left above: **After the bombing.** Hospital nurses look into the crater made by a Nazi high explosive.

Left centre: *'The Hospital in War-Time. Despite hits with bombs which have damaged four of the nine blocks of St. Thomas's Hospital, the medical and nursing staff are carrying on with their work, in spite of the difficult conditions. This picture was taken during a visit to the hospital and shows how the staff met the emergency. One of the patients in a bath-chair – she is an air raid casualty – views the damage to the hospital caused by the recent raids.'*

Left below: This child surveys the wreckage of his orphanage from his cot. The Children's Home was bombed in a night raid on 27th October.

Daily Mail

FOR KING AND EMPIRE

LATE WAR
NEWS
SPECIAL

BROWN & POLSON
CORNFLOUR

NO. 13,888   MONDAY, OCTOBER 28, 1940   ONE PENNY

A A GUNS POUR INTO BRITAIN

Canada Develops Mighty Arms Flow

AXIS SURPRISE LAST NIGHT

So The Captain WON'T Resign

By EMRYS JONES

THE electors of Marylebone, the London constituency famous for its Madame Tussaud's, continued to be puzzled yesterday by The Strange Case of Captain Cunningham-Reid, their 44-years-old M.P.

Some of them reflected sourly that it is difficult to put a man into the House of Commons, but it is more difficult—nay, impossible—to get him out of it before a General Election when he displeases his electors.

With simple faith, most of us argue that when we put a man to do a job, and he is paid for it, then if the job is not done to our satisfaction we should be able to put somebody in his place.

That, Member ***

BRIEF ***

Ca is this servative Union cause he sented the fuses to Indeed which the Saturday, third time on as M.P.

As is a were harn

Council ing the should originally supporters terly dis the wrong

The tr ***

TANKS, SHELLS, CARS ON WAY

From WALTER FARR, Daily Mail Special Correspondent

OTTAWA, Sunday.

SHELLS at the rate of a million a month and masses of new guns are pouring into British ports from Canada to add to the already tremendous power of the anti-aircraft barrages defending London and the great industrial centres of Great Britain.

This is just one heartening piece of news given to me to-day by Mr. Howe, Canadian Minister of Munitions and Supply, in a special statement for The Daily Mail.

It was explained to me that this great torrent of arms has been made possible because of a new plan of co-operation between Canada and the United States.

Canadian plants are working in close collaboration with United States plants in ***

HITLER SACKS ARMY CHIEF IN FRANCE

THE chief of the German military administration in France, General Streccius, was replaced by General Stulpnagel on October 25, the official German News Agency announced last night (says Exchange).

General Stulpnagel presided at the Franco-German Armistice Commission at Wiesbaden. He was formerly in charge of the Third Reserve Corps at Berlin.

8 Down

EIGHT German 'planes were shot down yesterday. Six of our fighters were lost, but one pilot is so far reported safe.

FIGHTERS DESTROY NIGHT RAIDERS

Heavier raids on England have been ordered by Göring within the last two days, stated the French radio, quoting a Berlin message, last night.

By Daily Mail Raid Reporter

A NUMBER of German bombers are believed to have been shot down off the north-east coast during last night's raids.

British fighters chased some of the raiders back over the North Sea, and both the fighters and A.A. batteries are believed to have scored some successes.

German 'planes were also re-ported over Merseyside

Hitler May Meet Mussolini To-day

Hitler and Mussolini will meet to-day, according to reports in Rome last night, says B.U.P. These reports said the Duce and other members of his Cabinet had already set out for the meeting place. Mussolini ordered the March on Rome anniversary celebrations, due to be held to-day, to be advanced a day to enable him to leave Rome.

By WILSON BROADBENT, Daily Mail Diplomatic Correspondent

ON the latest information available in London last night, it appears that the agreement announced between Hitler and Marshal Pétain is not of a far-reaching character.

Much depends, of course, on the further discussions, but for the present it seems that Hitler, in search of some diplomatic triumphs for propaganda purposes, put forward various proposals, all of which Marshal Pétain has not yet seen fit to accept.

Up to the present it may be that the marshal has not done much more than agree to make

LATEST

HITLER'S PLANS FOR FRANCE

Vichy, Monday. — French radio, commenting on Hitler-

Children carry on with their lessons in shelters during air raids:

Above: A drawing lesson at a boys' school in North West London.

Below: A shelter knitting lesson in progress at a girls' school in the same area.

Aerodromes Attacked

29th October, Tuesday

The Luftwaffe showed they meant business in their first attack of the day in which a number of aircraft dropped their bombs on West and Central London. Further raids kept the defenders busy during the day and more bombs hit South London. The strong RAF response during the day led to large clashes and many dogfights over London with resulting high Luftwaffe losses of 27 aircraft.

As on Sunday 27th, the Luftwaffe used much of their energies attacking RAF aerodromes as dusk approached. During the night, London got off reasonably lightly since the West Midlands was the main target with much incendiary bombing of Birmingham and Coventry. Liverpool was again attacked and its main telephone exchange put out of action.

30th October, Wednesday

In two main daylight attacks, each involving over 100 German planes, little was achieved by enemy raids.

Persistent attacks in the early evening threatened London and other targets in the Midlands but for relatively light damage, Luftwaffe losses of ten aircraft were high.

Increasing reports started to come through of small canisters, dropped from the air by German aircraft, only inches in diameter with a wire attached. They were described as looking like small Mills Bombs. The first SD2 anti-personnel fragmentation bombs fell in East Anglia in late October and would cause much damage and inconvenience in the years to come.

TICKETS STOP SLEEP-QUEUE

3 Years' Bread Assured

PRICES FIXED

CANADA has enough surplus wheat to last Britain three years and enough bacon for a year, said the Hon. J. G. Gardiner, Canadian Minister of Agriculture, in London yesterday.

Production was increased on the outbreak of war and the surplus is now much greater than expected.

Food news of the week ranges over many commodities, from cod fillets to carrots.

FROZEN COD FILLETS.— From Friday the Ministry of Food will become sole importers and will supply 60 per cent. to inland and 40 per cent. to coastal wholesalers.

Wholesalers will charge fish fryers and retailers a maximum of 11s. 6d. per stone, carriage paid. The maximum to the public will be 1s. 3d. per pound.

LEMONS.— From Monday the maximum price will be 6½d. per pound, or about 2d. each.

ONION CONTROL

ONIONS.— From the same day a maximum price of 4½d. per pound will operate.

TEA.— The public must not think the International Tea Committee's recent statement that next year 20,000,000lb. more tea will be available will mean an increase in the supplies of tea in this country.

OUTLOOK OBSCURE

"THE future's in a helluva mess since they put this anti-blast netting on my crystal."

—By Phipps

YOUR OPINION

Plea: 'Don't Demand

Bring In

Mrs. Lingis Has Her Shelter

Bed Reserved Now

By Daily Mail Reporter

DISTRIBUTION of "season tickets" for the big basement shelters in the City of Westminster began last night.

The first to secure the yellow square of pasteboard which will reserve for her and her family places in the refuge near their home was Mrs. Agnes Lingis, of Newburgh-street, W. I met her, her tailor-husband, and their two daughters in the basement shelter of a famous West End store.

"I can't say what a relief it is to get this ticket," she told me. "In the past we have had to queue up from as early as 2 p.m. to make sure of a place for our mattresses.

"My husband has either had to close his shop early or risk not getting a place at all. Now, they tell us, with these tickets, our places will be reserved for us, whatever time we arrive.

"When the bunks they promise us are installed it will seem almost like home!"

There were envious glances at the Lingises and the rest of the chosen few—all local residents—who received their passes last night.

But by the end of this week, I was told, 500 permanent tickets will have been issued for this store shelter, while within the same period 1,200 passes will have been distributed for fixed places in a big garage shelter.

Residents First

Arrangements are being made to accommodate between 20,000 and 30,000 ticket-holders within the next few weeks.

Mr. F. Copeman, shelter manager for the City of Westminster, told me:

"Three-quarters of the total shelter accommodation in the city will eventually be reserved for ticket-holders.

"The rest will be kept for casuals and the friends of residents temporarily in the district. First passes are being [...] people living in the [...] se to the shelters.

Speed-up

[...] hem, residents of other [...] the city will be given [...] finally, if there is any [...] mmodation, those living [...] estminster will be able

[...] ly, the passes will re-[...] ks for each holder. We [...] in bunks at the rate of [...] week.

[...] rs are also being quickly [...] with canteens, many of [...] already running."

[...] being issued with tickets [...] ave to show their iden-[...] as proof that they live [...] trict.

They Can't Count It

BRITAIN-AT-WAR is now spending more than ten million pounds a day.

Exchequer returns for last week, published yesterday, showed that £72,895,500 was required for supply services. The total spent was £73,997,397.

* * *

And if you have any adding or calculating machines you don't want, the Government will take them. Business firms are asked to "Give, lend, hire, or sell their machines and other office machine equipment."

WORST SHIP LOSSES

A BIG concentration of U-boats in one area of the Atlantic has caused the Allies' worst mercantile shipping losses in any one week of the war—apart from the Dunkirk evacuation week.

During the week ended October 20-21, the Admiralty announced yesterday, losses were: British, 32 ships (146,528 tons); Allied, 7 ships (24,686 tons); neutral, 6 ships (26,816 tons); total, 45 ships (198,030 tons).

The average for the previous 58 weeks was approximately 57,000, and in the week when Dunkirk was evacuated losses were 209,894 tons.

It is authoritatively admitted that the U-boats scored considerable successes, but, it is hoped, not entirely without loss to some of their submarines. Extra precautions have been taken with a view to preventing similar heavy losses in the future.

Left: 'The stage was the platform. The 'auditorium' was an electric railway line which a couple of weeks ago would have meant death to a human being. But Aldwych Tube Station is now an air raid shelter and members of the ENSA brought music, song and comedy to the shelterers last night.'
Daily Mail, 9th October 1940.

Organised Shelters

31st October, Thursday

On the day which is universally agreed to mark the ending of the Battle of Britain, there was little activity by the Luftwaffe, operations being hampered by rain and winds. Nevertheless, for Londoners the presence of any German aircraft spelled danger and the capital's inhabitants took to their shelters for the fifty-fifth night of unbroken aerial attack.

Time in the shelters was now part of everyday life. Wherever people regularly took cover, things were beginning to be more organised than in the early days of the Blitz. In public shelters sanitation had been improved, some sleeping bunks installed, even entertainment and canteens provided. Rules and regulations (often unofficial) now governed the behaviour expected in shelters.

In the past month, thousands more had been added to the list of homeless. Many of these people found new homes with relatives or people willing to open their homes to Blitz victims. Others went to Rest Centres. For more than 250,000 people now made homeless in the Blitz, the Rest Centres were supposed to be temporary – a 'resting' place for a few hours before being moved on to be rehoused. However, this was seldom the case and many people spent weeks in Rest Centres, often in school buildings, which were not really designed for long stays.

Overcrowding, inadequate washing or toilet facilities, lack of furniture and a basic and repetitive diet were endured with amazing calmness by many Rest Centre inhabitants. There was still much clearing up to be done before many of the homeless again had homes of their own.

Right top: **In late October, Westminster Council began providing bunks for the basements of private houses in the area.**

Right top inset: **Shelter notice reminds Finsbury residents of their need to register for tickets to their local shelter.**

Right centre: **These lightweight shelter bunks were the brainchild of a racing bicycle designer. They opened to provide three sleeping beds and closed to take up only four inches of space.**

Right bottom: **Issuing shelter tickets.**

NEWS SPECIAL

HELP-MEAT

H·P SAUCE

NG AND EMPIRE

NOVEMBER 1, 1940

ONE PENNY

SHELL

When the Bombs Fell in Leicester-square

A GERMAN bomb dropped in Leicester-square recently. The first pictures of the damage were released yesterday. This one shows the wreckage of a line of taxicabs. Another picture of Leicester-square in BACK PAGE.

Gale and Rain in the Channel

A wild, south-westerly gale howled and whistled through the Straits of Dover last night, driving heavy showers of rain before it. The sea was rough and covered by dense mist.

Two-hour Night Raid is London's Shortest

Daily Mail Raid Reporters

LONDON'S raid last night lasted little more than two hours—the shortest, with the exception of the night when the warning was in force for only some minutes.

Soon after the "Raiders Passed" signal was sounded tubes, buses, and trains were running to normal schedules.

The raiders dropped a few bombs and some incendiaries. They were met by a heavy barrage—and promptly turned home.

Two bombs fell in one district. One was near a surface shelter and some casual...

Coal May Go Up 1d. a Cwt.

Retail coal prices may go up by 1d. per cwt. as the result of an increase of 1s. 9d. per ton in pithead prices authorised last night. The pithead increase operates from to-day, and is made to meet the rising costs incurred.

A further increase of 1s. per ton...

LATEST

LONDON 'ALERT' THIS MORNING

London's first "Alert" to-da was sounded in the early hour of the morning.

MR. CHAMBERLAIN GOING TO U.S.

From Daily Mail Correspondent

New York, Thursday. New York Daily Ne despatch from London says M Chamberlain plans to lea England soon for Californ...

Roosevelt

A Break in the Night Blitz for the Capital

1st November, Friday

German attacks on London were heavier than on the previous few days and nights but not classed as severe, although the capital's casualties were more than 300 – of which 65 were fatal. Heavy attacks were directed at the Midlands, the East Coast and Scotland during the night. The Luftwaffe continued using Messerschmitt Bf109s as fighter-bombers flying at high altitudes to avoid AA and RAF defences.

2nd November, Saturday

Substantial numbers of aircraft – fighters and fighter-bombers – attacked London and the surrounding area during the day; the Home Counties also suffered. Casualties after another day and night of attacks amounted to 100 dead or injured in the London area. Damage was classed as slight, although the raids, as was invariably the case, left some road and rail communications blocked and a serious fire at the well-known department store, Barkers of Kensington.

3rd November, Sunday

This was the first night since 7 September that no bombers attacked London. Extremely bad weather made flying over the south of England impossible, so the capital escaped with only a few bombs dropped in daylight hours.

Further north, Aberdeen was the target of raiders based in Norway and most of the fatalities during the night were in Scotland.

Left: *'A German bomb dropped in Leicester Square recently. The first pictures of the damage were released yesterday. This one shows the wreckage of a line of taxi cabs.' Daily Mail*, 1st November 1940.

The closely cropped newspaper image showed limited street damage and not the actual site of the parachute mine explosion; we now see another part of the jigsaw making up the Leicester Square October bombing – the AA HQ building next to Thurston's, this time looking in a north-westerly direction.

Opposite: *'Bomb Crater With A Staircase – But Explosion Caused Only One Casualty. Although the explosion of the bomb had caused only one casualty – a broken arm – a crater in North London is so large that the men working on a sewer at the bottom have constructed a stone staircase down the side of the hole. This picture shows the staircase in the wall of the bomb crater.'*

Left: *'The old soldiers at Chelsea Hospital experience modern warfare when bombs landed on their home during recent indiscriminate bombing raids on London. The photograph shows Chelsea Pensioners surveying damage to the hospital buildings.'*

Below left: The Pioneer Corps salvaging furniture from a bombed house. They will go on to salvage bricks, timber and steel which can be re-used in the building of air raid shelters.

Below centre: Salvaging of a different kind! A Harrow schoolboy with some of his souvenirs – incendiary bomb fins which the boys swapped and sold among themselves.

Below right: Pensioners from the Royal Hospital at Chelsea washing crockery salvaged from the damaged building.

READY!
Housewives'

BACK FROM BERLIN— 2 VERSIONS

First Day a

BACK from Berlin—to a "well-done" greeting. A Hampden bomber, one of the R.A.F.'s most successful night raiders, makes its way over the British coast at dawn, wheels down to land after a raid on the German capital.

BACK from Berlin—to this. A pilot officer D.F.C. looks over the ruins of his home, bombed while he was "over enemy territory." With him are his father and sister, who were slightly injured. They were the only casualties. The pilot officer—veteran of many flights over Germany—might have been in the house at the time . . . . but he was "held up" on the journey home.

And so the Horse Had a Few...

[With apologies to Damon Runyon.]

MORE '35'

...YOUR OPINION...
Shooting for Looting

POST-BAG ANALYSIS: "Attack Italy; bomb Rome." This is still the principal theme of correspondents, many of whom believe that there are secret influences at work to prevent this action. Prevention of looting is a new problem dealt with to-day.

SIR,—Looting, scrounging, and stealing are one and the same. In war-time people who do this should be shot, especially those who are entrusted with the defence or help of those whose homes have been bombed. It is an action of the enemy and should be treated as such.—**R. F. Pringle**, Teddington.

SIR,—It is pitiful to realise that looters are merely sent to prison with or without hard labour. Why not sentence them to the cat? Only cowardly scoundrels steal the belongings of those who may be beneath the wreckage.—**Horace Bayers**, Aylesbury, Buckinghamshire.

For the Defence

SIR,—Mr. Duffield's article in *The Daily Mail* on looting is very narrow in outlook. Our main job is to win the war, and not to sour the feelings of non-property owners, soldiers, and A.R.P. workers with savage sentences for taking things which the Government and local councils neglect to salvage.

Take the case of the men who recently saved St. Paul's. They stole articles costing 1s. 6d. One day they were hailed as heroes. The next, like Lucifer, they fell, and became followers of Charles Peace.

A great paper like *The Daily Mail* could find a stouter dog to kick than A.R.P. workers, who at least do save lives as well as property.—**R. Wyeth**, Kensington, London, W. 11.

Mr. Wyeth seems to have the wrong idea that soldier, and A.R.P. workers are accused of wholesale looting in stances in these Services are exceptional. There is strong reason to suspect that organised gangs of looters are at work—possibly posing as A.R.P. workers. Even Mr. Wyeth might change his tune if his own possessions were bombed and scrounged.—*Looting Editor.*

4th November, Monday

Any hopes held by Londoners that the previous night's cessation of night-time bombing would last were quickly dashed. After some minor attacks by day, the night raiders returned, concentrating on Scotland in the early evening. Bombing was fairly severe during the early hours of darkness and although the weight of the bombardment later eased, raiding continued until after dawn on Tuesday morning.

5th November, Tuesday

The Luftwaffe was active by day across the south of England while at night London was on Alert from dusk until after dawn on Wednesday 6th. There were no daylight casualties in London. During the night, despite the lengthy Alert in the capital and widespread enemy activity across the country, bombing was not severe, nor were damage or casualties.

Winston Churchill addressed the House of Commons after the second month of the Blitz: 'Fourteen thousand civilians have been killed and 20,000 seriously wounded, nearly four-fifths of them Londoners.' But, he went on: 'None of the services upon which the life of our great city depends – water, fuel, electricity, gas, sewerage – not one has broken down. On the contrary, although there must inevitably be local shortages, all the authorities concerned with these vital functions of a modern community feel that they are on top of their job.' His speech acknowledged that the agony of the Blitz was not London's alone and he included the other major cities of Birmingham, Liverpool and Manchester. His timing was appropriate as November would see the scaling up of Luftwaffe attacks on Britain's key industrial cities.

Below: 'Back from Berlin – to this. A Pilot Officer DFC looks over the ruins of his home, bombed while he was 'over enemy territory'.' Daily Mail, 2nd November 1940.

King and Queen tour Merseyside

Left: King George VI and Queen Elizabeth inspect Liverpool Cathedral during their morale-boosting tour around the city and its environs on 6th November.

Below right: *'Their Majesties the King and Queen today visited Merseyside where they inspected air raid damage and casualties, chatted to the victims, first-aid parties and A.R.P and A.F.S. personnel. The picture shows the Queen sheltering under an umbrella chatting to demolition workers during their tour.'*

Below left: *'Families looked down from terraced flats as the Queen spoke to Mrs. Helen Thomas, of Liverpool, who has lost four of her children in a raid.'*

6th November, Wednesday

Again, minor but extensive attacks across the country during daylight hours were followed by heavier raids in the early hours of darkness, focusing on London and the South East then with sustained lighter bombing until dawn the following day.

7th November, Thursday

By day most of the Luftwaffe's attacks were concentrated on coastal shipping around the Isle of Wight and Thames Estuary with some seaside towns bombed.

Under cover of darkness until around midnight, numerous bombs were dropped on London, causing damage to St Pancras Station and blocking a number of railway lines.

8th November, Friday

More daylight attacks on shipping in the Thames Estuary; these were part of the Nazi strategy to cut off Britain's maritime supply lines – the episode of World War II known as the 'Battle of the Atlantic' in which German U-boats, surface ships and aircraft attempted to sink the convoys bringing essential supplies of food and raw materials from the USA and Britain's colonies. For this campaign the Stuka fighter bomber came back on the scene; German losses on this day were high, indicating the same level of success at sea as the Ju87 previously enjoyed with land-based targets!

Raids at night were widespread throughout the London area and, in a period characterised as comprising mainly nuisance raids, it's sobering to consider London's casualties for the night – 43 killed and 228 injured.

9th November, Saturday

A change in the pattern of attacks from the last two days saw raiders attacking London, as well as making the Luftwaffe presence felt across the country during the day, although none of the raids was severe. Night raids were again fairly light.

10th November, Sunday

No daylight attacks on London and, in the rest of the country, isolated appearances of single aircraft in coastal areas.

In the early evening there was widespread bombing across London that affected railways and hit a number of utilities and factories giving rise to significant casualties. Outside London, Birmingham and Portsmouth were raided though one of the worst incidents was a direct hit on the Star public house in Swanscombe, Kent; here a well-attended darts match was in progress. The death toll was 27.

Above left: *'Why, Sir, it is difficult to settle the proportion of iniquity between them': Dr. Johnson, one leg cut by the bomb splinter, still declaims from his pedestal in the yard of damaged St. Clement Danes Church.*

Below left: *'The Sappers Are On The job. Men of the Royal Engineers working at high pressure on the clearing of air raid debris in London.'*

Shelter Census

NO. 13,901

25 Down—13 Italian

THIRTEEN Italian 'planes and 12 German 'planes were shot down by the R.A.F. yesterday. Two British fighters were lost. Seven of the Italians were destroyed while trying to attack shipping off the Thames Estuary.

'Vengeance Raids' on London Fail

11th November, Monday

Attacks by day resumed with enemy aircraft in some number flying over southern England, but the targets were mostly shipping. Night raids lasted for just a few hours after dark and the skies were clear of raiders at 21.00. This day was noteworthy for the appearance of the Italian Airforce in some numbers, joining the ranks of the Luftwaffe raiders; both Germans and Italians suffered more losses than usual while casualties across the country were very low.

12th November, Tuesday

Very minor German bombing activity took place outside London by day but was followed by a night of regular bombing raids until around dawn the next morning. In the worst incident of the night, a single bomb penetrated Sloane Square tube station where hundreds were sheltering. Collapsing concrete destroyed a train pulling out of the station and of the 79 casualties over 20 died.

By this period of the Blitz everyone in London had adapted to life under continual threat of air attack. So much so that most people were able to get more than four hours' sleep at night, despite the sirens, AA guns booming, aircraft noise and bombs dropping. Some people even claimed to sleep through bombs dropping right outside their sheltering place, wherever that might be. A 'Shelter Census' had taken place in early November and found that on most nights, 4 per cent of London's population was sheltering in the Tube, 9 per cent in public shelters and 27 per cent in domestic, mainly Anderson, shelters. Of the remaining 60 per cent, some would be on duty but many would be sheltering in cupboards, under the stairs or sleeping in ground-floor rooms.

13th November, Wednesday

A day and night of light bombing. During the day, German raiders crossed the Channel in significant numbers but gave more attention to Birmingham, Gloucestershire and Dover than London. Only 25 bombers raided London at night, dropping 28 tons of high explosive (HE), far short of the nightly average of 201 tons of HE and 182 incendiary bombs. Casualties and damage reflected the minor nature of the raids.

Left above: '*London Silhouette. Air raid blaze in the City: the glare of the flames spreads across the scene, silhouetting the varied roofs and domes, with the spire of the famous Bow Bells Church standing out in the centre.*'

Left below: Civilian workmen and soldiers working on a deep crater in Charing Cross Road.

Top: 'The restaurant and the Palm Court of the Carlton Hotel were hit recently by a German bomb. Picture shows some of the damage. It is hoped to open the residential section very soon. Guests have been put up at another hotel.' The famous high-society haunt suffered a direct hit on 14th October: an HE bomb exploded in the library over the restaurant which was occupied by diners who were able to make their escape. The 28-day rule applied to this story and details were finally released a month afterwards.

Left: 'Famous London Terrace Bombed. It can now be revealed that Carlton House Terrace was damaged during one of the night raids on London recently.' One of the capital's most prestigious residential addresses, designed by John Nash with views over St James's Park, it also housed, at numbers 8-9, the residence of Germany's ambassador, the most recent being Herbert von Dirksen, who succeeded Joachim von Ribbentrop when he was recalled to be Foreign Minister of the Third Reich in 1938.

Above: 'Air Raid Damage at Famous Club. Blocks of smashed masonry and a wrecked car outside the Carlton Club after a recent night attack by enemy bombers on the London area.'

Coventry Blitzed

14th November, Thursday

Any daylight attacks on this momentous date pale into insignificance against the actions of the night that was to follow when the Luftwaffe carried out a massive raid on Coventry, revealing their latest campaign of the Blitz – 'Moonlight Sonata' – which aimed to eradicate the production capability of Britain's industrial cities, many of them in the Midlands and North, with a sequence of raids timed with the full moon. The Coventry Blitz marked not only a stepping up of the bombing campaign outside London but also highlighted a number of issues.

First was the development of the tit-for-tat escalation that now characterised the struggle between Britain and Nazi Germany: on 8th November RAF bombers attacked Munich where Hitler was preparing for one of the important dates in the Nazi calendar – in the time-honoured fashion, in a Bierkeller drinking beer and making speeches. Hitler's answer to this gesture by Bomber Command was the storm of devastation visited on Coventry – a medium-sized but important industrial hub and a city contributing much to the British war effort.

Other critical factors in this event were the increasing productivity of secret intelligence achieved by Ultra at Bletchley Park and the scientific research being carried out on Germany's guidance system whose radio beams enabled bombers to arrive over their designated targets and release their bombs. No doubt the musical reference in the operation code name connected the moonlight conditions with the *Knickebein* navigation system which delivered an audio signal to the Luftwaffe bomber crews headsets, indicating that they were on course.

By mid-afternoon the target of the rumoured heavy raid was known to be Coventry: Ultra intelligence gave a code name 'Korn' to the target, which was unknown to military intelligence but the directional beams located intersecting over Coventry gave ominous confirmation. There was little the authorities could do in the time available: the city had been prepared for bombing and in recent times its defences had been tested. As in many other cities, great numbers of the civilian population trekked out from the town before dark to avoid the night raids. But nothing could have prepared the citizens of Coventry for this night.

The full moon rose early in the clear evening skies and the first pathfinder bombers following the directional beams dropped their huge bombs with over 10,000 incendiaries at 19.20, launching an all-night attack that lasted until 06.00 the next day. It was a text-book operation from the initial blasts that blew the roof tiles off and exposed the beams to the fury of the IBs that turned Coventry into a burning beacon visible to the waves of bombers a hundred miles distant. With perfect navigating conditions the carefully phased bombers avoided RAF night fighters and bombed continuously through the night on a conveyor-belt principle.

Left: *'Coventry Raid. Piles of bricks where once there was a street.'*

Below: This was once a busy shopping street in Coventry.

Bottom: Less than 48 hours after the raid on 14th November 1940, the people of Coventry go about their business through the city's smouldering ruins.

THIS IS COVENTRY CATHEDRAL — GAPING WALLS . . . RUBBLE

ONLY the tower and steeple and a shell of the walls now remain . . . this graphic picture tells how Coventry's beautiful 14th-century cathedral was shattered. Incendiary bombs struck. These were tackled—until a shower of other incendiaries came.

Non-aggress

Gre
Enc
Kor

Axis St

It was
Athens (as
Exchange)
has been
Greek troo
communiqu
700 prison
heavy-calib
captured d

From TERE
Daily Mai

GREEK-YUGO

HEAVY
tense
the entire
Koritsa at t
that the Gr
had receive
the offensiv
for this i
base in Sout

Reports rec
that bitter
going on all
tions are co

In Retrea

At the poin
Greek troops
Ivan mounta
objectives th
their grip on

Already m
much of the
the operation
pleted it appe
will be unabl

The enemy

2' WINDOW CARDS

for All in
tten City

ly Mail Special Correspondent

COVENTRY, Friday night.

smitten by as heavy a night of
n London has suffered has shown

ty of good

Through
he well-to-d
hrown ope
ess.

Hundreds
whose homes
been welcom
they had nev

In worki
saw hastily s
of house afte
Room fo
Room for
Will take fo
en."

one who k
doors was
on. People
everything w
ete strange
me to shi
we've got
fterwards

COVENTRY—BRITAIN'S 'ROTTERDAM'

"I FOUND . . . a picture of hideous destruction," writes the Daily Mail Special Correspondent from Coventry. What he saw is told in this vivid picture in the Cathedral precincts. The graceful spire still stands, towering over the rubble heaps. In the littered streets the people pass, stopping for a glance—then carrying on with their tasks. Right: Picture-tribute to the unnamed heroes of Coventry who, like these citizens turned themselves into fire-fighters to save something of their home.

The Bombed Arms City

Continued from Page 1

BERLIN EXPLOSION 'AWED' NAZIS

RAF Raid Went On for Hours

A BOMBER pilot who took part in the great Royal Air Force raid on Berlin on Thursday night and early yesterday morning, told of one mighty explosion.

"A building was the centre of the biggest of several fires blazing when we arrived," he said. "Then came a terrific explosion. The whole structure went sky-high. The explosion lit up the inside of our machine, though we were thousands of feet above."

We Lose Five Trawlers

Shock and Disbelief

A total of 449 German planes dropped 503 tons of HE and 30,000 incendiary bombs on Coventry. Many parachute mines were deployed as well as quantities of the Luftwaffe's largest weapons – five SC1800 and 11 SC1400. Of the 250,000 inhabitants of the city, an estimated 568 were killed and 863 seriously injured. Coventry's heart, including its 600 year old cathedral, was almost totally destroyed by high explosives and raging fires that exhausted the water supply of the AFS defences; the population was left stunned and terrified in the immediate aftermath. Nevertheless, the King's visit on 16th November boosted morale considerably and, despite the privations of their wrecked city, its inhabitants returned to life with renewed determination in their local industry; few people were untouched by personal death or loss.

With a third of Coventry's industry put out of action and the city centre little more than rubble, the Luftwaffe considered their job done and the new word 'Coventration' (Koventrieren) entered the dictionary of the Third Reich. Britain's war leaders were mystified that the Luftwaffe did not complete their destruction of the city – it would have been easy to do with a heavy follow-up raid – but the German military machine moved on to the attempted devastation of other cities later in the month.

Both sides learned from the Coventry experience and in the years to come Nazi Germany would harvest a bitter whirlwind sown by them over the English Midlands in November 1940.

On the Allied front, the Coventry raid had at least two unexpected outcomes: first the USA, attempting to stay neutral, now saw the Nazi threat in a different light and great sympathy for Britain flooded America; secondly the ability of the Luftwaffe to mount such a raid, unopposed in the night sky was the seal on the fate of the Commander-in-Chief of Fighter Command, Hugh Dowding, who was removed from his position in the middle of the month to be replaced by Sholto Douglas who officially took office on 25th November.

Above left: 'The King, with Mr. Herbert Morrison, Minister of Home Security, inspecting the ruins of Coventry Cathedral today, November 16th, after the devastating raid on the midland town.'

Centre left: 'King Inspects Devastation In Coventry After Large-Scale Nazi Raid. The King – accompanied by Mr. Herbert Morrison, the Minister of Home Security – is seen here inspecting the tremendous air raid damage in Coventry after the large-scale Nazi raid on the city.'

Below left: 'They queued for water from a street hydrant, bringing pots, pans, kettles – and smiles that showed this was a minor inconvenience.'

Above: The ruins of
Coventry Cathedral

Left: A hundred and
seventy-two victims from
the raid on Coventry
were buried in a
communal grave.

Moonlight Attack Coda

15th November, Friday

After the relative quiet in London the night before, while Coventry took its pounding, a daylight raid was made on the capital during the afternoon and there was considerable activity over the South East. Despite poor weather the Germans launched a huge night raid on London as a follow-up to Coventry's night of terror. The bombing of the capital was almost as severe as the attack on 15th October but casualties were lower at 142 killed and 430 injured. Over 400 tonnes of HE caused enormous damage across the city: although some aircraft were guided by the *Knickebein* beam system, others 'found' their targets by dead reckoning – cloud cover making results inaccurate, though the massive delayed action SC1800 'Satan' bomb that fell on GPO's Mt Pleasant sorting office was a successful hit that caused the Bomb Disposal Squad a major challenge.

Despite the severity of this latest Moonlight Sonata attack, it did not have the same impact on Londoners as on the people of Coventry – the citizens of the capital were too used to such raids and besides, while the heart had been ripped out of Coventry, London was simply too big for the Luftwaffe to achieve an equivalent effect here, although later in the year it would come close.

While the Luftwaffe were bombing London, 200 RAF bombers were dropping 2,000 fire bombs, in addition to high explosives, on Hamburg in the first of two consecutive night raids in reprisal for the bombing inflicted on Coventry where once again this night a small secondary attack was mounted with little effect.

16th November, Saturday

Daylight activity by the Luftwaffe, hampered by poor flying conditions, was mainly reconnaissance and minelaying. Despite poor weather, German aircraft managed to drop over 100 tons of HE on London through the first part of the night and early morning and although damage in London was not too severe, on the south coast, Southampton received six parachute mines that caused considerable damage and many casualties.

Above left: *'London Church Damaged in Last Night's Air Raid. 500 people sheltering in the crypt escaped injury, although the bomb fell alongside it. The picture shows a general view of the damaged church.'*
The church was St Martin-in-the-Fields overlooking Trafalgar Square and pictures of the damage were not passed for publication until two weeks after the raid damage which took place earlier in the month.

Below left: Bomb damage to the National Gallery from a raid on 15th November.

17th November, Sunday

Intelligence had indicated that Coventry, Birmingham and Wolverhampton were about to be singled out for heavy attacks. This intelligence was part of a blurred picture which interpreted German movements and signals as the planned invasion of Southern England. However, little or no intelligence warning was given on the next target of Operation Moonlight Sonata – the city of Southampton – which suffered heavy raids that began in the early evening and continued through the night until 07.25 next day. Despite poor weather, 159 aircraft dropped 198 tons of HE that included 28 parachute mines and 10,000 incendiaries over Southampton causing little damage to the docks or industrial areas but considerable devastation to residential districts.

Over London, the weather conditions for flying were even poorer but a number of bombs found their targets across the capital – including Battersea Power Station.

18th November, Monday

Thanks to unfavourable weather there was very little daylight activity by the Luftwaffe throughout Britain, and although London was harried from just after dark until about 06.00 the following day, only about five tonnes of HE were dropped, causing little damage and few casualties. In other areas around the country, Liverpool, Southampton, Birmingham and Coventry were subject to light raids.

Left above: *'Fire Follows Raid in London Area. Firemen playing water on wall of a building after last night's raid.'*

Above: Inspecting the damage to the Dress Circle caused when Drury Lane Theatre was bombed.

Left: *'The familiar figure of Mr. Churchill strides on. He was leading the way across a plank bridge during his tour of the coast defences that are 'ready for any eventualities' – due largely to the efforts of the man who bridged the gaps in them and at the age of nearly 66 remains Britain's active leader.'*

Relentless Raids on Birmingham

19th November, Tuesday

Low cloud during the day reduced Luftwaffe daylight activity. At night, Birmingham – Moonlight Sonata code name 'Regenschirm' – was the principal target for the latest massed attack while London suffered relatively minor bombardment. Soon after the Coventry raid, which 80 Wing had tried to jam, the physicist and military intelligence expert RV Jones discovered a fundamental oversight in British surveillance and, although on this night the jamming signal 'Bromide' was working correctly to counter the X-gerat beam, the bombers found many of their targets; the payload of over 400 tonnes of HE and almost 30,000 incendiaries dropped by nearly 400 bombers stood a good chance of success. The heavy bombs used included 48 parachute mines and damage was widespread and severe, made worse by raging fires that directed more incoming bombers to their targets. 450 civilians were reported dead with 540 injured.

Elsewhere around the country widely scattered night raids took place.

20th November, Wednesday

A very similar pattern to that of Tuesday. As weather conditions improved with darkness, Birmingham was again the principal Luftwaffe target, with London in receipt of minor raids throughout the night. Around 116 aircraft attacked Birmingham dropping 130 tonnes of HE and around 10,000 IBs compared with the 48 tonnes of HE and 1,100 incendiary bombs dropped on the capital. Planes arriving at Birmingham were guided by the fires still burning from the night before and aided by clear aiming conditions their bombs caused great damage to residential areas. Failures in navigation led to considerable stray bombing across the Midlands and isolated bombs fell across many parts of the country.

21st November, Thursday

Poor weather inhibited the Luftwaffe by day and during the night the City of London and Westminster were the main targets for minor raids from dusk until dawn. Birmingham was again raided but less severely than on the previous two nights. Southampton, Coventry and Bristol were all bombed.

Following a hunch that Wolverhampton would be next after Birmingham, RV Jones asked for additional AA guns to be moved to the city codenamed 'Einheitspreis'. When the attack failed to materialise, Jones' critics enjoyed his discomfort until around a week later, much to Jones' relief, Luftwaffe POWs were overheard discussing a raid over Wolverhampton that had been cancelled because of the buildup of AA reported by German reconnaissance.

Top: *'Midland Town Bomb Damage. Firemen and rescue squad at work among the debris of houses wrecked by Nazi bombs during the large scale attack on a Midlands town last night.'*

Above right: Firemen and ARP workers clearing debris from a London school building – used as a welfare centre and tuberculosis dispensary – that was bombed and destroyed by fire.

Above left: Salvaging the contents of a home wrecked in a raid on Birmingham.

BLITZ TOWNS KEEPING AT IT

500 'Planes Drop 500 Tons of Bombs on Birmingham—Berlin Claim

By Daily Mail Reporter

DESPITE the big attack made on them during nine hours of Tuesday night the Midland towns were "going to it" at full speed again yesterday. It was the severest raid the Midlands have had, yet the bombed towns are almost "back to normal." The casualties are not heavy for so big an attack.

The fire, rescue, and casualty services did magnificent work. Now all the homeless have been found accommodation and everyone has been fed.

Berlin is trying to magnify the raid which, they claim, was directed at Birmingham "as a reprisal for attacks on Hamburg, Bremen, and Kiel."

The fires and explosions, the Nazis say, were "even more widespread than those in the raid on Coventry."

The German Official News Agency alleged last night that 500 tons of bombs were dropped by 500 'planes on Birmingham, and added:

"The British A.A. fire was strong and continuous, but absolutely unsuccessful."

In fact five German bombers were brought down during the night—at Wolveygate, near Nuneaton; at East Wittering, Sussex; in marshes near Barking, and in the sea off Portland and Yarmouth, Norfolk.

"Coventry was also attacked again," they say.

Yesterday, in daylight, the Germans sent a reconnaissance bomber back to the Midlands to look at the damage. It took a look, was chased

VICTORY ON YOUR PLATE

Food Is Guns

GOOD food will send up Britain's arms production—and help the winter war on infection.

Lord Woolton, Minister of Food, and Professor J. C. Drummond, one of his scientific advisers, said this in London yesterday.

Lord Woolton said:

"If we look after the stomachs of the workers the output will look after itself.

"Don't make canteens dreary places. Make them attractive, give the people music, and decent crockery.

"Make them into places in which people, when they are eating, will not be associating their minds all the time with their work.

"Do them as well as you expect the workers to produce their shells and munitions."

Cold Beaten

Professor Drummond said:

"Food is probably the most vital factor in maintaining the security and efficiency of the Home Front.

"If people were properly nourished cold and unhygienic conditions would be of much less importance.

"If food in canteens and hostels were well-balanced and nutritious, it would have a profound effect on health, resistance to infection, and disease during the winter."

Professor Drummond disclosed that the Ministry of Food was shortly to make available wholemeal flour at the same price as

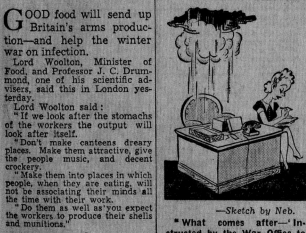

—Sketch by Neb.

"What comes after—'Instructed by the War Office to examine your new hand-grenade'?"

William Whiteley's Widow Dies at 95

Mrs. William Whiteley, widow of William Whiteley, founder of the Bayswater stores bearing his name, died at Worthing yesterday. She was 95.

Mrs. Whiteley was widowed in 1907. Her husband was murdered in his office at the stores by a man who claimed to be his illegitimate

BLITZ TOWN KEEPING AT IT

"Birmingham Bombed"—Berlin Claim

Guns and Victory on Your Plate

GOOD food will send up Britain's arms production—and help the winter war on infection.

Lord Woolton, Minister of Food, and Professor J. C. Drummond, one of his scientific advisers, said this in London yesterday.

Cheer Up

"Don't make canteens dreary places, when they are eating, will not be associating their minds all the time with their work.

"Do them as well as you expect the workers to produce their shells and munitions."

Professor Drummond said:

"Food is probably the most vital factor in maintaining the security and efficiency of the home front.

Cold Beaten

"If people were properly nourished cold and unhygienic conditions would be of much less importance.

"If food in canteens and hostels were well-balanced and nutritious it would have a profound effect on health, resistance to infection and disease during the winter."

Professor Drummond disclosed that the Ministry of Food was shortly to make available wholemeal flour at the same price as white flour.

MRS. RANSOM TO APPEAL

Mrs. Florence Iris Oudis Ransom, aged 35, of Piddington, near Bicester, Oxfordshire, who was convicted at the Old Bailey of the

VITAL 4 HOURS IN MURDER

Daily Mail Correspondent

BOLTON, Wednesday.

A reconstructed police photograph showing 17-years-old Minnie Stott as she looked on the night before she was found strangled in a garage yard of a main street here was issued to-night in the hope of getting more data about the girl's last movements.

The picture shows Miss Stott in the clothes she was wearing when she left her mother at 8 p.m. on Saturday. She was found dead four hours later.

People who may have seen the girl after eight o'clock will probably recognise the photograph. If so, they are asked to get in touch with the police at once.

Detective Inspector Hodgson, head of Bolton C.I.D., told me to-night that the police were still pursuing the new line of inquiry mentioned a day ago.

Widespread search is being made for a green crêpe de Chine scarf

Town Undaunted

In spite of the intensity of the attack—the most severe the Midlands area has experienced and the most widespread

How Miss Minnie Stott was dressed on the night of her death: A photographic reconstruction issued by the police last night.

"REPRISAL FOR HAMBURG"

By Daily Mail Reporter

A FOLLOW-MY-LEADER chain of Nazi raiders attacking continuously throughout the night for nine hours gave the Midlands area the heaviest bombing it has yet experienced. The raid did not end until the early hours of yesterday.

Berlin's version of the raid was that "Birmingham has apparently suffered the same fate as Coventry. Nazi officials said 500 'planes were used and 500 tons of bombs were dropped.

Large numbers of incendiary bombs and many high-explosives, including some of very heavy calibre, were scattered indiscriminately.

Fierce anti-aircraft fire turned many of the raiders away from their targets, and at least one was brought down by anti-aircraft fire.

This bomber crashed at Wolvey Gate, near Nuneaton. Two members of the crew were killed, a sergeant pilot was captured by an air-raid warden, and the fourth German staggered to the main road, held up a night lorry with his torch, and surrendered to the driver.

Houses and shops suffered most of the damage. Many fires were started. One hotel was completely demolished, and another had to be evacuated because of damage.

Fatal casualties are described as not heavy, having regard to the severity of the raid.

These men are part of the new "Go To It" and North-West area who responded to the call workers to take munitions drive. Among are many middle-aged who have been among the years. They come walks of life, and if adaptable it means of a new career, being trained in most of engineering, and schooling will last four weeks. Now

N. Eyland (left) started work in a chemist's shop and became assistant dispenser. Also had a mixed business, but before taking up the training scheme was an insurance agent. He is working a pneumatic drill with James Sandford, a spinner from Oldham, who was unable to find work in the mills.

YOUR OPINION
No Truce

Where Ins

By

ELEVEN weeks attack—the most severe. It is just announced that for nation-wide against air-raid property.

Left: *'The Pioneer Corps at work among the wreckage of a Midland town.'*

Glow from Burning Southampton Visible from France

22nd November, Friday

Again, poor flying conditions during the day kept German activity slight but clearing skies by night brought yet another heavy raid on Birmingham – its third in four consecutive nights of bombardment: 209 aircraft dropped 227 tonnes of HE and 16,000 IBs during 11 gruelling hours. Hundreds of fires were started and AFS reinforcements had to be called in the next morning from Manchester, Bristol and Cardiff. The damage from this attack wrecked the water supply and transport systems as well as destroying many homes. Over 300 died and 500 were seriously injured; large numbers of the population had to be evacuated after the destruction of their homes and the ongoing threat of the many UXBs.

London suffered a secondary attack by night which targeted the City and Government buildings while elsewhere isolated attacks across the country followed the pattern of previous nights.

23rd November, Saturday

During daylight hours three attacks were made on London but were mainly intercepted by Fighter Command though some bombs were dropped. Among the aircraft involved in this attack were some from the Italian Airforce; they proved to be no match for the RAF fighters but continued intermittently to join Luftwaffe attacks in London, East Anglia and the South East.

At night German bombers returned to Southampton in force: soon after 18.15, 120 aircraft dropped 150 tonnes of HE along with 16,000 IBs. The resulting fires which were both intense and widespread could be seen from Cherbourg. Damage to government offices, residential areas and infrastructure was considerable with broken water mains hampering the AFS. Over 70 people died and 130 were seriously injured.

Elsewhere a minor attack took place on London again, damaging the City and Whitehall; scattered bombing raids were widespread across the country.

Left above: **The aftermath of Birmingham's 22nd November, 11-hour raid. As a major manufacturing centre the city was an obvious target. Transport and telephone systems were severely affected but it was damage to the water system which caused the most urgent problem – firefighters had to rely on pumping water from the canals or leave some fires to burn themselves out. Here the struggle continues to extinguish the fire in this factory.**

Left below: **The Pioneer Corps work their way through wreckage in a Midland town.**

Opposite left: *This sign, snapped in Regent Street, emphasises the 'business as usual' attitude. In fact, all three major stores were open as usual.*

Opposite right: **A London taxi almost buried by debris.**

...ike After Chase

SHIPS ...PLED

...has struck another
...as the Italian ships

...o class—latest and most
...by Swordfish aircraft

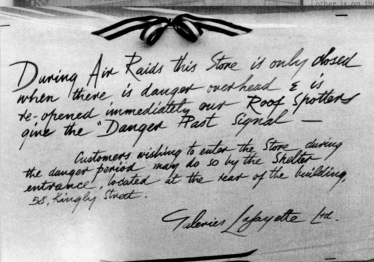

Merseyside Defences Beat Night "Blitz"

FAMOUS N.W. CATHEDRAL HIT

THE people of Merseyside are hoping this morning that for the first time it can be said that a German attempt to wreck a town in a one-night "blitz" had completely failed.

Wave after wave of bombers which came over the area for several hours were scattered by the fiercest A.-A. barrage yet heard in the district.

The first attackers used the now familiar technique—shoals of incendiaries and a few explosives to light the way for the succeeding wreckers.

Some fires were started. But though the following bombers did their best to drop their cargoes in the light of the fires the damage reported this morning was comparatively slight.

One of the largest blocks of luxury flats in Liverpool was hit by a large bomb. A number of people were still trapped after rescue workers had been labouring for some hours.

Fierce Barrage

A large suburban road-house was hit and more people were trapped. There were a number of casualties from house fires.

Bombs fell in a number of Liverpool suburbs and houses were damaged. Some were completely demolished. There were some casualties when a high-explosive bomb burst near a public shelter in a playing field.

Fires which were started in houses and commercial property were quickly extinguished.

But the number of bombs dropped in the district was small

Turn to BACK Page

ONE MAN STOPS BIG STRIKE

Daily Mail Correspondent

SOUTHPORT, Thursday.

A NATION-WIDE strike of half a million engineers, mostly shipyard and arms workers, was averted at the meeting of the National Committee of the A.E.U. here to-day by a vote of 25 to 11—and by the moving plea of one grey-haired delegate.

Several delegates called for strike action to secure a 3d.-an-hour increase. Others wanted a policy of "go slow."

Many speeches were made, some bitter in the extreme. Then Mr. Owen Jenkins, a 48-years-old engineer in the Royal Dockyards at Portsmouth, rose.

He spoke simply but with deep feeling.

"I have two sons in the Forces. One is in the R.A.F. in Greece, perhaps bombing the Italians. The other is on the North Sea...

"BOY WONDER" SHOT DEAD

New York, Thursday.—Jessie L. Livermore, one-time "boy wonder" of Wall-street, who made £2,000,000 from £2 and was afterwards declared bankrupt four times, was found shot dead in a hotel here to-day.—Reuter.

CUDAHY RESIGNS

Washington, Thursday. — Mr. Cudahy, United States Ambassador to Belgium, personally gave his resignation to President Roosevelt to-day. He stated that he intended to devote his time to writing. A few months ago Mr. Cudahy, on a visit to London, made a statement defending King Leopold.—Reuter.

During Air Raids this Store is only closed when there is danger overhead & is re-opened immediately our Roof Spotters give the "Danger Past" signal —

Customers wishing to enter the Store during the danger period may do so by the Shelter entrance, located at the rear of the building, 58, Kingly Street.

Galeries Lafayette Ltd.

Bristol's First Heavy Air Raid

24th November, Sunday

Fog over France by day reduced Luftwaffe activity but as this cleared, along with good weather over Britain at night, a major attack was mounted on Bristol – its first heavy raid of the war – when over 100 aircraft followed a familiar pattern of attack: lighting with a mix of HE and IBs in the first wave, which then created a beacon for the inbound aircraft. Much damage was sustained to the city centre and large numbers of the population had to be temporarily rehoused when bombed out and left without water or functioning drainage. Damage to the main targets – the docks and industrial areas were reported as insignificant but 200 were killed and 163 injured.

Elsewhere, the London area and a number of RAF airfields in the south of England were subjected to minor raids.

25th November, Monday

Fog and drizzle across Western Europe by day and night meant virtually no Luftwaffe activity except for a raid by nine Heinkel IIIs over Avonmouth guided by X-Verfahren, targeting the docks. Damage was light and casualties were few. London had its first bomb-free day and night since the Coventry attack on the 14th.

26th November, Tuesday

Most of France and the Low Countries were under fog and drizzle by day and night, limiting the Luftwaffe to flying missions from their Britanny bases; four He IIIs bombed Avonmouth, missing their targets but causing minor damage. A brief attack on London in the early evening by six Dornier 17s lasted little more than half an hour and caused little damage. No casualties were reported anywhere across the country.

27th November, Wednesday

Insignificant Luftwaffe activity during the day despite clear weather over Britain. By night Plymouth received a major attack with London a secondary target. 107 German aircraft dropped 100 tonnes of HE with 6,000 IBs on Plymouth. resulting in minor damage and few casualties.

The London raid was heavier than for some nights with 57 aircraft dropping some 60 tonnes of HE but there was little damage and suprisingly few casualties.

Above: The Savoy Hotel was bombed early in November. This picture shows the scars to the building after the bomb debris and rubble have been cleared away.

Left: 'The top part of the Savoy Hotel after bombs had fallen. The damage was at the back of the building. A few people were injured.'

28th November, Thursday

Daylight sweeps across the south of England and an isolated attack on shipping at the Isle of Wight gave way to a heavy night raid on Liverpool – the city's most intense of the war to date. As Britain's largest and most important Atlantic port area Merseyside was frequently raided with considerable casualties. On this raid over 320 bombers targeted Liverpool and Birkenhead dropping 356 tonnes of HE and over 30,000 IBs in an attack that started at 19.15 and ended eight hours later. Poor visibility may have impeded the accuracy of visual bombing but with an enormous target of docks and warehouses it's hard to understand why more damage was not done to buildings crucial to the war effort. In fact the damage to Merseyside's civilian life was huge – mostly on residential and commercial buildings, as well as the transport and utilities networks. Casualties were high, largely because of a direct hit by parachute mine on a school in whose basement shelter several hundred people were taking refuge; 164 of them died, bringing the death toll to nearly 300.

The secondary night attack on London was minor; although 21 aircraft made their presence felt, damage and casualties were not significant. Elsewhere the country was beset by bombers who, having failed to find their designated target, dumped their bombs on 'targets of opportunity'.

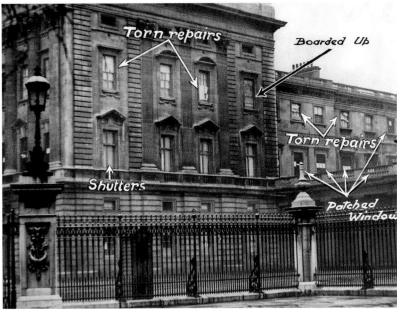

Left above: *'Bomb Damage in Liverpool. A bomb was dropped on a Liverpool junior school recently.'* Reporting like this enforced by the censor caused much distress if read by those who went through the terrors of the bombs: this was Edgehill Technical School, Durning Road and the tragedy of those 164 killed in a direct hit on the building, whose basement was being used as a shelter for hundreds of people, went down as one of the worst events in Merseyside's wartime history. The magnitude of the disaster could not be allowed to give joy to the enemy but the denial of fact hit civilian morale – especially in Liverpool.

Left centre: *'The King's Windows. Buckingham Palace and the smallest home rank equally in the matter of repairs after air raids. This photograph was taken yesterday. Note there has been no priority call for glass to replace broken windows.'* This picture of Buckingham Palace on 23rd November showed that the King and Queen suffered the same frustration as everyone else trying to repair bomb damage – the materials for repair were simply unavailable.

Left below: Business as usual! The sign on the stall reads *'Oranges came through Musso's Lake'*, referring to the Mediterranean Sea over which the Axis Powers of Mussolini's Italy and Hitler's Germany claimed control, having occupied all the countries, except neutral Spain, surrounding it.

New Moon Raid on Southampton

29th November, Friday

During the day the Luftwaffe flew many sorties across southern England with no notable incidents but during the night of the new moon there was an intense attack on the capital involving over 330 aircraft dropping nearly 400 tonnes of HE and 30,000 IBs. Of the nearly 400 casualties, over 130 were fatal.

30th November, Saturday

Fog affected the airfields of RAF Fighter Groups 11 & 12, allowing enemy fighter bombers unchallenged access to central London, where bombs fell on Piccadilly and Westminster.

By night the Luftwaffe bombers turned their attention back to Southampton in a very heavy raid. Although it was still a new moon, the firelighter formations illuminated the city from 18.00 hours using flares, IBs and a range of heavy bombs that included two SC1800 'Satans'; 128 aircraft continued the attack until 00.55. Over 150 tonnes of HE and 20,000 incendiaries fell, creating enormous fires which could not be controlled because of the shortage of water. The areas to suffer most were the city centre where an estimated two thirds of the shopping area was destroyed. The telephone system was put out of action, cutting off the city's communication with the rest of the country. Damage to the Port and the city's factories was insignificant but in the attack 70 were killed and 120 injured.

Left: 'Signing the Visitors' Book at a London shelter!' Throughout the Blitz the civil defence organisations, particularly the ARP, were faced with the enormous task of keeping track of the living, the injured and the dead. Notes also had to be made on damage to buildings which might receive multiple damage in recurring raids. These notes would support claims for compensation and repair. A direct hit on a shelter was the hardest thing for the rescue teams who would try to identify the casualties – sometimes from a single body part.

Above: 'Their Majesties the King and Queen made a visit to inspect some of London's air raid shelters. The Queen is shown here chatting to children in their bunks in a deep shelter in Southwark, South London.'

Worst Raid Yet on Southampton

THOUSANDS NOW HOMELESS

From Daily Mail Correspondent

SOUTHAMPTON, Sunday.

THOUSANDS of people are homeless as a result of the raid here last night—the worst that Southampton has known. For more than seven hours successive waves of raiders carried on the attack.

The fire brigade had to deal with outbreaks in many different parts of the city. By daybreak most of the big fires were out.

The centre of the city this morning is a scene of desolation. Business premises, with few exceptions, were completely flattened. Where they were not shattered by high-explosive bombs only burned-out shells remain.

The destruction of these commercial premises has temporarily thrown hundreds of Southampton people out of work, including large numbers of shop assistants and clerks.

Military units to-day helped the police in dealing with traffic. Ambulances stood by while rescue workers, thick stubble on their chins, worked incessantly—as they had been doing since the first bomb fell.

Mobile canteens served tea and coffee to relays of auxiliary firemen, A.R.P. workers, and soldiers. American Red Cross ambulances helped in the rescue work.

Evacuation Demand

A strong feeling is expressed in Southampton that the women and children should be compulsorily evacuated from the town.

Councillor G. Bennett Bascomb, Chief Labour Supply Officer for the area, told me to-night that all non-producers should be evacuated and that workers, their shifts completed, should be transported out of the area, housed and fed in communal rest places, and brought back the following day.

"It is only by such means that

BACK Page, Column ONE

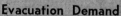

MISS MAY JAMES, aged 50, who has been arrested by the Gestapo in Paris on charges of espionage and the illegal possession of a wireless transmitting apparatus.

When the Germans entered Paris Miss James stayed to care for the 40 British and

LATEST

SOUTHAMPTON AGAIN, SAY NAZIS

Berlin, Monday.—Southampton was again raided last night, according to the German News Agency.

The agency adds: "While one party of German bombers attacked Southampton, another proceeded to London to continue the work of annihilating British public services and supply services."—Reuter.

GREEKS REACH COAST

Budapest, Sunday.

Greek forces in the south Epirus sector have reached the coast north of Corfu, according to a Greek radio report picked up in Budapest.—B.U.P.

5

1st December, Sunday

By day, widespread misty conditions kept Luftwaffe activity limited to sweeps over southern England but with nightfall, bombing raids commenced on Southampton around 18.15 and continued to 22.55. The 123 German planes dropped a deadly mixture of 147 tonnes of HE and over 20,000 IBs, rekindling major fires smouldering from the pounding of the previous night. Although a flour mill and a couple of major factories including Supermarine at Woolston were hit, little damage was done to the docks area but 40 died and the psychological damage to the population that had suffered four devastating heavy raids in a fortnight was significant, despite the ever-optimistic reporting. Patterns of Luftwaffe bombing outside of London were becoming much more damaging to the civilian population and Southampton was reported to be showing cracks in morale.

London received a minor attack between about 19.00 and 23.30; casualties were few and damage was slight.

2nd December, Monday

A sweep by 70 Bf109s took place over the South East during the morning but weather conditions worsened during the day. Night operations were launched against Bristol during the early evening and first part of the night in order to get the German bombers back to base before morning mist and fog obscured their bases in mainland Europe.

Bristol was heavily hit with a payload similar to that on Southampton the previous evening: as well as 120 tonnes of HE, 22,000 incendiaries caused many blazes and 31 deaths. Damage to industry was slight with most destruction being effected on residential property and public buildings. London had another quiet night.

While the active defence of Bristol had little effect on the German raiders, for the first time in the Blitz two new defensive decoys were deployed near the city: 'Starfish' was the codename for diversionary fires created near to Luftwaffe targets. This night the two decoys attracted a reported 66 HE bombs – a good outcome for the new measure.

Above: A bombed-out church in Southampton symbolises the experience of the local population under Luftwaffe bombardment: shocked, burned, part-destroyed, but still standing.

THE KING SEES FOR HIMSELF

Germ
in Pa

14 GERMANS DOWN YESTERDAY

Big Night Raid on Nazi Guns

*From EDWIN TETLOW,
Dover Area, Thursday.*

TO-NIGHT, after a day of air battles around the South-east coast which cost the Germans 14 planes for the loss of two British planes and one pilot, the Nazi big guns opened fire along the French coast.

The enemy appeared to be using batteries dotted along the coast all the way between Boulogne and Dunkirk.

Biggest flashes of all came from one emplacement of several guns near Cap Gris-Nez, which has been consistently sending the heaviest shells to the Dover area.

A quarter of an hour after the first German shells had dropped, the R.A.F. joined in the fight.

R.A.F. Go in

From a cliff top I saw a cluster of enemy searchlights at Calais suddenly stab the sky. A moment later another cluster shot up near Cap Gris-Nez.

Apparently one section of our bombers were concentrating against the biggest gun of all.

SMOKE was still rising from smouldering ruins as the King walked through Southampton yesterday—his latest visit to the bombed provinces. With him are Mr. Herbert Morrison and the Mayor. An Alert sounded as the King drove past docks. A raider was over the district. The King told his chauffeur to drive on.— See BACK Page.

Roosevelt Visits Jamaica Base

From Daily Mail Correspondent

NEW YORK, Thursday.

PRESIDENT ROOSEVELT to-day visited Jamaica and inspected the site of the proposed U.S. base

duction for weeks to come. In ports—Antwerp, Ostend, and ais—were also heavily bombed. ian radio admits severe damage veral Turin factories. Last night e R.A.F. planes attacked the my's ports across the Channel.

Top: '*The King with the Mayor of Southampton – wearing chain of office – and Mr. Herbert Morrison M.P. – wearing trilby hat behind His Majesty – walking down one of the bombed streets in Southampton today, December 5th, when His Majesty paid a visit to the 'blitzed' south coast port.'*

Above: '*This is bombed Southampton: yesterday's Daily Mail picture of gutted buildings in the business centre of the city.'* The picture was taken on 2nd December.

Birmingham Hit Again

3rd December, Tuesday

Poor weather continued by day but during the night London suffered a minor night raid while Birmingham was visited by 55 enemy raiders during the evening, dropping over 50 tonnes of HE and 16,000 IBs. Nine large fires resulted and damage was caused to a number of factories. Observers noted an uncanny three-mile band of flame which was interpreted as following the X-Verfahren beam intersecting Birmingham over a north-south axis. Damage to London was slight but harassing bombs fell on Westminster and the City.

By this period of the Blitz nearly all raids were carried out at night as the Germans had found that British defences were considerably weaker by night. However, the RAF was beginning to be supplied with a new plane, the Beaufighter, which carried improved radar equipment and heavier guns and was intended to be a better counter to night attacks.

4th December, Wednesday

With little change in the weather, Luftwaffe operations were confined mainly to darkness with bombing missions flown to Birmingham, London and Southampton. Although the bombing was heavier on Birmingham and London than the previous night, less damage was done and the raid on Southampton by seven aircraft had little impact.

5th December, Thursday

The Luftwaffe managed to mount two fighter sweeps during the day then from the early evening turned their attention to Portsmouth for the 25th time. 74 aircraft dropped nearly 90 tonnes of HE and 5,000 IBs causing widespread but not catastrophic, damage. 44 people were killed. Damage to London from the attack that focused on the City was relatively light.

Top: *'Mothers and babies had a remarkable escape when bombs hit the maternity ward of a hospital in a London suburb on Saturday night. The nurses' home also suffered, but there were no casualties. The picture shows three nurses, helped by medical students, salvaging twisted cots and babies' gas masks from the maternity ward. Fifty-six expectant mothers and mothers with 38 recently born babies were in the ward when the bombs dropped.'*

Above: *'A convent in the London area used as an air raid shelter was hit – and a number of casualties are feared – during night raids on the London area. This picture shows Sisters of the Convent inspecting the wreckage.'*

One Night of Respite

CITIES START ANEW

MR. Herbert Morrison, Minister of Home Security, went to Southampton last night to see the bomb damage.

He immediately went into conference with the Lord Mayor and city officials. Their talks were still continuing early this morning.

Southampton, Birmingham, and Bristol—Britain's big-raid cities—are working day and night to bring life back to normal.

Mr. Robert Bernays, M.P., deputy regional commissioner, is staying in Southampton until the situation is normal. His chief task is to co-ordinate the work of the civil and military authorities.

Hundreds of people whose homes and businesses were destroyed found that they have been able to salvage much more of their belongings than at first seemed possible.

The work of demolishing unsafe buildings goes on from dawn till dusk. Dynamite helps the work.

Shops which appeared to be completely wrecked now show notices proclaiming "Business as Usual."

In some cases their only counter was a small table standing on the pavement laden with goods salvaged from the disorder inside.

Students Help

Boys from the Department of Navigation at Southampton's University College, half of them Polish students, are helping with demolition work. They are using their own tackle.

Bristol business firms have registered new addresses with the Chamber of Commerce.

A terrific drive is under way to clear up shattered streets and

ONE of the bombed landmarks in the centre of Bristol—the centuries-old Dutch house.

Right above: *'Last Night's Bomb Damage in London Area. Several people were rescued alive after four houses had been demolished by an enemy bomb last night.'*
Houses turned to rubble in Ilford on the night of 5th December.

Right: *'Last Night's Bomb Damage in London Area. Rescue squad salvaging furniture.'*
On site in Ilford: the ladders and stout props used by the rescue teams to secure unstable buildings can be seen sticking out from the back of their truck.

NO. ... th Year   LONDON: WEDNESDAY, DECEMBER 4, 1940   5.21 p.m. to 8.21 a.m.   ONE PENNY

NIGHT ATTACK ON BIRMINGHAM AREA

FOG & MIST CHECK THE ENEMY BOMBERS

100 London People Under Debris of a Convent

NUNS SAVE WOMEN AND CHILDREN

IT was officially revealed in London this afternoon that the raid on a Midlands town last night was in the Birmingham area. Like the attack on London, it was small in comparison with recent nights. There were relays of enemy bombers, but casualties and damage were small. Most of the bomb-loads were merely incendiaries.

Fog, Mist and ... Aerodromes

R.A.F. BOMB THE RHINE RAILWAYS

It was learned in London to-day that a small force of R.A.F. bombers last night bombed railway communications in the Rhineland.

BERLIN BOASTS AGAIN

"More and More Raids on Britain to Come"

"The British say that German fuel supplies will soon be exhausted and large-scale raids on Britain will therefore cease," said a Berlin announcement to-day.

"We must disappoint them. Such raids will continue in increasing numbers."—B.U.P.

At the Bombed Convent

"Fires Were Soon Under Control"

The official communiqué on the night raids, issued early to-day, stated:

LAST night the enemy attacked London and the Midlands, and bombs were also dropped at various scattered points between these areas and the coast.

The attacks were not on a large scale, nor of long duration, and ceased soon after 10 ...

In 6 Years Her Husband Left Her 22 Times

The Belgian Premier, M. Pierlot, watching one of the craftsmen at work.

LONDON HAS A DIAMOND WORKS

£500,000 OUTPUT FOR EXPORT EXPECTED

By a Special Correspondent

WHEN Germany invaded Belgium the diamond merchants of Antwerp and other cities took as much as possible of their stocks and fled in cars, on bicycles and on foot across France for London.

They carried hundreds of thousands of pounds worth of diamonds "in the rough"; diamonds that had neither been cut nor polished.

With the merchants were their expert cutters and polishers.

Site a Secret

To-day the employers and the employees opened in London a new factory—the first war-time factory for Allied refugees.

For many reasons I am asked not to reveal the site of this factory. Undoubtedly the enemy would like to know the whereabouts of this new London industry, which, the experts say, will produce at least £500,000 worth of diamonds for export within the next 12 months.

Wives Hid Gems

The factory has the backing of the British Government and of the British diamond merchants in London.

At its head are such men as Mr. ...

Greeks Press On: Mussolini Calls Up Another 250,000

Greece is keeping the Italians on the run. Latest news is that the Greek armies have now advanced to within a mile of Santa Quaranta, Italy's "invasion" base in Albania.

As the Greeks advance Mussolini looks around for more men to throw into the battle.

It was announced in Rome to-day that the 1922 class, comprising 250,000 youths of 19, has been called to the colours.

The only exemptions to the call-up are priests and men already enrolled in the Fascist militia or police.—B.U.P.

The Greek advance: See BACK PAGE.

R.A.F. BOMBER DOWN

Reported Capture of the Crew in Spain

Reports from Rome, quoted by the Berlin Radio to-day, say that a British bomber made a forced landing in the valley of the Ebro in Spain.

The crew were captured. Maps of Spain, France, and Italy were in the plane, according to the announcer.—B.U.P.

HE'S NOW A D.S.O.

RECTOR: 26 CASES PROVED

HE SAYS, "I SHALL CONSIDER APPEAL"

From Our Own Correspondent
BEDFORD, Wednesday.

THE 57-year-old Rector of Blunham, Bedfordshire, the Rev. William Henry Hopkin, was to-day found guilty of 26 of the remaining 36 charges against him at St. Albans Consistory Court at Bedford.

The findings were announced by the Chancellor (Mr. K. Macmorran) after he and his assessors had been absent nearly two hours.

They found eleven charges of drinking, nine of resorting to taverns and ale-houses, and six of accosting women proved.

The other ten charges were not proved.

Crowded Court

Originally there were 43 charges, but seven were dropped. All the allegations were denied by the Rector.

The court was again crowded with parishioners to-day when Mr. G. O. Slade made the final speech for the prosecution.

Mr. Slade said the importance of Miss Barbara Lloyd's evidence lay in the fact that even the Rector had admitted it sounded true.

[Miss Lloyd said the Rector came up to her in Bromham-road, Bedford, and held her hand until she managed to meet him.]

6th December, Friday

Gale force winds affected the British Isles in the restricted hours of daylight but they didn't prevent yet another heavy attack on Bristol by 67 bombers that exploited clear skies and light AA to drop their bombs on target, despite Starfish decoys being deployed. The city experienced widespread damage to homes and public buildings as well as the utilities and transport network. Numerous other bombers missed their targets, dropping bombs in the nearby countryside. Other isolated bombs were dropped in the Home Counties but none in the London area.

7th December, Saturday

No bombing anywhere in Britain: the Luftwaffe, nervous about the extremely cold weather feared the danger to their aircraft from icing up of the wings and instruments. Under much kinder conditions, German planes had been known to break up in mid-air due to icing. However, RAF Bomber Command did fly missions to Dusseldorf and the Channel Ports; notably on this night, German long-range nightfighters infiltrated the returning RAF raiders, accompanying them across the English coast to choose their moment of attack.

Left above: 'A view of a church in the Birmingham area damaged by bombs during the latest Nazi night 'blitz'.'

Left below: 'Houses were damaged during night raids on the London area when bombs were dropped by German raiders. This picture shows members of a rescue party searching among the debris.'

Above: An evening class in first aid in a London shelter at the beginning of December. The casualty rate during the Blitz had reached a point where the rescue services (often victims themselves) needed all the help they could get. Often people sheltering in basements could be trapped for many hours before rescue would come. First aid knowledge was essential in these life and death situations.

Middle Temple Blasted

8th December, Sunday

The lull in bombing of the previous night was shattered when, in reprisal for the Dusseldorf mission by the RAF the night before, London was raided by 413 aircraft from 18.00 on Sunday until 06.00 the next day. It was the biggest raid on London since 15th October. Around 250 people died and more than 600 were seriously injured in a night that saw damage to the Houses of Parliament, Broadcasting House, the Middle Temple, the docks and a great deal of commercial and private property. The bombload included nearly 400 tonnes of HE and approximately 115,000 IBs. Parachute mines were again in evidence.

9th December, Monday

Atrocious weather with cloud cover, high winds and rain grounded most Luftwaffe aircrews and there were no bombing incidents.

10th December, Tuesday

Continuing poor weather suspended bombing operations by the Luftwaffe.

Right above: **The parachute mine which caused this damage to the Middle Temple Law Library fell on 8th December, but this picture was not passed for publication until 20th December, in keeping with the restricted information on these bombs permitted by the censor.**

Right below: *'A bomb fell in Trafalgar Square. One of the buildings hit was Hampton's Store. This picture shows firemen at work on the damaged building.'*

Below: *'Damage to famous library in last night's raids. The picture shows the salvaging of books from the damaged library.'*

Old Tavern
TOBACCO
1/4½ AN OZ.
THE SIGN OF SMOKING CONTENTMENT
TV25b

The Evening News

LARGEST EVENING NET SALE IN THE WORLD

NO. 18,373   Sixtieth Year   LONDON: MONDAY, DECEMBER 9, 1940   ONE PENNY

TO-NIGHT'S BLACK OUT
5.19 p.m. to 8.26 a.m.

LATE EXTRA

CITY

ALMOST EVERY LONDON BOROUGH BOMBED

"700 Tons of H.E's and 100,000 Fire Bombs" Says Berlin

SEVEN HOSPITALS, HOTELS, CONVENT, AND FOUR CHURCHES HIT

Germans Say "All Our Bases In France, Belgium and Holland Used"

TWO RAIDERS DOWN

Hoping to catch London by surprise after the week-end lull, hundreds of German bombers during the night carried out one of the biggest raids of the war.

They used a large number of heavy calibre bombs, which caused most of the casualties.

THE Germans themselves say that their pla...
aerodro...

Soon...
were dro...
bombs, a...

Very...

Man...
few minu...
were stil...
the more...

S...
gener...

Four...
two hote...
post wer...

"A...

Here...
Security...

During...
aircraft...

BOMB KILLS P.C. FIANCE OF BARONET'S DAUGHTER

A spotter on the roof of a London building during the night phoned "Look out, there's a big one coming down right beside us." As he spoke a bomb hit the side of the building and exploded in the road.

Two policemen were killed and many people were injured.

One of the policemen was P.C. John Charles Vaughan, 23-year-old Welshman, whose engagement to Miss Jean Orr Ewing, a daughter of Brigadier-General Sir Norman Orr Ewing, Bart., D.S.O., of Cardross, Stirling, was announced just over a month ago.

Doors Wrenched Off

P.C. Vaughan met Miss Orr Ewing, who is 22, when he went to inquire about a light showing from a hostel.

The bomb blew out almost every window in the building and doors were wrenched off their hinges. Some people inside were injured by flying glass and debris—most of them only slightly.

Three fires broke out on one floor, presumably started by a short circuit.

At one time they looked so serious that all who could not assist were ordered to leave.

Rooms Flooded

Twisted fragments of the air raider which crashed in Epping Forest.

FIREMEN SAVED
...SANDS

...S ALL
...NING

...espondent
...d he
...ervice
...nt.
...ver
...n n
...everal
...ous—
...who
...said
...gnific
...case
...es in
...y m
...prop

P.C. John Charles Vaughan, who was killed by a bomb in the night.

Mr. Percy Trentham, City Sheriff, was killed in a recent raid. See Talk of the Day.—Page Two.

DUSSELDORF GETS IT AGAIN

R.A.F.'s FIRST BOMBING OF BORDEAUX

THE R.A.F. have battered Dusseldorf, great industrial city in Western Germany, again—for the third time in five nights.

An Air Ministry communique issued this afternoon stated:

Last night R.A.F. bombers renewed their attacks on industrial and military targets in the Dusseldorf area.

Other forces of aircraft bombed the submarine base at Lorient and the shipping and harbour installations at Bordeaux and Brest.

Among other targets attacked were the ports of Flushing, Dunkirk and Gravelines, and several enemy aerodromes.

Two of our aircraft are missing.

Vast Fires Raged

In a raid on Dusseldorf on Saturday night, vast fires that astonished even the R.A.F. pilots were left blazing in the city's blast-furnaces, steel works and railway yards.

Last night's raid on Bordeaux was the first carried out by R.A.F. bombers on the city itself.

Attacks have previously been made on oil refineries at Bec d'Armes, oil storage plant at ...ic, and the aerodrome at ...nac, all of which are within ...miles of Bordeaux.

...MY SCROUNGING
...e Is None To-day Says ...R.A.S.C. Officer

...ere is no scrounging in the ...to-day," said an R.A.S.C. ...giving evidence at Hendon

...NCHMAN EXECUTED
...of Violence Against
...a German"

...ed to death by a German ...al for committing an ...ence against a member

WOMAN "THE REAL BRAINS"

STORY OF RUSE TO TRADE WITH ENEMY

A WOMAN was described by the Solicitor-General (Sir William Jowitt) at the Old Bailey to-day as the "real brains behind transactions which have benefited the Germans while her country was at war."

Charges of trading with the enemy were brought against three company directors, Doreen Grant Gibbons, whose age was not given, Louis Frances Szilagy, aged 66, and Thomas Ogle, aged 55.

They all pleaded not guilty and entered a similar plea to charges brought against a limited company, Metal and Electro-Chemical Products, Ltd., of London.

£84,000 Assets

The charges alleged that the three directors transferred assets worth £84,712, in accordance with an agreement between Metal and Electro Chemical Products, Ltd., of Stockholm, a firm under enemy control, by making a contract with the Stockholm firm to pay £10,350 to A.S.A. Berlin and by transferring into enemy control three other assets worth £12,500.

There were also charges of having commercial dealings for the benefit of the enemy, by trading with the firm of A. F. Tudor, of Stockholm, then under enemy control, in quantities of crepe rubber and antimony valued at more than £6,000.

"Men Just Signed"

Sir William Jowett said that the two men were really in a subservient position. The real brains, the person responsible, was Miss Gibbons.

"If you arrange with a Swedish company to give it assets provided it will pay a debt which you owe to Germany, in that way you are indirectly paying your debt to Germany instead of paying it to the custodian of enemy property," he adds.

"That is the scheme which Miss Gibbons evolved and the two men obediently 'signed on the dotted line' because the line was drawn by her.

"In that way, they have succeeded in doing a great disservice to their country."

ENGAGEMENT RING

Woman Sold It As Old Gold: Dealer Gaoled

Leon Bernstein, 62-year-old bullion buyer, of Hereford-road, Bayswater, called on Mrs. Christian Young, of Hampstead-way, Golders Green, and asked if she had any old gold for sale.

Mrs. Young produced a five-stone diamond and gold engagement ring. Bernstein took it, gave her 10s. deposit and said he would bring the balance from £5 in a few days.

He did not turn up, and at Hendon to-day he was sentenced to six months' hard labour for stealing the ring as a bailee.

...QUADS MUCH BETTER

5 C
B
Five
by bo
night
Elizabe
son—
Mr
daugh
Patri
don.
H.E.
Count
Six
demo
Angli
lieve

JAPA
IDEA

Far left: 'Air Attacks on London Renewed. After a period of comparative quiet London faced another night attack from enemy raiders. Photo shows:- Men of the Pioneer Corps clearing debris from a block of flats damaged during the night raid on the London area.'

Left: Two women were buried for several hours when rubble and earth covered their Anderson Shelter. The rescue squads got them out.

Parliament Hit

11th December, Wednesday

Improved weather brought light daytime activity from Luftwaffe fighter sweeps. The night was more intense with 384 aircraft setting out to bomb targets in Britain; 278 reached Birmingham dropping nearly 300 tonnes of HE and 25,000 IBs in two waves of attack that occupied most of the night. The full moon aided accurate bomb aiming and the city centre was badly damaged along with industrial targets and the rail network; 95 were killed and 235 seriously injured.

In London, Westminster's largest UXB of the war fell this night, landing close to the Serpentine. The 4,000 pound monster took 90 days to recover and make safe; the bomb squad's difficulty was that the bomb kept sinking into the watery ground but finally the engineers prevailed.

In other parts of the country isolated bombing incidents took place. It is interesting that 126 British night fighters were in the air but only two opened fire on enemy raiders.

Left: *'Bomb damage to Cloister Court, House of Parliament, during a recent raid.'*
The Member's Cloakroom, where an HE bomb fell is in the bay behind the guard to the right of the picture.

Below: *'Looking into damaged Cloister Court with a camera. The picture shows where one of the high-explosive bombs fell.' Daily Mail,* 24th December 1940.

House of Commons Has Been Hit By Two Bombs

The top picture sho... the damage in Cloiste... Court, the second pic... ture the Members... Cloakroom.

CLOISTERS AND M.P.s' CLOAKROOM DAMAGED

IT can now be revealed that the House of Commons was damaged in a recent raid.

The House was not sitting at the time and no one was hurt. The Debating Chamber was untouched.

Two bombs—an oil bomb and an H.E.—fell on the Private Bills Office only ten minutes after custodians had completed one of their several nightly patrols.

Cloisters Hit

The ancient Cloisters—built by Dr. John Chambers, physician to Henry VIII in the sixteenth century—were considerably damaged.

Fallen masonry and debris from the Cloister court temporarily closed the entrance to the famous crypt, where a flight of stone stairs collapsed.

The secretaries' room and an old staircase leading from it to the Debating Chamber were destroyed.

The Members' cloakroom adjoining the Cloisters was badly damaged, the stone staircase leading from the Members' Lobby to administrative rooms was destroyed and several stained-glass windows in the outer Lobby were broken by blast.

Near Premier's Room

The roof of the Members' Lobby next to th...

The bomb...
examined...

The bomb...
from the C...
from the P...

One "i...
large piece...
from the ro...
soft groun...

In the d...
for a time...
nearby roo...
ated.

Later a...
the hole a...
was a piece...

The...

This is...
one of th...
named b...
recent...

TURKEY TIME WITH CHICKENS

'COVENTRY' RAID

Flats, Hospitals, Churches, Convent H...

FIRE RING LIGHTS UP THE CAPITAL

By Daily Mail Raid Reporters

LONDON was lit up by the bright glow of raging fires last night as waves of heavy German bombers carried out a long and heavy attack on the capital. Three hospitals, churches, a convent, a big block of flats and many buildings were hit. Berlin claimed this morning that it was the biggest raid on London since September.

The attack grew in ferocity after the earliest London night Alert ever sounded. It ended a quiet spell which had lasted for two days and a night.

The heaviest barrage for more than a fortnight rocked London as the attackers came in at high speed. Some very heavy guns were in action and the whole skyline was constantly lit by gun flashes. Searchlights swept the sky.

The raiders tried Coventry tactics. The first flares were followed by incendiaries and then by high explosives.

Some machines carried out dive-bombing attacks —screaming down for thousands of feet before discharging their bombs. Roof-spotters and wardens heard the growing scream of the diving machines followed by the shriek of the falling bombs.

After bombs had been dropped on another district, people heard several bursts of machine-gun fire, which may have been fired by an R.A.F. night fighter.

One of the damaged hospitals was hit by a high-explosive bomb. It wrecked the massage department, but no one was hurt.

A delayed-action bomb struck the nurses' home of a children's hospital.

20 Explosions

Raided City Mass of Flame

4,000 Fire Bombs On One Target

FIRES that astonished even the R.A.F. were left raging in Dusseldorf, Germany's great industrial centre, after it had been raided on Saturday for the second time in four nights.

One pilot said "largest fire ever" was blazing when he left.

Blast furnaces, steelworks, gasworks, railway yards, and Dusseldorf's inland port were attacked.

'CAVELL' CHARGE

FIRST picture, radioed from New York last night, of Mrs. Elizabeth Deegan, the American woman held by the Nazis in Paris. Mrs. Deegan, 35-years-old clerk of the United States Embassy, was arrested by the usual Gestapo tactics is understood to be accused of helping British officers to escape — Nurse Cavell's "crime." The United States authorities are taking "energetic measures" to get her released.

Athen... Goes N... with J...

Britons Ch...

From CHRONIS PROT... Daily Mail Corres...

ATHENS, S... A THENS we... with joy... when the occup... Argyrokastro, ma... base in southern... was officially ann...

Church bells ran... thronged the moon... They carried Bri... jackets shoulder-hi... and British soldier... arm-in-arm.

Searchlights playe... balcony of the Hellen... George of the Hellen... with British Navy, ... Air Force officers... ledge the cheers of th... We want the... chanted, "We want...

2 Generals Ki...

And, while Athen... the Italian people, ... rapped by constant ... and bewildered by ... signations of Army... leaders, received a new...

Two Italian genera... general of the Air ... learned, were killed du... when a military... members of the Italia... Commission to Fra... during a flight from Ro...

The dead Air For... General Albo Pellegrin... nation was delivere... Pietro Pinto.

Their plane crashed... in the province of Pie... cause "has not yet ...ished."

CYCLES

Left top: *'Bomb damage done in a recent raid on London to 145 Piccadilly, the famous home of the King and Queen when they were Duke and Duchess of York.'*

Left centre: New Bridge Street – a rescue party at work after raids on the night of 8th December.

Left bottom: Bicycles in Grose's sports shop on New Bridge Street after a bomb had fallen.

Left: Sheffield's centre in ruins.

Below: Sheffield United's Bramall Lane stand wrecked.

Bottom: After the raid on the night of 12th December, virtually every tram car in Sheffield was left with some degree of damage – 31 were totally destroyed.

Opposite: Troops assist in clearing the debris in Sheffield after Thursday night's major raid.

Moonlight Sonata Continues on Sheffield

12th December, Thursday

Little daytime activity by the Luftwaffe, doubtless in preparation for another heavy night during the period of the full moon. The Moonlight Sonata code of 'Crucible' was given to Sheffield and by late afternoon Fighter Command had received intelligence that the iron and steel producing hub of Britain, hitherto left alone, would be the target that night.

The Sheffield raid was intended to be another Coventry and could have been more successful had not intelligence and countermeasures improved. Of the 406 bombers sent out only 336 claimed to have arrived on target. The others dropped their bombs indiscriminately in isolated incidents.

Amongst the 355 tonnes of HE, 18 He111s released 36 of the largest 1,000 kg parachute mines. The city suffered many fires from the 16,000 IBs devastating the centre and industrial areas. Sheffield's tram system was made inoperable with every tram damaged or destroyed. In the worst casualty incident of the night, over 70 people sheltering in the basement of the city centre's Marples Hotel were buried when the building collapsed on them; astonishingly, seven survived, released from the rubble at 14.00 the next day. Despite the heavy damage, the Germans were unable to destroy Sheffield's industrial capacity, even after another 'Doppelganger' raid three nights later.

13th December, Friday

Daylight activity by the Luftwaffe was restricted to minelaying and there were no bombing raids during the night.

NIGHT ATTACK ON SHEFFIELD AREA

MINOR ATTACK ON LONDON

CHILD KILLED WHEN FAMILY ARE BURIED

IT is officially stated to-day that bombs fell in the Sheffield area last night during widespread enemy activity over Britain.

Although there is at present no official confirmation, it is believed that two, and possibly three, German bombers taking part in the attack on the Sheffield area were destroyed.

Baled Out

There are also reports that Germans were seen to bale out, but again there is no official information of these airmen having been taken prisoners.

Children Can Still Be Re-Evacuated Free

MANY London children who were evacuated early in the war and then returned to London before intensive air raids began have now been re-evacuated.

Parents who have wanted to send children back to the same place they stayed in before have found that to do so they must pay the fares.

Under the Government scheme children must go to any reception area where billets are available.

They Go Quickly

Any child who has been evacuated and has returned can be sent out again free in this way within two or three days of registration.

Parents are now being asked to give a written undertaking not to bring their children back from the reception areas until the whole school party returns.

SMILING THROUGH .. *By LEE*

[No. 1,960]   KNITTING FRONT

Parachute Mine Terror in Chatham

14th December, Saturday

Fog and wintry conditions limited Luftwaffe operations, giving Britain a second quiet night with the most notable incident being in the early evening when a pair of parachute mines fell in close proximity around 18.30 killing 15 and injuring 123 in Chatham's worst casualty incident of the War. The Heinkel He111 could carry two of the largest parachute mines and when released together they would cause a huge zone of devastation. Later in the early hours of Sunday two raiders penetrated London's IAZ but dropped no bombs.

15th December, Sunday

Minimal daytime activity by the Luftwaffe – again the result of bad weather. From 19.00 for nearly three hours, 94 bombers released 80 tonnes of HE and almost 22,000 IBs on Sheffield causing a number of large conflagrations as smaller fires connected. Although in some respects this attack on Sheffield was less severe than Friday's, damage and casualties were considerable and the combined attacks left 750 killed or missing and 500 seriously injured. More than 6,000 were made homeless and 1,200 business premises were damaged. However the city recovered with determination, its civil defences working well and industry returning to increased output of war material relatively quickly.

Elsewhere in Britain, separate bombing missions targeted Bristol, Southampton, Dover and Plymouth while isolated bombs were widespread over the country and the capital.

AT ETON : Demolishing an unsafe chimney stack after the bombing of Saville House recently.

Top: Eton College boys removing their belongings from buildings damaged when the school was hit by stray bombs.

Above: Eton College suffered two bombings in December, the first involved over 200 incendiaries; the second, two HE bombs: one of them, delayed action, caused considerable damage to the Upper School buildings designed by Christopher Wren and destroyed most of the stained glass in the famous chapel.

Left: 'Famous City Church Bombed. The Church of St.-Mary-le-Bow, famous for its 'Bow Bells', has been bombed in recent raids. The famous bells are still in being. The pulpit was not damaged, although the sound apparatus was smashed.'

SIR O. LODGE ON DEATH MESSAGE

CHILDREN WARNED OF BOGUS CLAIMS

REFERENCE to the secret message he left in a sealed envelope deposited with the Society of Psychic Research was made by Sir Oliver Lodge, scientist and spiritualist, in his will, published to-day.

Sir Oliver, who died at his home near Salisbury on August 22, aged 87, left £27,899 (net personalty £27,730).

Sir Oliver Lodge

In his will, he said :

"I advise all my children to be cautious about accepting bogus messages as authentic but to be receptive of such genuine communications as have identifying points in them, and to consult with the Society of Psychic Research about the treatment of my posthumous package deposited by me in their custody in May, 1930, the contents

Etonians clearing out belongings from bombed buildings.

LOST FOR SEVEN
WEEKS—IN A CRYPT

Man Found Wife Because Traffic Light Was Red

Mrs. Jane Lummes is the wife of a City van-driver. They have six children. They live in Welham-road.

BOMBS ON THE PLAYING FIELDS OF ETON

WEMBLEY CUP FINAL PITCH HIT, TOO

HARROW'S 200 FIRE BOMBS IN NIGHT

IT was revealed to-day that among recent targets for German bombs were

Eton College and the Cup Final pitch at Wembley Stadium.

It was also disclosed that at Harrow School, already known to have been raided, more than 200 fire bombs fell in one night.

At Eton, fire bombs started a number of fires, but a time-bomb which exploded later caused the real damage—to parts of the College dating back to the 15th century.

One of the oldest buildings, Upper School, built by Sir Christopher Wren, was seriously damaged. So was the school memorial to 1,157 old boys who fell in the last war.

No One Hurt

Much of the valuable stained

Top: The King during his visit to a bombed area of Buckingham. The King and Queen tirelessly visited the ravaged cities of Britain. The royal train would often lay up on a siding in what was hoped to be a safe location for the night. Regular appearances at some sidings meant that local people knew when the Royal pair were in the area and would get as near the train as possible, sometimes to receive a royal wave.

Above: 'During the King's visit to Bristol. on Monday he met hospital staff who continued to do such heroic work during the raids.'

Right: 'Standing on the heap of blackened ruins that was her Bristol home are Mrs. Beatrice Herbert and the King. Mrs. Herbert, 29, held her young baby as she told the King how they escaped when the bomb struck. 'I have been lucky,' she said.'

16th December, Monday

Continuing poor weather conditions resulted again in light harassing attacks on London, Birmingham and Manchester by the Luftwaffe, with some nightfighter raids in Eastern Counties. However, the weather did not stop the RAF mounting a major attack on Mannheim in Germany.

The War Cabinet had been reticent to sanction the same sort of raid as Germany had directed against London, Coventry, Southampton, Bristol and other British cities – namely an attempt to destroy a whole area regardless of whether it contained military or war production targets. In response to the recent heavy attacks on British civilian targets Bomber Command despatched 134 RAF bombers to Mannheim on this night but lacking the navigation aids enjoyed by the Luftwaffe, their bombs were scattered to little effect.

17th and 18th December, Tuesday, Wednesday

Very bad weather grounded all fighters and bombers.

19th December, Thursday

Slightly improved weather conditions brought another minor attack to London, aimed again at government offices and the City. Outside the capital there were isolated raids confined to the South East of England.

LT. MELVILLE SMITH
is on Page 2

P

TUESDAY, DECEMBER 17, 1940

Editorial

320,000 FED NIGHTLY IN LONDON SHELTERS

BRITAIN ASKS
U.S.A. FOR
DOLLAR HELP

NO details are yet available in Washington of the British request, through Sir Frederick Phillips, the British Treasury envoy, for financial help from America.

A statement issued by the British Press Service in New York said "British official circles, when asked for their reaction to reports received in London from Washington stating that a 'formal application for financial assistance has been made to the United States and that this assis-

HE WAS BORN AT
BRIGHTON

NOW HE MAY BE U.S.A.
ENVOY TO LONDON

WASHINGTON, Tuesday.

Mr. Norman Armour, one of America's leading diplomats, who was born in England, may be Mr. Joseph Kennedy's successor at the embassy in London, it is reported. His name is believed to have

MORE FOOD
CENTRES

LONDON REGION HAS
150 ALREADY

LORD WOOLTON, the Food Minister, said to-day that it was part of the war effort of any town to arrange community centres for the feeding of people bombed out of their homes.

"I sent round to the Mayors and Corporations before the blitz started on the provinces, asking

Preparing Christmas Treats for Children

Merseyside's Christmas Blitz

20th December, Friday

Despite improved weather conditions, German planes were few over Britain in the short hours of daylight. When night fell, a series of raids on Merseyside inaugurated three nights known locally as the Christmas Raids when 365 died in intensive bombing attacks. This night German bombers were active over Liverpool and Birkenhead for eight and a half hours from 18.30, dropping over 200 tonnes of HE and nearly 30,000 IBs. With a clear view of the city quickly illuminated by an inferno in the centre, subsequent bomb aimers hit their targets until they were obscured by a massive plume of smoke over the city. Considerable damage was inflicted on the city centres, docks and warehouses of Liverpool and Birkenhead. In one of the worst incidents of the night, in Bentinck Street, a bomb hit the railway viaduct whose arches were 'sheltering' around 100 people – resulting in 42 deaths. London had a quiet night but German aircraft roamed widely during the night making seemingly random attacks.

21st December, Saturday

Clear skies by day increased Luftwaffe activity over England. Following the Doppelganger strategy the Luftwaffe returned to Liverpool in force with almost 300 aircraft. In addition to 280 tonnes of HE, over 30,000 IBs were scattered across Merseyside, re-igniting disastrous fires across the cities on either side of the Mersey. German bomber crews compared the damage inflicted on Merseyside with the success of Coventry. Although Liverpool was the principal target, London received special attention from two Heinkels, one of which dropped the first recorded SC2,500, the Luftwaffe's heaviest HE bomb of the Blitz, nicknamed 'Max', causing considerable damage to Victoria Station and its vicinity.

Opposite: **Liverpool and the Birkenhead area suffered two nights of heavy attack on 20th and 21st December 1940. This picture was taken after demolition squads had worked to make the shattered ruins stable.**

Left above: **Damage to Big Ben.**

Left centre: **Cleaning away bomb debris at Savoy Hill.**

Far left below: **A Christmas concert given by ENSA in a public shelter decorated for the occasion.**

Left: **A burning school fired by incendiary bombs in a raid just before Christmas.**

RUM

is the most "POPULAR ISSUE" this Winter

Civilians appreciate it as much as the A.R.P. and the Fighting Forces.

RUM WARMS YOU AND KEEPS YOU WARM

Height of
the Raid in
Manchester

SLAVS I

Christmas R

THESE Daily Mail pictures tell the story of Manchester's heavy raid—the first large-scale bombing of the city. The shot above was taken from the roof of the Daily Mail office while bombs were falling and fire swept the centre of the city. You can see the glare in the background and flames shooting up on the right. Manchester's fire-watching plans were criticised by the North-West Civil Defence Commissioner.—See Page THREE.

Young
Men for
the H.G.

—AS OFFICERS

By LT.-COL. T. A. LOWE,
D.S.O., M.C.,
Daily Mail Services Correspondent

AT first sight the names of the 11 highly distinguished officers who will be responsible for the granting of commissions in the Home Guard might indicate a barrage through which not even the most ambitious prospective subaltern might creep.

The list, when seen together, seems as formidable as the Army Council—but such is not the case.

There will be as many different boards as there are names. The claims of men will be examined locally and pinned down to their work rather than their influence.

I understand the first names to

DAYLIGHT, and fires were still burning. Hosing the flames while smoke poured from a building gutted during the night. Manchester's firemen were on duty throughout the raid as wave after wave of bombers swept over. Rescue squads were still at work yesterday.

Manchester Hit by Doppelganger Raids

22nd December, Sunday

A day of light activity by the Luftwaffe gave way to the first major attack on Manchester in the first of two consecutive nights – following the by-now familiar doppelganger strategy. This night, in two main waves of attack, 370 aircraft dropped around 300 tonnes of HE and almost 40,000 IBs resulting in 400 fires. Water was plentiful for the fire-fighters but there was simply not enough of them since many of their number were on loan to Liverpool. German pathfinder aircraft had navigational beams to guide them but the still-burning fires of Merseyside made Manchester unmissable. Damage to the city centre was considerable and fires raged in the docks and industrial areas.

London had another quiet night, enjoying a respite which would prove short-lived.

23rd December, Monday

After another quiet daylight period Fighter Command successfully predicted another major follow-up attack on Manchester and on this date 171 aircraft homed in on the city centre to drop a lighter load of bombs than on the previous night but enough to cause significant damage: It is hard to imagine the impact of 18 Heinkel He111s each releasing two of the largest parachute mines over the city centre and the repercussions and shock waves of the ensuing massive explosions.

The death toll from these two nights amounted to 376 and an even greater number were seriously wounded. As well as the many commercial and industrial properties affected, an estimated 15,000 were made homeless in the Greater Manchester area.

Elsewhere the City of London and the capital's government offices were targeted. Further south, the second 'Max' of the Blitz was dropped by a single aircraft attacking Portsmouth, causing an enormous flash and deafening detonation that made a huge crater and broke windows up to a mile away.

24th December, Tuesday

Christmas Eve and the beginning of an unofficial truce in the Luftwaffe's aerial bombing campaign.

Opposite: *'Manchester Blitz. Scene of wreckage. Shop Window cheer.'* The caption writer's irony delivers an understated invective.

Left above: This photograph, which shows the same scene as opposite page of destruction in Manchester centre, is taken from a slightly different angle and before the demolition squads have knocked down the still-smouldering shop building.

Left centre: In Cannon Street workers walk to work past burnt-out buildings and fire tenders.

Left: With a second wartime Christmas approaching, food rationing and shortages were becoming severe – although this picture of poultry on display in the City might suggest otherwise, but turkeys were 'off the ration'.

Christmas Peace

25th December, Wednesday

Christmas Day and no German bombs fell anywhere in Britain. It was the second Christmas Day of the war and families sat down to whatever meat or poultry they could manage to find and afford, and to vegetables they had probably grown themselves; followed by a Christmas pudding made with precious eggs and fruit or substitute dried egg and grated carrot, parsnip or mashed potato. People exchanged Christmas presents: home-made from recycled materials or treasured items of food such as a banana, an orange or a bar of chocolate. There were a few, limited supplies of children's toys and games since not all factories had yet turned to war production.

26th December, Thursday

Another day of calm in the unofficial Christmas truce, which the RAF brought to an end when it bombed Luftwaffe bases in France.

27th December, Friday

The Luftwaffe gave its answer the following night in a major attack on London, bringing the Christmas peace to a very destructive end as more than 100 German bombers unloaded over 100 tonnes of HE and 11,000 IBs on the capital. As on previous occasions when heavy damage was caused in the bombing of British cities, the He111s of I/KG28 which carried the dread heavy parachute mines took part in this raid that badly affected transport. A single hit on a Southwark shelter caused 50 casualties with a night's toll of 141 killed and 455 seriously injured.

During the evening, outside London, one of the least effective defensive countermeasures were deployed: the untethered balloon barrage called Pegasus was released into the air with an explosive device attached to each free-flying balloon, ready to tangle with enemy aircraft and explode on contact. Unfortunately, the failsafe devices on many of the balloons failed when they landed, leading to ARP reports of explosions across the South East.

28th December, Saturday

After a quiet day, a small but elite Luftwaffe force raided Plymouth with a high concentration of IBs. The attack lasted around 50 minutes and the widespread fires were all under control by midnight. Casualties were not heavy and little damage was done to military or naval establishments though shops and houses suffered. Ominously, London was left alone.

The 29th December would be one of the worst nights of the Blitz for London's churches: these pictures illustrate a few of the finest of London's historic churches which were ruined in that dreadful raid.

Left top: St Bride's Church, looking toward the belfry.

Left centre: St Lawrence Jewry

Left bottom: *'Last Night's Fire Raid on London. The gutted interior of the Church of St. Andrew-by-the-Wardrobe, Queen Victoria Street.'*

Above: 'The War's Greatest Picture' – St Paul's stands unharmed in the midst of the burning City.

Far left: Fire-fighters battle to prevent the spread of the fire beneath St Paul's.

Left: Filling petrol cans for the water pumps.

London's Second Great Fire

29th December, Sunday

For Londoners this night would be one of the most dramatic of the War when a major attack ignited the 'Second Great Fire of London' and challenged the capital's fire service to an unfair battle that would see 16 of its men die with 250 requiring hospital treatment.

In a relatively brief attack between 18.00–21.30, 136 Luftwaffe bombers navigated to a point over the City to drop 127 tonnes of HE and more than 10,000 incendiary bombs. This was not the heaviest bombardment directed on London but the fires that erupted rapidly threatened to turn the City into one huge conflagration thanks to an unfortunate set of coincidences.

Sunday nights were regularly the occasion of major air raids because Civil Defences were deemed to be at a more relaxed and less alert level. More to the point, the commercial premises targeted for raiding were empty of people and in the case of this night, their doors were securely locked, thereby denying access to the few fire-watchers on duty in the City. In other words the vital early action by fire-watchers in dousing IBs was absent. In the case of Paternoster Row, a repository for around six million books, this would prove fatal and like many of the City's historic areas by morning it was a shell and would disappear forever.

In addition, the Thames this night was experiencing a neap tide so the river was particularly low, making it extremely difficult to access water for the 2,300 pumps operated by 9,000 fire-fighters, assisted by countless soldiers and civilians who, nonetheless, fought until dawn in their attempt to get the blazing City under control.

If these unusual factors were not enough, the gentle southwesterly wind of the early evening built up to gale force, no doubt encouraged by the updraft from the flames. The result was a furnace-like firestorm.

Terrible damage was inflicted on the City and casualties were high: as well as the many offices, warehouses and commercial buildings destroyed, the fifteenth-century Guildhall was gutted, eight Wren churches were destroyed and with more practical consequences, the Central Telegraph Office was destroyed and the Wood Street telephone exchange was burnt out – a serious disaster when most defence communication was by telephone.

The greatest miracle of this hellish night was captured by *Daily Mail* photographer Herbert Mason who surveyed the bombardment from the roof of the newspaper's building. As the smoke of the many fires engulfed the city he captured the moment when the smoke swirled away to show the undamaged dome of St Paul's Cathedral lit up by the blaze. This photograph would become the iconic memento of the London Blitz and a great symbol of hope and deliverance for the nation.

Top: *'Last Night's 'Blitz' on London. London had one of its heaviest raids last night and a number of fires were caused. The picture shows workers outside their 'blitzed' premises in London. Only a skeleton of the building remains.'*

Above: Workers walk to work past burnt out buildings in the heart of the City.

Opposite: St Paul's Cathedral: the north side viewed from Stationer's' Hall looking east. The picture dates from after 29th but shows the devastation surrounding the iconic cathedral and reveals its extraordinary survival.

The Evening News

LARGEST EVENING NET SALE IN THE WORLD

NO. 18,390   P   SIXTIETH YEAR   LONDON: MONDAY, DECEMBER 30, 1940

TO-NIGHT'S BLACK OUT
5.27 p.m. to 8.38 a.m.

ONE PENNY

LATE EXTRA

Old Tavern TOBACCO 1/4½ AN OZ
THE SIGN OF SMOKING CONTENTMENT

GIGANTIC GERMAN ATTEMPT TO SET THE CITY OF LONDON ABLAZE

Guildhall in Flames: St. Bride's a Blackened Ruin: Old Bailey Damaged: St. Paul's Saved Just in Time

SEVEN FAMOUS CITY CHURCHES DAMAGED

Flaming Buildings Had To Be Dynamited

Guildhall Treasures Had Been Removed

R.A.F. ATTACK RAIDERS

FIRES DAMAGED THESE FAMOUS BUILDINGS

R.A.F. BOMB NAPLES AGAIN

Rome Says:—

RAIDS OVER GERMANY AND THE PORTS

Naples was bombed by the R.A.F. last night, according to to-day's official Italian communique.

Two waves of aircraft are said to have dropped bombs and leaflets. Buildings were damaged and a number of

CITY CA~ DA~

H.E. bomb ton Club r and did co~ club and e~ Some o~ glass windo~ Mary Wool~ Heavy ~ damaged.

GERMAN ATTACKS ~

German ~ campaign to ~ velt not to ~ Britain—r~ dent of Swe~ ten to-day~

TWO R~ M~

Later ~ munique ~ R.A.F. ra~ aircraft ~

127

Shocked Nation
Braces for New Year

30th December, Monday

As City workers turned up to their offices on the Monday they were met by astonishing scenes of devastation and among them the exhausted fire-fighters still battling to dampen down the smouldering fires. Fortunately bad weather suspended German bombing operations all day and during the night.

31st December, Tuesday

Continuing severe weather again suspended all German attacks. However there was little time for New Year celebrations for Civil Defence workers in the City who bent their backs to the major task of clearing up the ruins and rubble.

In an evening broadcast to the nation, Home Secretary Herbert Morrison answered one of the questions on the minds of the people – how could the country survive such fearsome attacks – when he announced new legislation, with compulsory fire-watching as well as volunteer groups. At this point the civil defence fire-fighters were called the Auxiliary Fire Service and it was formed of volunteers.

Above left: **Coventry**, pictured at the end of the year in which most of the city centre's buildings were destroyed. The spire of the Cathedral Church of St Michael still rises above the wrecked streets and the scattered remains of buildings. Perhaps Coventry was not the worst in terms of the volume of destruction but it certainly came near top of the league in terms of scale, relative to the city's size. And in a year where such scenes of destruction had become commonplace, what is extraordinary is not the panorama of devastation but the purposeful, seemingly normal behaviour of the populace. Coventry, like St Paul's, symbolised the unconquerable spirit of the nation.

Left: A Salvation Army girl giving a welcoming cup of tea to the fire-fighters.

Far left: *'Blitz Returns After Nearly 80 Hours Quiet. The German airmen, after nearly 80 hours of silence, returned last night with new tactics. Their fierce concentrated attack, lasting in the region of four hours, was as heavy as many of their all night raids. As usual, a hospital and working class houses were their objectives. This picture shows the inside of a shelter with Christmas decorations still hanging, showing the slight damage.'*

Hitler Planned Monday Swoop

London was to Blaze First

By NOEL MONKS,
Daily Mail Air Correspondent

HITLER meant to start the second Great Fire of London as the prelude to an invasion.

This was the belief held in well-informed quarters in London yesterday.

The Nazis planned to set big fires burning all over London before midnight.

Relays of bombers laden with H.E. would then have carried out the most destructive raid of the war. The New Year invasion was to have followed.

The R.A.F. have given more attention to the invasion ports this past week than for two months or more. Clearly there are sound reasons for supposing that Hitler is still going ahead with invasion plans.

Yet during last night no raid was reported from any part of the country.

THE FACTS

Here are the real facts of Sunday night's fire-raising raid, as told to me yesterday :

It was one of the biggest night attacks on Britain since September.

No R.A.F. night fighters were operating over the London area, though some were doing so between London and the coast.

Soon after 10 p.m. the German Air Command sent out instructions for all the bombers then engaged to return to their bases, as the weather had taken a turn for the worse and fog was blotting out their aerodromes.

It was the weather, then, and not our night fighters, that saved London from an even worse attack. The view is held that the assault was intended to be the fiercest of the war.

Up to 1,000 bombers were to have been used during the night.

One explanation given for the sudden silence of London's inner A.A. barrage is that in the light of the fire by which most of London was lit up, to continue firing would have disclosed the positions of the guns.

Some of the German fighter-bombers came down to a lower height over London than ever before. They were able to do this because

(i) The guns had stopped firing, and
(ii) Flames lit up the barrage balloons, and the raiders could fly between them.

It is estimated that more than 10,000 incendiary bombs were dropped on the capital within three hours.

Because of bad weather across the Channel most of the R.A.F.'s operations on Sunday night had to be cancelled.

Churchill Sees London's Ruins

MR WINSTON CHURCHILL, accompanied by his wife, visited the ruins of London's famous Guildhall yesterday and spent two hours walking through the City.

As they walked along people cheered. One man shouted : "God bless you, sir." Mr. Churchill smiled and lifted his hat.

They inspected a deep, underground shelter. To shouts of "Good luck" from the crowd Mr. Churchill replied : "Good luck to you."

As they left this shelter a woman ran forward and asked : "When will the war be over?"

Mr. Churchill paused, turned to the woman, and said : "When we've beat 'em."

Mr. Churchill looked grim and

WAR'S GREATEST PICTURE: St. Paul's Stands Unharmed in the Midst of the Burning City

ROAR of gun barrage mingled with roar and crackle of flames ; raiders droned overhead. Daily Mail cameraman H. A. Mason stood on a City roof to get this awe-inspiring picture of the second Great Fire of London—St. Paul's Cathedral ringed with flame. "I focussed at intervals as the great dome loomed up through the smoke," he said. "Glare of many fires and sweeping clouds of smoke kept hiding the shape. Then a wind sprang up. Suddenly the shining cross, dome, and towers stood out like a symbol in the inferno. The scene was unbelievable. In that moment or two I released my shutter."

Here is his picture, one that all Britain will cherish—for it symbolises the steadiness of London's stand against the enemy : the firmness of Right against Wrong.

.*. Other pictures showing the raid havoc are in the BACK Page.

HAVOC COULD HAVE BEEN SAVED

By Daily Mail Reporter

MANY of Sunday night's fires in the City of London could have been avoided if fire-watching regulations had been properly observed.

That is the opinion of Commander A. N. G. Firebrace, the London Fire Brigade chief, who has just been transferred to the Home Office to help in organising local brigade duties through the country.

"It should be a point of honour," he declared. "For every firm to say ' I will not let this place burn down, both for my own sake and for the sake of my neighbours.'

"It is terrible to see a little fire start, and then in half an hour to see the whole roof ablaze.

"What is needed is not merely

Fire Spotter Off: Firm Fined £20

The Central Manufacturing Company, Ltd., of Elliott-street, Rochdale, were fined £20 at Rochdale yesterday for failing to secure that a person "who had undertaken to act as fire watcher was at all times present on the premises."

Mr. R. S. Clegg, for the firm, submitted that the regulations did not require a firm to engage a fire watcher but that somebody should undertake that duty.

It was only when somebody undertook this, he added, that responsibility arose for the firm to see that he was on the premises at all times.

100 to 1 Backing for Roosevelt

From Daily Mail Correspondent

WASHINGTON, Monday.

PRESIDENT ROOSEVELT is "tremendously pleased" at the reaction to his speech, in which he pledged more aid to Britain and declared that the Axis could not win the war.

The President's secretary, Mr. Stephen Early, said to-day that the address had brought a greater response than any previous Roosevelt talk.

Within 40 minutes of its end the President received 600 messages. They were 100 to 1 in favour.

This is how it was received by Senator Alben Barkley, leader of the Democratic Party in the Senate : "A magnificent clarification of our objectives.

Senator Warren R. Austin, leader of the Republican Party Minority in the Senate : "A remarkably fine presentation of the situation."

The New York Sun : "Deadly

Arms Flow Has Begun

From Daily Mail Correspondent

NEW YORK, Monday.

The United States Defence Commission announced to-day that they had approved arms contracts worth £2,500,000,000.

Monthly production had now risen to 2,100 aircraft engines, 700 warplanes, 100 tanks, and 2,300

SPECIAL LATE EDITION

London Flat Mystery

By Daily Mail Reporter

SCOTLAND YARD early this morning were investigating the mysterious death of a man and his wife at their luxury flat in Bickenhall Mansions, Baker-street, W.1.

The dead couple, Mr. and Mrs. Arthur Spottiswoode, aged about 50, were found seated in the drawing-room of the flat after a charwoman had failed to gain entrance.

Mr. Spottiswoode, dressed in his pyjamas, was seated in an armchair near the fireplace. His wife, in a dressing-gown, was on a settee near him. Sunday newspapers lay unopened behind the door.

"Mr. and Mrs. Spottiswoode lived here for about two years," a porter told me, "and were a very happy couple.

"It seemed to me that they were worrying about something."

There was no sign to indicate the causes of death.

LATEST

£62,500,000 FOR ARMS

Ottawa, Monday.

The Finance Minister announced to-day the sale of £62,500,000 worth of short-term notes to Canadian Chartered Banks, the money to be used for war purposes.—Exchange.

MORE U.S. AID FOR GREECE

Washington, Monday.

Mr. Morgenthau, Secretary of the Treasury, indicated to-day that President Roosevelt may extend his "loan or lease" plan to Greece and China, in addition to Britain.—Exchange.

LONDON LULLABY

1. I am a draughtsman in a "hush-hush" department. One night I stayed late and got back to my digs to find I wasn't allowed in—time-bomb near. Dead tired, I dragged myself to my cousin Jack's.

2. Jack's family were in their cellar shelter. He kept turning on the light. His wife Mary made endless cups of tea. And the children were restless. I slept bad. I didn't get much good out of my sleep.

3. I felt fit for nothing in the morning and it took me over an hour to get to the office, standing the whole way, first in the long queue at the bus-stop and then in the bus itself. I wasn't so fresh when I arrived.

4. I couldn't do my work as well as I should. I don't blame the chief when he said I wasn't exactly helping to win the war. "What shall I be like after months of this?" I wondered.

5. Johnson, at the next drawing board,

6. Then next morning

Devastation shocks the Capital

1st January, Wednesday

The New Year commenced with snow and wintry weather over Britain and Europe. In London by day, the clear-up and inspection of the immense damage continued. Despite poor weather the Luftwaffe managed to mount some isolated raids against the capital, Manchester and Birmingham with parachute mines causing casualties and disruption.

2nd January, Thursday

Improved but unsettled weather kept the Luftwaffe away during the day only to come out in strength to attack Cardiff by night in two phases during which over 100 aircraft dropped 115 tonnes of HE and almost 15,000 IBs. The city was prepared for the attack and met the bombers with aggressive AA. In addition to the 103 deaths and 168 seriously injured, the attack caused considerable disruption aggravated by numerous UXBs. Despite many fires, the city's civil defence worked well and the new priority given to fire-watching seemed to pay off in combating this major attack and reports were quick to emphasise this. Damage to the docks and installations of importance to the War effort were played down but widespread destruction in the shopping centre and the bombing of Llandaff Cathedral were openly admitted.
London had a quiet night.

Left above: **Clearing debris around Tower Hill with the Tower of London in the background.**

Left: *'Among the historic churches and chapels which were destroyed by the fire bombs dropped during Sunday night's raid was the famous City Church of All Hallows, Barkingside, the home of 'Toc H'. The picture shows the wrecked interior of the 'Toc H' Chapel with the Foster Memorial (given by Lord Foster, a President of 'Toc H', in memory of his son killed in action in 1916) and the altar on which stood the Lamp of Maintenance.'*

A Busy City Street Ran Through Here

THIS is part of the shell of Alder-manbury, one of the City streets that were wrecked out of recognition in the second Great Fire. The Daily Mail cameraman chose this spot to show one of the few buildings that still stand—almost undamaged, some windows intact. Aldermanbury is one of the worst spots in the trail left by the Nazi vandals. It was here that the beautiful Wren church of St. Mary the Virgin was devastated.

Top: The Banqueting Hall of the Guildhall after the 'Great Fire'.

Left and below left: The Lord Mayor toured the City on New Year's Day seen here viewing the damage in the ruined Guildhall and amid the rubble of Aldermanbury.

Seen from St Paul's

3rd January, Friday

The mixed weather continued but became bitterly cold by night. As with the previous night's attack on Cardiff, the RAF listening organisation Y-Service's intercepted radio transmissions gave advance notice of a planned major raid on Bristol. 178 bombers dropped 154 tonnes of HE and over 50,000 IBs in partial moonlight and clear skies that allowed visual aiming. The attack in two separate raids was the longest on Bristol to date and 149 were killed including 12 people who died when a YWCA hostel took a direct hit. Over 2,000 homes were damaged and a large granary destroyed in the docks area.

In an attempt to combat the bombers, RAF night fighters flew around the city from about 19.00 for a couple of hours seeking Luftwaffe targets without success. January would see positive developments in RAF night fighting tactics but in situations such as these, the silence of the heavy AA guns, which had to cease firing while the fighters patrolled, increased the feeling of threat in the populace.

Minor raids took place on London and various places around the country.

4th January, Saturday

A similar pattern to Thursday, with Bristol and Avonmouth receiving the predictable 'follow-up' heavy raid by 103 aircraft, many of which dropped their bombs wide of their targets, as far away as Weston-super-Mare where the incendiary fires continued to attract more bombs. In all, the damage and casualty rate in Bristol was much lower than the previous night.

Elsewhere, London was attacked and bombs fell on scattered targets across the country.

Opposite: Looking north-west from St Paul's at the gutted buildings and the lingering haze. The other survivors in view are the dome of Old Bailey and the tower of St Sepulchre-without-Newgate.

Above: *'Just how the City of London was battered and scarred on Sunday is best shown in this* Daily Mail *panorama by cameraman W.R. Turner from the dome of St. Paul's Cathedral yesterday. It gives what the man in the street cannot see – a proper perspective, revealing the true extent of the damage. Let the eye travel east across the City boundaries to Newgate Street, where the spire of Christ Church stands out. The ruins in the foreground first dominate the scene. But one other fact is shown. Look across to the edge of the City – London's skyline is still London's skyline.'*

Below: *'Remember the famous picture in the Daily Mail on Tuesday of St. Paul's surrounded by fire? This is the aftermath picture – the ruins surrounding St. Paul's. It was taken from the golden gallery surmounting the cathedral dome, looking north-west towards Newgate Street.*

Those hollow shells of brick in the foreground are part of the business centre of St. Paul's Churchyard. As the eye travels slowly towards the background it sees still more ruin, emphasising how providential was the cathedral's escape.'

City Workers Search for New Offices

with **H·P SAUCE**

FOR KING AND EMPIRE

STOCKINGS
Finer – Stronger

NO. 13,942   WEDNESDAY, JANUARY 1, 1941   ONE PENNY

FIRE WATCH CONSCRIPTION

Cabinet Decision on All ARP Services

RUSH TO ENROL AFTER BIG RAID

By Daily Mail Reporter

CONSCRIPTION is to be introduced for every branch of the Civil Defence Services. Following the tragedy of Sunday night's great fire raid on the City of London, when scores of buildings were destroyed for lack of fire-watchers, fire-watching on all factory and business premises, large or small, is to be compulsory.

Severe penalties are to be introduced for those who fail in their obligation.

These important Cabinet decisions were made known last night in a broadcast by Mr. Herbert Morrison, Minister of Home Security.

Details are being worked out, and the new regulations will be brought into force as soon as possible. The scope of these regulations is expected to be very wide.

Where any town or city finds itself short of A.R.P. workers, and unable to fill the gaps with volunteers, it will be empowered to apply to the Home Office for help.

Ironside is made

New Year

Who are the Wise Men by
your cot, New Year?—
Sorrow and Toil and Penury
and Fear.
Sorrow shall teach you sympathy, and Toil
Repay you with the riches of
his soil,
And Penury for dross shall
give you these—
The song of birds, the glory
of the trees,
And you shall learn that life
is very dear,
Clasping the cold but kindly
hand of Fear.
These four shall bid the guns
of horror cease,
And you shall walk in wisdom . . . and in peace.
BEE.

Offer to Rebuild Guildhall

By Millionaire

By Daily Mail Reporter

THE Lord Mayor of London may to-day receive the greatest New Year gift ever made to the City—an offer to rebuild the charred and broken Guildhall, which was ravaged by the German fire raisers in their raid on Sunday night.

The offer is contemplated by a British multi-millionaire, whose name at this stage cannot be revealed.

All I can say is that the man who is to give back to London its beloved Guildhall is one of Britain's younger millionaires. He has contributed thousands of pounds to the rebuilding of devastated areas in the last few months.

He is shy. He hates publicity.

'FOOD IN PERIL': A WARNING

LORD WOOLTON, Minister of Food, yesterday gave a grave warning to the nation. The danger to our food situation due to enemy sinkings, he said, is much worse than it was in the last war. Last night Lord Woolton issued a special appeal to housewives to help conserve the nation's food. Meals, he said, must be planned with renewed care, making the fullest use of home-produced foods. Community kitchens should be set up in every town throughout the land. He went on: "We must conserve our supplies, and I believe the public will accept such restrictions as are necessary." —See BACK Page.

Raiders Maroon 500 on Islet

SINGAPORE, Tuesday.

FIVE hundred people—passengers and crews of ships sunk in the South Pacific by enemy raiders—were put ashore by the raiders on the lonely island of Emirau, in the Bismarck Archipelago, off the coast of New Guinea.

To-night—ten days after they were landed on the island—it was officially announced in Singapore that they had been rescued.—B.U.P.

It is possible that one of the raiders is the ship which recently shelled Nauru, the phosphate island about 1,000 miles east of Emirau.

The Bismarck Archipelago is

'Four Italian Ships Sunk'

'Peace to Italy'

SAYS ROOSEVELT

WASHINGTON, Tuesday.

PRESIDENT Roosevelt has sent a message to King Victor Emmanuel of Italy expressing the hope that "the Italian people may be enabled to enjoy the blessings of a righteous peace in the coming year."—B.U.P.

France's Plight

Daily Mail Radio Station

Marshal Pétain, in a midnight broadcast last night, said 1941 would be a difficult year.

"We will be hungry. The war has ravaged our crops, and the blockade prevents arrivals of the cargoes from our colonies."

LATEST

FRANCE WILL TRIUMPH—DARLAN

Vichy, Tuesday.—"France, under the high authority of Marshal Pétain, will surmount all difficulties she is undergoing—and with honour, dignity and respect for her obligations."—Admiral Dar-

5th January, Sunday

London had its heaviest raid since the 'Great Fire' of 29th December: by night, parachute mines were dropped – 28 people died and 124 were seriously injured – a relatively high casualty list considering the attack was on a relatively small scale. Elsewhere the Luftwaffe visited targets in the north of England including Manchester.

6th, 7th, 8th January, Monday, Tuesday, Wednesday

Very bad weather and poor flying conditions ruled out night flying, confining the Lufwaffe to small scale daylight intrusions

Opposite left top: *'A.F.S. girls carry welcome refreshment to London's firemen engaged in a night-long, day-long effort to extinguish burning buildings in the City of London. Bomb debris and damaged buildings scarred City streets after last night's big fire raid.'*

Opposite right top: *'Traffic light posts held notices of business removals – here is a picture in Fore Street, in the city today.'*

Opposite left below: Refreshments for the firemen.

Opposite right below: Carrying their books and ledgers, office workers make enquiries as to the whereabouts of their new offices.

Left: *'The famous Temple, already bombed many times, was hit again during a recent night raid on London. This picture shows some of the barristers' chambers that were damaged.'*

Below: The Duke of Kent tours the City with the Lord Mayor of London on 6th January.

This page: 'R.E.s give a long pull and a strong pull. They are helping the City of London to clear up and carry on by demolishing buildings rendered unsafe during the recent Nazi fire blitz.'

Manpower, in this case the Royal Engineers, was the principal tool of the demolition squad.

Pulling Together: The Great Clear Up

By day the clearing-up operations continued. It was an almost never-ending task in some areas which were hit time and again. In the early days of the Blitz it had become obvious that there were not enough men for the demolition squads and troops had to be called in to assist with the job of shoring up buildings, removing debris, salvaging personal belongings and building materials that could be reused, and knocking down unsafe masonry. For the soldiers engaged in such work it may have been hard labour, but for many it was preferable to the boredom of being confined to barracks and the endless round of drill and training which, at this time, was the lot of a high percentage of the British Army. For while the seaman and the airman during this period of the war was almost constantly on active service, the soldier, since the retreat from France at Dunkirk some eight months earlier, had few opportunities to be involved in fighting.

Left: Royal Engineers (REs) laying a charge ready for demolishing a dangerous wall.

Below: Blasting unsafe buildings in Newgate Street in the clear-up of the City.

Manchester Centre in Ruins

9th January, Thursday

Improved weather gave the Luftwaffe access to the skies by day and a major attack was launched on Manchester by night, with London as the secondary target. From 17.35 the first of over 300 German aircraft commenced the attack with 143 bombing Manchester in good visibility. Damage reports for both cities this night are not specific but the bombers headed for Manchester carried 26,000 IBs and those for London 16,000, plus the usual mix of HE. Based on Ministry of Home Security reports, the Luftwaffe were very distracted from their principal targets with bombs reported falling widely across many cities around the country with a death toll of 73.

10th January, Friday

Very little Luftwaffe activity by day. Radio intercepts indicated a 'doppelganger' raid would take place on Manchester, however Nazi direction-finding beams were picked up intersecting at Southsea indicating Portsmouth was the main target for the night. The bomb-load originally destined for Manchester had numerous large bombs including two SC2500 – the deadly 'Max'. 153 bombers dropped 140 tonnes of HE and an incredible 40,000 IBs. As might be expected, the large fires that ensued did tremendous damage to the city centre and could be seen from the other side of the Channel. Included in the destruction was the Guildhall and many other public buildings and private homes in Portsmouth, Gosport and Southsea with 68 killed and 161 injured. By contrast, London enjoyed a peaceful night

Opposite above: **A view of the damage to buildings in Mosley Street, Manchester, after the raid in early January.**

Opposite below left: *'Manchester 'Blitz' damage. The interior of the burnt out Free Trade Hall.'*

Opposite below right: *'Manchester 'Blitz' damage. A damaged hospital.'*

Right above: **This photograph shows the near-complete destruction of Manchester's superb Royal Exchange. When the interior of this third Exchange building was remodelled in the thirties it had the largest trading room in England, from where the textile commodities for which Manchester was noted were bought and sold.**

Right: *'Bare pillars stand of the Guildhall, Portsmouth. The interior is gutted. Picture made after the building had been bombed, after a recent raid.'*

Catastrophe at Bank Underground Station

11th January, Saturday

After a quiet day over the country, a major attack on London. Between 18.30 and 21.00, 144 tons of HE and over 21,000 IBs were dropped by 137 aircraft. Low cloud meant their loads were released according to dead reckoning and radio beam. There was a significant amount of damage with one of the worst incidents at Bank Tube Station, where the booking hall received a direct hit. leaving an enormous crater in the road above that would not be repaired for many months; more than 110 shelterers and travellers were casualties. Two other stations were hit – Green Park Underground and Liverpool Street where 6 and 43 people died respectively..

12th January, Sunday

Continuing poor weather in daylight hours kept the Luftwaffe grounded but, after dark, 141 aircraft dropped 155 tonnes of HE along with nearly 30,000 IBs. The period of the full moon inevitably brought the Luftwaffe back to its main target, London, and following by now standard tactics, made it a double. Most of the damage took place around the south and south-east of London and the Thames Estuary. A total of 46 were killed and 102 injured.

13th January, Monday

Fog over Britain during the day kept the Luftwaffe away and weather conditions similar to the night before governed the timing and location of German bombing. As with Sunday night, early morning fog was forecast requiring the raiders to get back to their French bases before the fog fell.

Once again the target was Plymouth and Devonport and in an attack lasting just under four hours, 50 aircraft dropped 21 tonnes of HE and almost 27,000 IBs. In a typical variance of reporting, German crews reported successful visual aiming of their dock-area targets, while Home Security claimed the damage was mainly to public buildings, shops and offices and houses. A quiet night in London.

London Once Again—and Portsmouth

THESE pictures show how the German raiders hit again at London on Saturday, and the night before at Portsmouth—raids that cost them seven planes. Left: Wreckage of a London bus, bodywork torn off the chassis. Right: London firemen deal with a building swept by flames in the big fire raid. They quickly got it under control. In the centre is the week-end scene in Portsmouth— sailors helping to clear up débris among hosepipes in the streets. Germany admits six planes failed to return from Portsmouth. One, it is officially stated, was shot down over London.

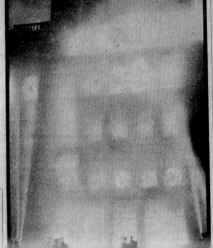

Guns Saved Industry
from Raids

DIG FOR VICTORY

This & opposite page: 'A.M.P.S. and rescue parties at work on the London subway which received a direct hit during a recent raid.'

The unimposing crater seen above concealed a much larger problem that is revealed in the picture of the excavation far left which became known as the largest bomb crater in London (the picture was not passed by the censor). The bomb that caused this brought about huge disruption to surface transport as well as the Underground. The banner 'Dig for Victory' lends a certain irony in this context.

Saving the City's Ledgers

14th January, Tuesday

Severe weather conditions over Britain and the Continent prevented any night flying by the Luftwaffe. In a service at St Martin's-in-the-Fields, the life of Amy Johnson was commemorated: the legendary aviator, and lately ATS volunteer, bailed out over the Thames Estuary after running out of fuel earlier in the month and was lost.

15th January, Wednesday

Again, not much daytime activity by the Luftwaffe but from around 18.30, 49 aircraft dropped 59 tonnes of HE and a small load of IBs, on Derby, home of the Rolls Royce aero engine. The attack on Derby was not very successful, largely because its factories provided a regular pall of smoke making the bomb-aimer's life difficult. Other cities around Derby experienced overspill from the bombing. Over London, two Stukas made a surprise appearance to drop their single bombs. Casualties in the Midlands included 26 dead, while in London the worst incident of the night – a direct hit on a boarding house – left 37 dead.

16th January, Thursday

By day the Luftwaffe mainly confined its attention to shipping. Despite the continuing full moon, early evening cloud disrupted the initial attack by 126 aircraft on Avonmouth's docks area. The clouds eventually dispersed to give more accurate visual aiming. A total of 124 tonnes of HE, most of it in the form of very heavy bombs, and an immense 53,000 incendiaries were unloaded. Casualties and damage in the target area were reportedly surprisingly light and the fires were well controlled; bombs fell indiscriminately around the Bristol area while others targeted factories, particularly aircraft works in the region.

Elsewhere a few minor incidents of bombing were reported in the London area and generally across the South of England and Wales.

17th January, Friday

Wintry weather by day kept the Luftwaffe from intrusion over Britain. There was little aid for the navigation and bombing by the 88 German bombers that shed their 89 tonnes of HE and over 32,000 IBs on Swansea. Intercepts by Y Service and 80 Wing alerted civil defence, AA and Fighter Command, none of which had much effect on the German attack that caused some serious damage to the docks. Poor weather was probably responsible for a large number of bombers failing to find their targets and isolated bombing was widespread during the night.

Again, London got off lightly with only two or three reports of bombs falling in London, at least one of them being a re-appearance by a Stuka.

18th January, Saturday

By night, Luftwaffe planes were grounded by bad weather; a few raids on East Anglian airfields took place during the day.

MONDAY TO FRIDAY: 8.30 AM TO 5.30 PM
SATURDAY : 8.30 AM TO 2.30 PM
SUNDAY : CLOSED

KING EDWARD BUILDING
KING EDWARD STREET E.C.1   OPEN ALWAYS

POST OFFICE HERE

TELEGRAMS ACCEPTED

Above: 'Moorgate Post Office, destroyed in the City fire, begins afresh at Eldon Street, E.C. It looks like a one-man show in the picture, but the premises are there all right.'

Far left: Blocked roads in the City force workers to move salvage from their wrecked offices by cart.

Left: To overcome difficulties with telephone and telegraph communications, still not properly restored since the 'Great Fire' of 29th December, the Post Office instituted a 'street telegram service'. 'Messengers advertising their function paraded the streets ready to receive and dispatch telegrams.'

Opposite top: 'Every day books and files are recovered from the wreckage of the office premises destroyed during last Sunday's wanton fire raid on the City. Here is a typical daily scene showing workers salvaging records etc.'

Opposite centre: 'Salvaging papers from a ruined City office.'

Opposite bottom 'Clearing up after the fire blitz.'

Winter Weather Halts the Luftwaffe

19th January, Sunday

Poor weather continued by day but the Luftwaffe made their presence known over coastal Britain. Intelligence picked up German traffic that indicated a major raid on Plymouth but as evening arrived it was London and Southampton that were attacked – the former by 56 German aircraft which dropped 48 tonnes of HE and over 5,000 IBs. The raid was inaugurated by two Stukas dropping single SC 1000 bombs, closely followed by two He111s guided by *Y-Verfahren* to drop their 'Max' bombs on Beckton Gas works – a popular target. Reports of damage and casualties indicate they were insignificant.

The raid on Southampton also seems to have been relatively ineffective despite 62 aircraft dropping 57 tonnes of HE and 11,000 IBs. Many bombs were widely scattered owing to very difficult navigating conditions.

20th January, Monday

Bad weather prevented any bombing attacks by German aircraft, a situation which virtually prevailed until 29th January. Apart from a few daylight raids, mainly on coastal areas, the Luftwaffe was paralysed.

21-27th, January, Tuesday-Monday

Continuing poor weather severely limited Luftwaffe operations. Even though RAF planes were scrambled no raiders attacked the capital.

Photographs for publication were by now subject to the '28-day rule'. This meant that pictures of bomb damage to an area or building could not be published until 28 days after they were taken, but if they were struck again within the 28-day period the first set of photographs could be published. This was to prevent the Germans from linking the pictures with a specific raid and so gaining knowledge about the accuracy of their bombing.

Left above: 'Prime Minister Visits Home Fleet. The Prime Minister goes ashore, well wrapped up and smoking a Churchillian cigar. Note how surely he grasps the rails. Obviously he is in no need of help to get down those steps. He had been on a visit to the Commander-in-Chief the Home Fleet, Admiral John Tovey, and is leaving the battleship at a northern base.'

Left below: The camera captures the reaction of people in the street to the explosion of a delayed action bomb in one of London's suburban areas.

Daily Mail

Culmak

FOR KING AND EMPIRE

NO. 13,963   SATURDAY, JANUARY 25, 1941   ONE PENNY

NEWS SPECIAL

After 3 Tablets The Pain Had Gone

ROOSEVELT MEETS HALIFAX

State Conference on Board President's Yacht

Rumania: Hitler Growing Anxious

Rebels Hold Out

By Daily Mail Balkan Correspondent

WHILE General Antonescu last night claimed to be master of Rumania it was clear that fighting was still going on in the provinces and that anxiety was growing in the Wilhelmstrasse.

Neutral correspondents in Berlin say that German hopes of a peaceful settlement have suffered a severe shock at a time when an undisturbed Rumania is important to Germany for military and economic reasons.

The Wilhelmstrasse, it is said, will "lend General Antonescu all necessary support" to put down the revolt.

General Antonescu is apparently gaining the upper hand, although his success may prove to be only temporary. He yesterday ordered the Army to deal with the insurgents, the "limits of patience having been exhausted."

At least two important towns, Jassy and Brasov, were last night believed to be held by the rebels.

A few hours after General Manfred von Killinger, new Nazi envoy to Rumania, reached Bucarest yesterday, Berlin took the trouble to issue a denial that war was to be declared.

"Sofia radio statement should be given and then.

'Skipper' Churchill at the Helm

THE man at Britain's helm "takes over" the wheelhouse of the drifter in which Lord Halifax started his sea trip to America. Britain's new Ambassador is seen (right) going aboard. Mr. Churchill went first, leaning out from the bridge to welcome his colleague. Lady Halifax went with her husband, travelling in the powerful new battleship King George V. *Platform conference—picture BACK Page.*

Crushing RAF Raid on Sicily

WAVELL IN TOBRUK

WHILE the British forces in Libya yesterday pushed on well over 40 miles

Big Arms Drive to Start

U-BOATS WAITED FOR WARSHIP

From DON IDDON, Daily Mail Correspondent

NEW YORK, Friday.

PRESIDENT ROOSEVELT and Viscount Halifax had a dramatic conference to-night in fog-bound Chesapeake Bay aboard the yacht Potomac in which the President had gone five miles out to meet the new Ambassador arriving in the battleship King George V.

Mr. Roosevelt's spectacular gesture of friendliness is without precedent and it has staggered Washington. No previous president has left the White House to greet anyone but the head of a State.

Putting all objections aside, Mr. Roosevelt ordered his yacht to be ready at Annapolis, Maryland, and ordered his car for one o'clock.

He set out from the White House punctually on his one-hour drive over ice-covered roads. Storm warnings were posted on the coast, with sleet, hail, and snow gales moving up through Virginia.

Mr. Roosevelt took the front seat beside the driver of his car. Cabinet Ministers and military and naval aides sat behind.

A car full of Secret Service men and four cars full of Government officials followed. Motor-cycle police rode with the cars.

CADET GUARD

A marine guard of honour

5 NIGHTS WITH NO RAID

Daily Mail Air Correspondent

LONDON was without an alert last night for the fifth night in succession—the longest bomb-free period the capital has known since September 7.

Weather and a reorganisation of the Luftwaffe following the total collapse of the Italian Air Force in Libya and Greece are the main reasons for the record lull in Nazi night raids on London and Britain generally.

Northern France has been in the grip of winter for the past two weeks, and it is known that most of the aerodromes used by the Germans for their raids on this country have been unserviceable.

Dense fog shrouded the Straits of Dover last night and there were occasional rain showers.

His Steam-Roller Beat Bomb

A STEAM-ROLLER driver, George William Paveley, of Chelmsford, who used his steam-roller to drag three unexploded bombs out of their craters, has been awarded the George Medal.

He had first dug through concrete floors and many feet of earth with a pneumatic drill in order to reach the bombs.

Two of them, said the *London Gazette* last night, were of exceptionally heavy calibre.

Nurse Mary Felicia Thomas, of Woolwich A.R.P. casualty service, wins the George Medal for crawling three times under tons of wreckage to give morphia to a trapped man and woman.

Heroes of Raids—See Page FIVE.

LORD HALIFAX IN WASHINGTON

Washington, Friday.—Lord Halifax arrived in Washington at 9.15 p.m. (3.15 a.m., Saturday, British time).

Before leaving Annapolis he said : The more quickly your generous help can be effective, the sooner we will be able to break Nazi power that is trying to enslave Europe and world.

"We assuredly have rough and difficult, and perhaps very long road before us, but British people are united as never before, and I have no doubt that with your help we will win through, and so save causes on which your civilisation and ours depend." — Reuter and B.U.P.

Left: Damage to the BBC caused by a bomb that fell in the first week in January.

Far left: *'The Union Jack still flies across the entrance to the Langham Hotel only a short distance from the BBC Headquarters in Broadcasting House – which was bombed during a recent raid.'*
Daily Mail, 15th January 1941.

The 28-day rule meant that the paper had to use a picture from a December raid to illustrate the story of January's attack.

The *Daily Mail* of 25th January reported five nights with no raid but the big news was the growing engagement of the USA with Britain's predicament.

28th January, Tuesday
Despite the continuing miserable weather, the Luftwaffe made what were soon to become very common:, 'hit and run', or 'tip and run', daylight raids. On this occasion 13 aircraft flying in the cover of low cloud were plotted by RDF with at least one reaching London, causing very slight damage and a single casualty. During the night, nine raiders braved the weather to lay mines in the Bristol Channel. Three of the returning bombers were damaged or destroyed on landing back at their base.

29th January, Wednesday
Although poor weather restricted Luftwaffe mssions by day, during the night they mounted the last heavy raid of the month, on London. Initially a force of German fighter bombers set out to attack Bomber Command airfields hoping to catch the aircraft taking off. However there was no such opportunity so the raiders diverted to London in the first part of the evening, causing light damage and shooting down seven barrage balloons.

   The main attack on London lasted a couple of hours from 19.30, involving 36 bombers that dropped 58 tonnes of HE and 2,500 IBs. The target was the Port of London but there was little reported damage.

30th January, Thursday
With the weather against formation flying by day or by night, solo raids were mounted by the Luftwaffe on a wide front across the country.

   Another countermeasure was explored on this day: 'Albino', an aerial minefield composed of explosive devices suspended by balloons was deployed by RAF Cardington, the centre of balloon technology and construction, near Bedford. Like 'Mutton', the parachute-deployed aerial minefield, 'Albino' was neither popular with the RAF, nor an effective deterrent.

31st January, Friday
As on the day before, the Luftwaffe was active with solo raiding: 95 separate attacks were mounted on London, RAF airfields and shipping. The raids were effective, killing 28 people and causing at least one big fire along with widespread damage. But by comparison with previous months, the Luftwaffe successes were down and the death rate, at 922, was at an encouraging low. However, the loss and damage to its infrastructure that Britain was experiencing under the Luftwaffe was threatening to become unsustainable. Winston Churchill was engaged in delicate negotiations with the USA to get material support for the war effort without which it was unlikely Britain could survive, never mind conquer. President Roosevelt's special envoy, Harry Hopkins accompanied Churchill to Southampton and Portsmouth on this day and recorded the enthusiasm in the bombed cities for their charismatic leader. Roosevelt was well aware of the continuing threat of a Nazi invasion of Britain.

Left above: *'On Wednesday of this week when Nazi planes again visited the Shetlands, they dropped six bombs in open country, no damage being done to any property, for the bombs just made big holes in open moorland. On a previous visit the German bombs had succeeded in killing a rabbit, but even this small success was denied them on this occasion. Photo shows: standing in one of the craters made by the Nazi bombs dropped this week on the Shetland Islands.'*

Top: After the 'Great Fire' the City attempted to carry on as usual. By the end of January most offices had been relocated and scenes like this one of workers collecting their wages in the street disappeared.

Right above: During a daylight raid policemen, neighbours and passers-by quickly rushed to help save belongings from homes threatened by fire.

Daily Mail

NEWS SPECIAL

★ BEAR BRAND

STOCKINGS
★ FINER—STRONGER ★

FOR KING AND EMPIRE

NO. 13,966   WEDNESDAY, JANUARY 29, 1941   ONE PENNY

GERMANS MASSING PLANES

U.S. Experts Tell of Big Invasion Armada

BOMB IN THE DESERT

Secrets for the King

18,000 MACHINES WILL CARRY AN ARMY

From JESSE ESSARY, Daily Mail Correspondent

WASHINGTON, Tuesday.

GENERAL GEORGE MARSHALL, United States Army Chief of Staff, predicted to-day that Hitler would most probably attempt to invade Britain in April or May. But, he added, with the aid of American supplies Britain would win.

EDWIN HARTRICH, former Berlin representative of the Columbia Broadcasting System, to-day sums up the position in the Reich by predicting the defeat of the Nazis. This is the third and last article of his notable series "Inside Germany."

Hitler Has Lost Already

By EDWIN HARTRICH

I BELIEVE Hitler's Germany has passed its peak and is on the decline. I believe Hitler has lost the war.

Those two sentences sum up my conclusions, based on an objective and dispassionate study of the internal situation — a study made possible and facilitated by the freedom to travel convinced myself that I am neutral.

I do not expect a crack-up, but it may appear.

Hitler is still a wonder man who will find a way to cross the Channel and smash Britain before "Uncle" Sam gets ... and ...

Information reaching the United States Government, I learn from other sources, shows that Germany has mobilised a powerful air armada to back up this supreme invasion attempt.

The Reich, it is reported here, is preparing for this assault with 31 divisions of aircraft, giving a total of 18,000 planes and 250,000 men.

Further, she has 100 per cent. reserves of both planes and men.

It is not believed here, however, that such a fleet can be put aloft under present conditions.

The Germans may possibly have all the aircraft claimed, but landing fields constitute a different problem.

NEW FIGHTER SURPRISE?

Adequate landing facilities, it is thought, cannot possibly be available for two or three months, when weather conditions will have improved.

There is one other thing in which the American

Blow at Libya by Free French

MUSSOLINI'S tottering African Empire was under attack from a new quarter yesterday. A Free French force, partly in cars and lorries and partly mounted on racing camels, have carried out a daring raid on an Italian air base in the heart of the Libyan Desert.

To attack the base, situated at Murzuk, in the Fessan Oases, the Free French had to travel 300 miles from the frontier of French Equatorial Africa.

They covered 100 miles a night, hiding by day.

The Italian garrison, though they greatly outnumbered the attackers, withdrew into a fort.

The French spent all day unhindered in destroying the aerodrome hangars and workshops and a number of planes on the ground.

Withdrew

The raiders withdrew at night ...

THE man who took this picture was only 50 yards away when the R.A.F. bomb exploded in the Libyan desert. Most of the Italian soldiers wisely threw themselves flat, but the machine-gunner on the left—in the absence of Italian planes to protect their troops—did what he could to cope with our attack. Booty from Bardia—Page SIX.

Boothby Will Explain to His Voters

By Daily Mail Reporter

MR. ROBERT BOOTHBY intends to explain his position to his East Aber-

Mr. de Valera on Radio To-night

Mr. de Valera is to broadcast from Radio Eireann at ten minutes past ten to-night.

He is expected to warn the people of Eire of the dangers which confront the country, particularly in the next three months.

NIGHT FIGHTERS

THE King and Queen discussed with R.A.F. night fighter pilots yesterday the new secret equipment with which their machines are being fitted to beat the night bomber.

The King turned to a young squadron leader and asked him his experiences.

"I think we are going to be much more successful in the future, sir," the officer replied.

The King and Queen also had a long talk with Air Marshal W. Sholto Douglas, Commander-in-Chief of the Fighter Command, about the difficulties of intercepting bombers at night.

At a bomber station where the King decorated 36 officers and men, one of the biggest of the new secret bombers of the R.A.F. filled the whole end of the hangar.

HITLER MAY SPEAK TO-MORROW

Berlin, Wednesday.—Hitler may make a speech to-morrow, officials in Berlin believe. The speech is unlikely to be officially announced until shortly before he speaks, and the locality will be kept secret until the last possible moment, it was stated.—B.U.P.

"METAXAS ILL"

Budapest, Wednesday.— General Metaxas, Greek Premier, is seriously ill, it is reported here. He has slightly improved after an operation and blood transfusion.—B.U.P.

Far left: A home-made shelter. Many people did not take refuge in officially approved shelters, preferring instead not to leave their homes. They built their own protection, although seldom as sophisticated as this!

Above and below left: Shelter comforts! The less pleasant aspects of shelter life – cramp and damp! Public shelters were originally intended to be used for a couple of hours at a time during the day. When the Blitz came they mostly proved uncomfortable for a whole night's occupation and the government sanctioned a massive upgrading of the standard of shelters, which was well underway by the end of January. More bunks, like the chicken-coop bunks pictured here, were installed – at first only for children; canteens run by the WVS, Salvation Army, local authorities or private firms like Marks & Spencer provided food. Gradually social life in the shelters made them more bearable, with organised games, evening classes and entertainment.

1st & 2nd February, Saturday, Sunday

A quiet weekend in London and across the country as poor weather limited Luftwaffe operations. February would generally be a difficult month for Germany to maintain aggressive attacks on Britain because of prevailing bad weather.

3rd February, Monday

Snow and wintry weather restricted operations; during the day and at night a few bombs were dropped by single aircraft flying over the Capital and the Eastern Counties.

4th February, Tuesday

Improved visibility, in better weather, brought out 159 German bombers to operate over Britain with Derby as a main target; here 40 aircraft claimed to have bombed the city with 28 tonnes of HE and 3,500 IBs. The Rolls Royce aero engine works suffered little damage as bombs fell wide and scattered thanks to deteriorating weather as the night progressed. London was also bombed along with Midlands and Eastern Counties towns, Southampton and Hull, but generally casualties and damage were light.

5th February, Wednesday

Poor visibility restricted Luftwaffe operations by day, confining them to attacks on shipping and sweeps over Kent. By night Chatham was the principal target for 26 aircraft loaded with 17 tonnes of HE in quite large bombs and nearly 4,000 IBs. Although intended for dockyard and manufacturing targets, the bombs were poorly aimed; also, numerous aircraft failed to find their target and jettisoned their loads – or found alternative targets – giving rise to isolated incidents around London, Kent and Essex. 15 were killed in Southend and 5 in London.

6&7th February, Thursday, Friday

Low cloud cover, fog and mist made flying difficult but a very few determined Luftwaffe pilots managed minor minelaying and tip and run raids. No bombs fell by night on either date.

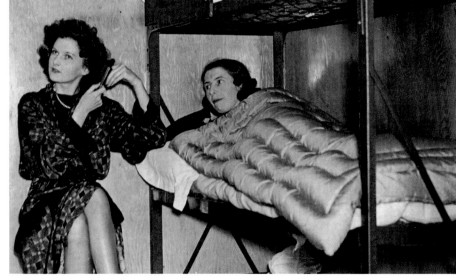

Right top: Shelterers asleep in their bunks while passengers wait for the last train of the night at Holborn Tube Station.

Right centre: Bunks in a shelter – in this case the shelter at the Berkeley Hotel. They look rather more comfortable than the chicken coop bunks pictured on the previous page.

Right bottom: An indoor domestic shelter given government approval.

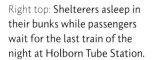

8-12th February, Saturday-Wednesday

A brief period of limbo where the continuing bad weather kept the Luftwaffe at bay. Missions were flown during this period but there were no major bombing raids and very little damage across the country. As the full moon rose on Wednesday night, the civilian population must have been wondering what was in store. However only 19 bombers carried out raids in the night, causing little damage but killing several people in the South West and Wales.

The Luftwaffe generally aimed their bombs visually but they did have navigational aids to help when visibility was poor. The first was dead reckoning, used by all airforces. It involved calculating the aircraft's position by taking into account such factors as height, flying time, wind strength., but was not terribly accurate.

The Germans also had a series of radio beacons all along the European coast facing Britain by which they could fix their position – direction finding. However, British defences could monitor these frequencies and possibly intercept the aircraft. As a counter to this, the Luftwaffe set up a series of more sophisticated and precise radio beam systems working on VHF frequencies. These systems were *Knickebein*, (the least accurate of the systems and available to all Luftwaffe pilots); the *X-Verfahren*, and the *Y-Verfahren* were limited to only small groups of specially trained pilots.

Above: **Even after five months of air attack Londoners had not given in to Hitler's attempts to terrorise them into surrendering. In fact the bombing merely seems to have strengthened civilians' resolve to win.**

Left: The largest bomb crater in London at Bank Tube Station – now spanned by a temporary road bridge. This picture shows the first traffic crossing after it was opened by the Lord Mayor. The *Daily Mail* received permission to publish the picture with the following proviso in heavy blue letters on the back: '*Must not be used unless entire background is painted out. Only roadway of bridge to be shown.*'

Massive Bomb Falls on Hendon

13th February, Thursday

The strange lull in Luftwaffe bombing ended abruptly for the people of Hendon in North London. Of 21 bombers raiding this night, a single He111 guided by *Y-Verfahren* navigation dropped an SC2500 'Max' on the unsuspecting residents of terraced houses in Ravenstone and Borthwick Roads, just before the air raid alert sounded. The ensuing destruction astonished the local people and ARP service who questioned whether the Luftwaffe had devised a deadly new bomb. 750 houses were affected in this neighbourhood close to the de Havilland works; 196 were totally destroyed. Casualties were very high with 75 killed and over 400 injured.

14th February, Friday

Despite continuing poor weather, the Luftwaffe returned to some semblance of its previous attacking style with a daylight sweep and isolated solo bombing raids. After dark over 20 aircraft attacked London to drop, in a first wave, 16 tonnes of HE and 3,600 IBs. A separate raiding party of five Heinkels from the elite 111KG/26, guided by *Y-Verfahren* and loaded with very heavy bombs, set out to attack de Havilland's aero engine plant in Edgware. It seems that one of the planes was carrying another Max which failed to find its intended industrial destination, instead exploding on open ground at Harrow causing some blast damage and killing one person. The effect that night of the other heavy bombs, four SC1800s, is not clear but a number of fires broke out in London, none of them serious.

Elsewhere in the country dispersed raids had insufficient concentration to do great damage.

Top: *'King George VI and Queen Elizabeth on a visit to bombed-out Salford, Lancashire.'*

Right: *'Fire Blitz on London. The ruins of St. Mary the Virgin, Aldermanbury.'*

Above: The Queen, deep in discussion with her guide, steps purposefully through one of Britain's damaged cities where her presence brought much moral support to the local people.

15th February, Saturday

Better daylight weather brought out Luftwaffe patrols to attack shipping and make isolated bombing raids on coastal towns.

Significant raids were planned for the moonlit conditions expected during the night, with the principal target Liverpool and the secondary the Hawker works at Langley. Aircraft under way were recalled after bad weather reports but about 30 continued to Liverpool; only 12 reported finding their target to drop a relatively light load on the city. However the other planes that set out that night bombed targets of opportunity or simply jettisoned their loads over a very wide area. Two aircraft managed to drop 3.6 tonnes of HE on the Langley factory.

One incident that took place this night is worth particular note: an attacking German raider, an He111, was intercepted and shot down by an RAF night fighter in what would become a more frequent success story as defence tactics improved. For some months, the development of a radar system that complemented the RDF early warning system had been underway in the background. 'Ground Control Interception' or GCI, started as a mobile radar facility based inland to monitor air traffic inside the RDF chain. Equipped with new technology that included the 'Plan Position Indicator' or 'PPI', observers could now view information about the strength, bearing and height of aircraft on primitive screens. In contact with night fighters, the 'GCI' unit could pass on the information to get the defender to within contact range of enemy aircraft where its onboard radar called 'Airborne Interception' or 'AI' would locate the intruder. It had taken many months of development to get all components effective: the organisation of trained crews; aircraft large enough to hold the equipment and fast enough to successfully track and attack German bombers; the communication systems; and, finally, the tactics. At last the RAF would start to be more successful in defending the night skies over Britain. On this particular night the night fighter crew gained their third victory in a textbook intercept, attacking from behind and below to bring the raider down near Totnes in Devon.

Secrecy shrouded the new technology; a press story about superior night vision through eating carrots was circulated and the new capability was alluded to as 'Cat's Eyes' so that nothing was given away. Germany concluded that RAF night fighters were simply patrolling Luftwaffe navigation beams to locate the raiders that were shot down.

Right top & centre: **The scene after a single massive bomb had fallen on Hendon on Thursday night. Rescue workers and ARP officials searching the wreckage for anything salvagable after hundreds of houses were either destroyed, made uninhabitable or received some structural damage. Around 75 people were killed, 150 seriously injured and 600 people made homeless.**

Right bottom: **The suburban streets took on a surreal appearance as bunker-like shelters occupied the roads. The designs became more sophisticated as the Blitz progressed and some of the problems they presented – damp, cold and a lack of sanitation – were partially addressed. The Anderson shelter may have saved lives but in many cases they were quite impractical: those in the devastated area of Hendon were sunk in clay and rarely used by the local people because they were poorly drained and invariably damp or flooded.**

90 Killed in Direct Hit on London Bridge Station

16th February, Sunday
Poor weather continued to restrict Luftwaffe operations by day and the country had a quiet night with no bombs.

17th February, Monday
Numerous Luftwaffe missions flew by day – mainly over coastal shipping. By night the largest attack for about two weeks was mounted on London; guided by *Knickebein*, 40 aircraft bombed the capital while on a separate raid directed by *Y-Verfahren*, six He111s aimed their SC1800 'Satans' on the docks of the Isle of Dogs and Millwall, causing damage and a number of fires. In total 42 tonnes of HE and 4,600 IBs were dropped. In most cases the night's bombing caused little damage but a direct hit on a shelter under a railway arch at London Bridge Station killed about 90 people and showed the inadequacy of the protection offered by some of the unofficial sheltering places.

Elswhere, nearly 100 other aircraft were deployed during the night, with a particular focus on the airfields of East Anglia.

18th February, Tuesday
Poor weather again kept daylight intrusions to a minimum and all the Luftwaffe's night bombing operations were cancelled.

19th February, Wednesday
Small scale operations by the Luftwaffe by day but clearer weather in the West during the evening offered the chance to make a sharp attack on Swansea. 61 aircraft dropped 54 tonnes of HE and almost 20,000 IBs with damage to the city centre and industrial targets; 48 died and 79 were badly injured.

In the London area a minor attack, lasting only about one hour, was targeted at Chatham and the docks but bombs were also dropped in other districts adjacent to the river. The worst incident of the night was when a bomb fell on St Stephen's Hospital in the Fulham Road.

20th February, Thursday
Little daylight activity but clearing weather in the West again allowed a second sharp attack on Swansea: in clear skies, over 60 bombers dropped 58 tonnes of HE and 20,000 IBs. Fires were started and damage incurred in the city centre, industrial and port areas.

The naval docks at Chatham were attacked again with a larger force in the later part of the night – over 30 bombers whose payload included 14 of the heavier parachute mines. The large bomber force flying this night led to many misplaced bombs across the country.

Right top: *'A direct hit on St. Stephen's Hospital in London during last night's raid buried many patients and nurses and rescue squads worked until early morning releasing the trapped people, among whom there were many casualties. The picture shows two wrecked wards at the hospital today.'*

Right centre: Rescue men worked all night and into the day to free a woman trapped under this pile of masonry.

Right bottom: Informing the public that all female patients were safe – unfortunately 19 male patients were dead.

21st February, Friday

Despite reasonable flying conditions, daylight activity was minor. At night, Swansea received its third night of heavy bombing in a row, following a similar pattern to Thursday night's bombardment; over 200 fires reported burning were brought under control. The combined raids left thousands of people homeless and prompted thousands more to trek out of the city by night. Despite a death toll of 219 and 260 seriously injured over the three nights, the people of Swansea were observed to be in good spirits.

Other parts of the country, including London, experienced minor attacks which caused no significant damage.

War historians have noted that the Swansea raids marked a new phase of Luftwaffe activity, with a greater focus on the ports and cities of the West and South West, the emphasis shifting from the industrial cities which had taken such punishment in the weeks before Christmas. The doppelganger tactic would be used with considerable effect on many occasions to come.

22nd February, Saturday

A quiet night in the Capital but Hull was the target for 17 bombers who unloaded 32 tonnes of HE and 17 parachute mines, 16 of which were the heavier type. Other bombs fell in the North East but overall damage was light and casualties few.

23rd February, Sunday

Light daylight activity was followed up by a return visit to the Humberside area, particularly Hull's docks. This was a much heavier raid by 49 aircraft whose 60 tonnes of HE included the horrific total of 24 parachute mines, only seven being the lighter LMA. Poor visibility meant little visual aiming and most bombs were dropped by DR, navigational beam or just guesswork. 14 people died on Humberside.

Elsewhere, three aircraft targeted Hawker's works in Langley while five more bombed London's East End.

24th February, Monday

Fog and cloud cover kept German flights to a minimum and, apart from isolated raids over East Anglia, few bombs fell this night.

Left above: *'The Premier looks out over a south coast beach across the channel to France. With him is General Sir Alan Brooke, C-in-C Home Forces. They were touring Britain's front line defence; they stayed to watch demonstrations.'*

Right above: The demolition squad at work.

Daily Mail

NEWS SPECIAL

FOR KING AND EMPIRE

NO. 13.985   THURSDAY, FEBRUARY 20, 1941   ONE PENNY

U.S. URGED 'IGNORE JAPAN'

New Battleships Ready Ahead of Time

NAVY READY FOR EMERGENCY

THE people of the United States were bluntly advised last night by their leading naval expert to pay no attention to any Japanese objections to United States naval dispositions in the Pacific.

The expert was Admiral Stark, Chief of Naval Operations. He declared "the U.S. Navy is on its toes and ready for any emergency."

The admiral's statement was contained in a letter which Mr. Carl Vinson, chairman of the naval committee, read to the House of Representatives as it was

Germany is 'Warned' by Russia

Daily Mail Radio Station

SENSATIONAL warn-

JAPANESE FLEET
LINE OF JAPANESE INFILTRATION
JAPANESE CONCENTRATIONS
POWERFUL BRITISH MILITARY & AIR CONCENTRATIONS
DUTCH
FRENCH

MAP shows clearly the

2 London Hospitals Bombed

Patients Killed

By Daily Mail Raid Reporter

PATIENTS were killed in their beds by blast when a high-explosive bomb made a direct hit on a L.C.C. hospital in London during last night's air raid.

A number of people are feared to have been killed and many injured by the bomb, which damaged severely wards in a large

'BRITAIN'S TOUGHEST'

BRITISH Paratroops badge—actual size. Wings are light blue, parachute white, background khaki.

Sky-Men Swim Fully Armed

By Daily Mail Reporter

DETAILS of Britain's newest, toughest Army—our paratroops—were released for the first time yesterday.

These men, trained to drop from low-flying R.A.F. troop-carriers, have gone through a hardening process

CANTEEN CUTS BY ARMY

By Daily Mail Reporter

MANY canteens serving the Army are being closed in the drive to end food waste.

This has been made possible by the hundreds of canteens started since the war began. Many cover the same area.

"In the days of the regular soldiers, with nothing but their Army pay to spend there was no room for overlapping," a man closely connected with Army catering told me.

"To-day there are scores of thousands of men getting pay from their offices in addition to Army money. If they wish they can eat in the men's mess and then for 9d. or 10d. have another complete meal in a canteen."

Hotel Meals Cut—See Page THREE.

LATEST

Hitler Escalates Attacks on Merchant Shipping

25th February, Tuesday

Little cloud over Britain and the continent but the risk of fog and mist forming inhibited activity by the Luftwaffe during the day. At night, Hull was again bombed – around 25 aircraft dropped a lighter load than the previous raid but still included ten parachute mines. Scattered incidents occurred around Humberside and further afield but damage and casualties were relatively small. The capital had a quiet night.

26th February, Wednesday

Cloudy weather by day was set to clear for night raids on London and Cardiff. 53 aircraft dropped 73 tonnes of HE and over 1,500 IBs on the capital, including 30 parachute mines of which 23 were the heavier type, giving London a severe battering in a typical end-of-the-month attack which, in the absence of moonlight, was illuminated by many parachute flares. Damage and casualties were at a greater scale than other nights during February: a military hospital canteen took a direct hit from a parachute mine killing 30.

The raid on Cardiff was carried out by 58 aircraft, the target also lit with parachute flares to allow visual aiming of 48 tonnes of HE and 25,000 IBs, killing ten people.

Numerous bombs fell outside the target areas, dropped by crews that were lost or had to abandon their mission. Compared with other end-of-month attacks, Britain got off relatively lightly and there would not be another heavy raid during February.

27th February, Thursday

Poor weather conditions grounded all Luftwaffe night bombing operations. Daylight activity was restricted to attacks on coastal shipping with the exception of two tip-and-run raids by single aircraft in different locations – the one on Grantham killing 15.

Luftwaffe attacks on shipping were a constant feature of their operations from the beginning of the war – either in the form of direct bombing of ships or in the dropping of mines in the waters around Britain. On 6th February Hitler had issued a directive to escalate attacks on British merchant shipping, ports and harbours in an attempt to break the supply of food and other goods from the USA and the Colonies.

28th February, Friday

Only three aircraft were over Britain at night dropping bombs on London, the Home Counties and East Anglia with little damage reported.

Right: A picture passed for first publication in the evening papers of Wednesday 26th February shows salvaged books in the Guildhall Library, cleared of the initial debris caused by the 'Great Fire' of 29th December.

Above right: Salvaging furniture and belongings, including toys, from a bombed-out house.

5-HOUR RAID ON SOUTH WALES COAST TOWN

Three Churches, Hospital, Convent and Schools Damaged : Berlin Says It Was Cardiff

A COASTAL town in South Wales was the main target of German bombers last night. The raid lasted five hours. Thousands of incendiaries were dropped with many H.E.s and delayed action bombs.

During the Alert, one H.E. bomb fell after midnight in a London district. It fell on open ground behind houses. There were no casualties and no damage.

"Damage Not Extensive"

The Air Ministry and Home Security communique, issued to-day, stated:

"Last night* enemy activity was not on a large scale. Bombs were dropped on a town in South Wales. where some fires were caused, but all were extinguished in the early hours of the morning.

"Some bombs were also dropped at a number of points along the North-East coast and South-East Scotland. Some buildings were hit, but damage was no-where extensive.

"A few bombs fell in other parts of the country, but with little effect.

R.A.F. BOMB TARGETS IN RHINELAND

It is learned in London that last night the R.A.F. attacked targets in the Rhineland.

The attack was officially admitted in Berlin to-day. A statement issued by the official German news agency (quoted by Reuter) said:

"Last night a number of British aircraft flew over Western Germany.

"Only a few H.E. bombs were dropped. The damage caused was insignificant and was confined to private property. Three persons were killed.

"Two enemy planes were shot down by A.A. fire."

Germany Claims—

"MANSTON ATTACKED"

It was claimed in Berlin to-day that a squadron of light bombers attacked Manston Aerodrome on

1st March, Saturday

Daylight fighter sweeps by the Luftwaffe gave way after nightfall to fairly busy but not very effective bombing missions carrried out by around 100 bombers supported by half a dozen night fighters. The main targets were Hull and Cardiff but heavy cloud cover forced many planes to seek other targets and 17 of the 37 aircraft sent to Cardiff ended up raiding Southampton. The heaviest of the attacks was on Hull where 16 parachute mines were dropped as part of a 29 tonne HE payload, delivered by 24 aircraft; surprisingly only four Hull residents died. The widespread incidents in the night included some minor damage in London but because of dense cloud cover, the lack of concentrated bombardment gave poor results for the raiders.

2nd March, Sunday

Negligible activity from the Luftwaffe by day or night, arising from adverse weather conditions at Luftwaffe bases in Europe.

3rd March, Monday

Clearer weather conditions brought about a busy day for the Luftwaffe, making minor intrusions over land and bombing Ramsgate; the bulk of their attention was on shipping and reconnaissance.

With the arrival of night, 68 aircraft set out for Cardiff, 47 arriving over the city to drop 52 tonnes of HE and almost 15,000 incendiaries. The main targets were the docks and industrial areas; numerous serious fires were started affecting the docks and the city centre including the cathedral. 48 people died. 14 other aircraft from the original attacking force bombed Southampton instead.

Further north, 22 aircraft attacked Tyneside, damaging parts of Newcastle and its outlying riverside docks and industrial installations. Isolated bombs fell elsewhere, including London, but with few casualties.

4th March, Tuesday

A similar pattern of activity to Monday's for the Luftwaffe with some 170 aircraft busy over the sea and coast by day and another concentrated attack on Cardiff – 61 aircraft with a slightly lighter load of HE but around 20,000 IBs. Fires in the dock area and city centre increased the toll of damaged and destroyed public buildings, but the damage was reported as being lighter than the previous night.

London and Southampton both received minor attacks.

Left above: The human cost of the Blitz was incalculable but generally people behaved with great stoicism; scenes like this reception centre in Southampton were repeated in all parts of the country as billets had to be found for the homeless.

Café de Paris Tragedy

Tanks and

LAST DANCE — FINALE

AN EXTRA HOUR OF SUMMER TIME FROM MAY 3

There will be an extra hour of summer time from the night of Saturday, May 3, to the night of Saturday, August 9.

Mr. Herbert Morrison, Home Secretary, announced this to-day.

"The addition during the summer months of an extra hour's daylight in the evening would be advantageous to the war effort in many ways," he said, "particularly by enabling loading and unloading of ships at the docks and the work at railway marshalling yards to be continued.

"In many factories it would also enable two shifts to be worked in daylight.

Farm Difficulties

"On the other hand, the change would cause difficulties in connection with farming which the Gov-

WHAT EXTRA HOUR WILL MEAN

WITH the clocks advanced a further hour, sunrise in London on May 3 will be at 6.28 a.m., and sunset at 9.27 p.m.

On June 21, mid-Summer Day,

THE band was playing in a packed London restaurant on Saturday night when the bomb struck. This was the scene yesterday when a Daily Mail cameraman went into the wreckage . . . the grand piano littered with débris; instrument cases hurled on top; page after page of music scattered throughout the wreckage on the dance floor.

RACING ON TO HARAR

5-7th March, Wednesday–Friday

Widespread fog, mist and low cloud over these three days and nights curtailed Luftwaffe operations, with virtually no night-bombing and very limited daylight raiding on East and South coastal areas and London.

8th March, Saturday

After the three-day lull in Luftwaffe aggression, bombing returned with a vengeance. Following very little daylight activity, a major attack was launched on London – the first since mid-January: 125 aircraft dropped 130 tonnes of HE and 25,000 IBs in a bombardment lasting around three and a half hours. A significant amount of damage was caused to the railway system, but the night's bombing was marked by two incidents which were widely reported.

One was a bomb which fell on the North Lodge at Buckingham Palace, killing a policeman; the other was when the Café de Paris in Coventry Street, Leicester Square, received a direct hit from two 50 kg bombs which passed through the Rialto Cinema above without exploding then detonated in the chic nightstpot that was crowded with fashionable diners. 34 were killed and around 80 injured. The Café de Paris, noted for its live musical entertainment, was frequented by officers and women from the wealthier classes and was believed to be one of the safest restaurants in London as it was underground. Among the dead was the popular bandleader Ken 'Snakehips' Johnson and one of his musicians, along with a number of the restaurant's staff.

Looting at the scene of the incident was a problem, as it often was where bombs wrought destruction. Often 'looting' was nothing more than picking up a cup or saucepan apparently abandoned among a pile of debris, however, at the Café de Paris the looting was of an altogether more distasteful sort as some people systematically worked their way through the dead and injured removing jewellery and other items of value. As a story guaranteed to damage public morale and the belief of 'all pulling together' in the face of adversity, the looting was of course not reported in the press. In fact the incident generally had a very low profile and went unreported in the *Daily Mail* until over two weeks later – probably because of the social impact of the tragedy.

Bombing was widespread during the night – across 50 London boroughs and elsewhere across the South and South East of England.

Opposite above left: *'Broken instruments, broken chairs, and music blown from stands: yesterday's clearing up scenes at the London restaurant Café de Paris bombed on Saturday night.'*

Opposite above right: Wreckage and reminders of the earlier revels at Café de Paris, struck by a bomb on the night of 8th March. At first the press could only refer to it as a 'London restaurant' – it was several days before the Café de Paris could be named openly.

Left above: *'Café de Paris. The band was playing in a packed London restaurant on Saturday night when the bomb struck. This was the scene yesterday when a Daily Mail cameraman went into the wreckage: the grand piano is covered with pages of music, scattered throughout the debris in the famous restaurant.'*

Left below: Buckingham Palace was hit again by bombers on 8th March.

Heaviest Raid of Year on Portsmouth

9th March, Sunday

By day activity was light but in a heavy follow-up night attack on London, German bombers dropped nearly 100 tonnes of HE and around 16,000 IBs; 22 boroughs reported bombs but the attack focused on the capital's North East districts. There was significant damage with the usual temporary interruptions to services – rail, road, water, electricity, gas and telephone.

Portsmouth was the main secondary target and isolated raids took place elsewhere from East Anglia to the Isle of Wight.

10th March, Monday

Little impact from minor daylight raiding but a massive night attack on Portsmouth dealt the naval port the heaviest raid anywhere in the British Isles since the beginning of the year. 238 aircraft released nearly 200 tonnes of HE and 46,000 IBs, starting major fires in the city and nearby Gosport. Things worsened for Portsmouth when oil and petrol storage tanks located in the dock area went up in flames. Bombs fell widely in the vicinity and 47 died.

Elsewhere, Eastern Counties took isolated hits while London had a quiet night.

Above right and below: 'Palace Escaped: Buckingham Palace has been bombed again, but the palace itself escaped. The Daily Mail picture below gives an idea of the damage done in this deliberate attack.'
Daily Mail, 13th March 1941

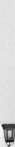

ON: WEDNESDAY, MARCH 12, 1941

Full Moon, to-morrow.

ONE PENNY

ks U.S.A. For Beat Nazis"

PILLARS SHATTERED by the bomb which wrecked the Palace lodge, a picture of which is on the Back Page.

Two days after the incident four canaries belonging to the lodge-keeper were rescued unharmed and two days after that his blue Persian cat was brought out of the debris, alive and apparently none the worse for its adventure.

BUCKINGHAM PALACE IS BOMBED AGAIN

POLICEMAN KILLED, LODGE WRECKED

BUCKINGHAM PALACE, it can now be revealed, was bombed again in a recent raid.

Bombs fell in a line near the front of the Palace building, three of them dropping in the forecourt, where the Changing of the Guard ceremony is held.

Another fell on the North Lodge, the low building on the right-hand side of the Palace next to Constitution Hill.

Safe in Shelter

The Lodge was wrecked, but the rest of the Palace buildings, including Royal apartments, are undamaged.

The porter of the Garden Gate, who lives in the Lodge with his family, was in an underground shelter.

A young policeman, of "A" Division, on relief duty at the Palace, was killed by falling masonry. He had sought shelter by the Lodge when the heavy bomb came down while he was looking for fire-bombs.

This is the third bomb attack on the Palace. In an earlier raid the private chapel of the Royal Family was badly damaged. Bombs were also dropped, in one of these raids, on the Royal Mews.

HIS WORRY AT 69

They Want Him to Go to Work

Philip Augustus Spencer, a 69-year-old photographer, was bound over at Marlborough-street to-day for offensive language at a Hyde Park meeting.

He said that all his apparatus was stolen from his house while he was in hospital. He was receiving unemployment assistance, zut the Labour Exchange had been "worrying old men like me" to go to work.

PASSPORT CHARGE

What Detectives Heard in West End

Two detectives who saw three

B.B.C.'s BAN ON ARTISTS

SOME CASES TO BE RECONSIDERED

THE B.B.C. Governors have been asked to reconsider the ban imposed on certain of the artists who supported the People's Convention.

This was announced in the Commons to-day by Mr. Duff Cooper, Minister of Information.

Mr. Duff Cooper, replying to Mr. Noel Baker (Soc., Derby), said it had been the policy of the B.B.C.

HE FORESAW TANK BATTLES IN 1913

F. BRITTEN AUSTIN, THE AUTHOR, DEAD

Mr. F. Britten Austin, author, playwright and military expert, who visualised the might of the mechanised army in a book published in 1913, died at the Royal West of England Infirmary, Weston-super-Mare, Somerset, to-day. He was 55.

He was a clerk at the Stock Exchange when his

ANZACS FROM ENGLAND REACH MIDDLE EAST

CONTINGENTS of the Australian Imperial Force and New Zealand Expeditionary Force have arrived safely in the Middle East from England, states the Dominions Office to-day.

When the troops left England, the Dominions Secretary, Viscount Cranborne, sent a message to the Australian Prime Minister, expressing the Government's "admiration of the Australian troops who are now leaving this country for

11th March, Tuesday

Birmingham was once more the target for a major night attack by 135 aircraft dropping over 100 tonnes of HE and 30,000 IBs. Most of the crews had no specific targets, just the city itself, but elements of the force were directed by *X*- and *Y-Verfahren* to a specific industrial area, others carried out visual aiming through breaks in the cloud or by dead-reckoning.

A substantial part of the bomber force that night re-routed to Manchester, doing considerable damage, while the secondary target of Southampton experienced a minor but concentrated attack with the raiders able to visually aim in clear skies. Bombs fell very widely across the country from Brighton to Caernarvon and included the London area. Fortunately, considering that nearly 200 raiding aircraft were operating, civilian casualties were relatively light.

On this day, the US Congress passed the Lend-Lease Bill with a resounding majority. President Roosevelt had fought his own campaign in support of his British friends, to prevail against the vocal anti-war element in the American electorate. It was this instrument that ensured Britain could finance its war effort, for the country's coffers were empty. The explicit support of the US now forced Hitler to realise that Britain would continue to be a force capable of resisting the Nazi Blitzkrieg. However, the US maintained its embassy next to the Brandenburg Gate in Berlin, though without an ambassador, until entering the War in December 1941 when the staff were interned.

Churchill, aware of the likely success of the Lend Lease Bill, was excruciatingly aware of Germany's improving record of destruction of Britain's merchant fleet in the Atlantic and in a speech on 6th March had announced that full attention would now be given to the protection of Britain's ports and shipping to ensure the safe transport of the vital supplies coming to the nation in support of the war effort.

Above: *'Mr. John G. Winant, the new American Ambassador to Britain, was the guest of honour at a luncheon given by the Pilgrims, and tasted for the first time 'Lord Woolton Pie', composed of carrots, parsnips, potatoes and pastry. The picture shows Mr. John G. Winant chatting with Mr. Winston Churchill, the Prime Minister, before the luncheon.'*

"YOU GIVE STRENGTH TO OVERWHELM TYRANNY"

American Army officers, in uniform, heard the loud cheers of M.P.s in the House of Commons to-day when Mr. Churchill thanked America for the Lease-and-Lend Bill, which he called "a new Magna Carta."

MR. CHURCHILL may also broadcast the nation's thanks to America.

Asked if he would do so, he replied: "I think I must try to choose the exact moment for such a broadcast."

"THIS MONUMENT"

In his statement on the signing of the Lease-and-Lend Bill by President Roosevelt last night, Mr. Churchill said:

"I am sure the House would wish me to express on their behalf and on behalf of the nation our deep and respectful appreciation of this monument of generous and far-seeing statesmanship. (Cheers.)

"The most powerful democracy have, in fact, declared in solemn statute that they will devote their overwhelming industrial and financial strength to ensuring the de-

NO. 18,451   S   SIXTIETH YEAR   LONDON: TUESDAY, MARCH 11, 1941

LARGEST EVENING NET SALE IN THE WORLD

Heavy Six-Hour Attack On Portsmouth Area

Clearing up wrecked shops in the South of England at a point where several bombs were dropped alongside a famous main road.

THREE, POSSIBLY FIVE RAIDERS DOWN

Hundreds of H.E. Bombs and Thousands of Incendiaries

LONDON'S 4 ALERTS

A heavy air attack was made on the Portsmouth area last night for the second night in succession.

R.A.F. BOMB

WEST GERMANY AND THE PORTS

IT is known that

LONDON SHIP WAS TORPEDOED	*Margate Is Annoyed*	*Balkans "Offensive"* MYSTERY OF

12th March, Wednesday

A major night attack on Merseyside, aided by the period of the full moon, proved that Churchill's concern for Britain's ports was fully justified. Since late February, the command of the Western Approaches, the term given by the Admiralty to the North Atlantic adjacent to Britain's shores, had been based in Liverpool after transferring from Plymouth. This night, 316 bombers dropped over 300 tonnes of HE and almost 65,000 IBs. Although the main target was the docks and warehouses of Birkenhead, the whole area was pounded by the aircraft, whose crews had good conditions for the visual aiming of their bombs. Casualties were very high, with the most deaths, 264, in Birkenhead; Wallasey was not far behind with 198 but Liverpool trailed with 49. Three and a half days after the bombing of Wallasey people were amazed when a young baby was pulled from the ruins still alive.

The huge Luftwaffe attacking force guaranteed widespread bombing across the country and many UXBs exacerbated the problems of the bombed population, forced to abandon their homes.

Reasons to be grateful were few that night but RAF night fighters did succeed in bringing down five raiders within a very short space of time. Guided by Ground Control Interception (GCI) – the new inland radar detection – this victory rate was a new departure for the RAF, however, as a percentage of the 261 sorties flown there was still some way to go before the tactics could be truly deemed successful.

13th March, Thursday

Taking full advantage of the full moon, the Luftwaffe pulled in every bomber they could to the night's raids, sending out almost 450 aircraft to attack Glasgow and Clydeside, Merseyside and Humberside. This was Glasgow's first major raid and it was a baptism of fire with 236 aircraft dropping 272 tonnes of HE and

60,000 IBs. The death toll was terrible but the overwhelming damage made it impossible to accurately assess the number of casualties before a second onslaught the following night.

It is astonishing to contemplate that with this major raid on Glasgow, two other concentrated raids could also be made in the same period on other cities; furthermore that collateral damage to targets of opportunity, misplaced bombs and UXBs could cause widespread damage over the country.

NO. 18,454 SIXTIETH YEAR   LONDON: FRIDAY, MARCH 14, 1941   Moon rises 8.40 p.m.; sets 8.12 a.m.   ONE PENNY

NIGHT FIGHTERS SHOOT DOWN 8 RAIDERS

HEAVY ATTACKS ON LIVERPOOL AREA AND CLYDESIDE

R.A.F. Batter Hamburg Again for Many Hours

EIGHT German raiders were shot down, all by R.A.F. night fighters, over Britain last night.

This is a record for the night fighters. With the nine brought down on Wednesday night and eight on Monday night, the week's total so far is 25.

In the light of the full moon, last night's raids were again fairly widespread. Clydeside was heavily attacked, and there was another "blitz" on Merseyside. The Germans claim much destruction to the food industry in Glasgow, Liverpool and Birkenhead.

Bombers of the R.A.F. during the night raided Hamburg for the second night in succession. The "successful" attack lasted for many hours.

FOUR YEARS FOR A SERGEANT-MAJOR

756 BOTTLES OF GIN AND WHISKY

Staff - Sergeant - Major Thomas Milton Bowden and Sergeant Harold Wilson Turner, both of the R.A.S.C., who appeared before a Chelsea court-martial in January, have been reduced to the ranks and discharged with ignominy.

Bowden has been sentenced to four years' penal servitude, and Turner to three years.

It was alleged against them that they obtained by false pretences 501 bottles of whisky and 255 bottles of gin valued about £450.

"A Gross Swindle"

The prosecuting officer at the court-martial said that the men carried out a "long-firm fraud," using War Office notepaper to write to wine stores in London, falsely stating that a sergeants' mess was being established. He described their activities as a "gross swindle."

Bawden's age was given as 47. It was stated that details of his previous military service had been lost by enemy action. He said that during the last war he was chief clerk to the Military Secretary at General Headquarters in France. Turner is 41.

SHE LOVED SABU

Actress Tried Suicide

A 17-year-old Indian actress tried to commit suicide in Hollywood because she fell in love with Sabu—and he did not love her. She failed.

At the age of 48, unusually old for a Service airman, Flight-Sergeant A. H. Bolton was awarded the Distinguished Flying Medal.

NO 'PITY THE POOR GERMANS' TALK

DUTCH PREMIER'S CALL

"There must be no after-victory pity or weakness shown to Germans," says Professor Gerbrandy, the Dutch Premier, in an interview in to-day's Vrij Nederland, the Free Dutch newspaper published in London.

The King Distributes More Awards

People decorated by the King at an investiture held recently included an air gunner who is 48 years of age, and a W.A.A.F. winner of the Military Medal.

Several of the recipients of honours took their little children to the Palace to see the ceremony.

Asst. Section Officer Elspeth C. Henderson, decorated with the Military Medal. She kept a special telephone line in operation when the R.A.F. Fighter Command. station to which she was attached was being bombed and the building in which she was working received a direct hit.

After receiving the O.B.E.—Mr. W. M. Scott, who is in charge of a Hornsey stretcher party, with his son Eric.

MASS ITALIAN ATTACKS SMASHED

MUSSOLINI LEAVES A SHATTERED ARMY

MUSSOLINI, who had hoped to return to Rome to-morrow with news of an Italian triumph in Albania, will leave behind instead a beaten and demoralised Italian army.

Instead of the great victory he had planned for the Italian offensive begun on Sunday, he has seen:—

Three Italian divisions wiped out:

Ten thousand of his crack troops killed, wounded or taken prisoner; and

Every Italian attack shattered.

"Appalling Slaughter"

The battlefields are strewn with Italian dead and wounded.

An Athens spokesman said to-day:—

"The great spring offensive which Mussolini, waiting patiently among his disillusioned generals at G.H.Q., was expecting to produce results by yesterday, has tailed off after appalling slaughter.

"The Italians," he added, "have failed to regain a single inch of the ground lost earlier this week, while the Greeks captured important strategic points approaching Tepeleni."

Fierce battles have been fought in the moonlight on these snow-capped peaks.

ITALIANS LOSE ANOTHER TOWN

Mass Attacks

14th March, Friday

Glasgow and Clydeside were again the target of 203 aircraft out of a force of around 500 sent out this moonlit night to attack Britain. The crews attacking Glasgow were jubilant at the accuracy of their aiming, sending 231 tonnes of HE and 28,000 IBs into Clydeside installations and docks.

Reporting of the two nights blitz on Glasgow, particularly by the BBC, was dispassionate, downplaying the damage and casualties. This caused great distress to the local population who were completely dazed and shocked by the ferocity of the attacks. Many thousands were made homeless and the Rest Centres could not cope with the numbers. Queues of thousands of people formed in the Glasgow Road awaiting transportation out of the city on Corporation buses. Although the deaths were reported at around 500 for the two nights, a few weeks later, Morrison owned up in a meeting that the death total had been closer to 1,100 with 1,000 injured. Damage and death on this scale could not be concealed from the local population or the country and the government was forced to reconsider its reporting of casualties. The people of Clydeside would have been neither shocked nor surprised by any revelations because they 'knew' the true casualty rate.

Sheffield was the secondary target of the night but in fact bombs fell widely around the Yorkshire area killing 52 in Leeds alone. Bombs fell all across the country from Plymouth to East Anglia.

15th March, Saturday

While the Luftwaffe night attacks met with so little effective resistance yet had such a dramatic impact, there was little point in meeting the RAF head to head during the day; so by night the Luftwaffe continued to scourge Britain. This night it was London's turn once more for a major attack in this new aerial bombing offensive by Germany. Clearly the Nazi regime wished to make up for the lost months of January and February. In little over two hours, a hundred or so bombers dropped 103 tonnes of HE and 14,000 IBs. Despite targeting the docks area, bombs fell widely around the suburbs of London and further afield in the Home Counties. The death toll in Greater London was about 50.

Elsewhere, a small force raided Southampton.

9 Night Raiders Destroyed : R.A.F. Plane Torpedoes German Destroyer: Biggest-Ever Raids on Germany

BRITAIN HAS SECRET WEAPON: LETHAL CABLES ARE ALSO IN OPERATION

FLASH "AS BIG AS HOUSE' AS DESTROYER IS TORPEDOED

A German destroyer was torpedoed by a Beaufort aircraft of the Coastal Com-

Bigger Bombers Over Berlin While Our New Beaufighters Shatter Raiders Here

BRITAIN'S new fighters and bombers were in action last night—and they struck some heavy blows.

Berlin, Hamburg and Bremen were bombed in the biggest-ever raids on Germany. Several of our new types

One of our Defiant fighters—

R.A.F. Night Blitz
MANY LARGE BERLIN FIRES
BREMEN WORKS AREA ALSO ABLAZE

RELAYS of R.A.F. bombers carried out last night's "heaviest ever" attacks on Berlin, Bremen and Hamburg.

Fire bombs and H.E.s were dropped on the three big German cities in raids which lasted for some hours.

Moonlight Bombing

It is learned in London that each of the three was heavily bombed in bright moonlight.

First reports show that many large fires broke out in Berlin. The industrial area of Bremen was also set well alight, and the target at Hamburg, situated in the dock area, is reported to have been heavily bombed.

One of our fither aircraft—

Above left: An artist sketches St Paul's while cleaning-up operations continue in the vicinity of the Cathedral.

Above right: A man salvaging clothes from his bombed-out home. It was vital for people to salvage whatever they could from their wrecked houses. The shops were virtually devoid of all household goods and clothes, so anything left in the house because it was slightly damaged or dirty could not be replaced even if there was the money to do so. Clothes rationing was to be introduced on 1st June 1941.

Left below: The 1941 dining room complete with a comfortable concrete and steel shelter.

Opposite: *'Outside a bombed London dance hall: the wreckage includes a laden bus.'*

Capital's Highest Death Toll

16th March, Sunday

The Luftwaffe turned its attention this night to Bristol and Avonmouth: 57 aircraft delivered just under 55 tonnes of HE and 23,000 IBs while a separate force of 105 aircraft dropped 110 tonnes of HE and 11,000 IBs. 208 people were killed but the ARP and fire-fighters were reported to have performed well to control fire damage. Starfish sites may have confused navigation resulting in widespread bombing dispersed across the city and its environs.

17th March, Monday

Night bombing operations cancelled due to poor weather.

18th March, Tuesday

After more daylight activity than of late, the Luftwaffe raised a massed force for a major attack on primary target, Hull, which spread widely over Yorkshire, including Scarborough. Initial reports put the death toll at 78 – low casualties for the bombload which included 316 tonnes of HE and 70,000 IBs dropped on Hull alone, where considerable damage was inflicted on the town's industry and homes. 378 aircraft participated in this raid out of a total of over 460 bombers operating during the night.

Southampton was the secondary target for 17 bombers manned by inexperienced crews with a relatively light load of bombs. London and the surrounding area also suffered raids by 36 aircraft, targeting the docks also providing an alternative target for some inexperienced pilots who failed to pinpoint Southampton, their designated target.

19th March, Wednesday

A massive attack on London by 479 aircraft. Some 470 tonnes of HE and a huge number of IBs – 122,000 – were dropped between roughly 20.00 and 02.00. It was estimated that no fewer than ten parachute mines were dropped along with four of the devastating SC2500 'Max'.

The attack, guided by *X*- and *Y-Verfahren* was illuminated by about 100 parachute flares and centred on the docks and the East End; many fires were started – 3 conflagrations, 10 major, 53 serious and more than 1,800 small. Public utilities and transport were all severely disrupted. In the Docks area many warehouses and their precious contents were destroyed and numerous public and private buildings were either destroyed or damaged. The death toll at 631 was the highest for any single night of the Blitz to date. In the East End, for the duration of living memory this became 'The Wednesday' – a true night of terror that wiped out entire streets for ever.

Right above: 'A Bren gun carrier races up a slope in England. One of the 'crew' looks out with a pleased smile – the King was enjoying his trip with 'Hell's Angels' (note the 'badge'). He was spending a day with Canadian troops training in this country.'

Right below: Damage at one of six London hospitals hit in the major raid on Wednesday 19th March. Here nurses are salvaging bedding.

HEAVY RAID ON HULL

LONG LONDON ALERT

HULL was the town that had a heavy raid last night. The attack lasted some hours.

On their way to bomb this area waves of German planes passed over London, causing the longest Alert of the year.

The Air Ministry and Home Security communiqué states: "The enemy's main effort during the night was concentrated on a town on the N.E. coast [afterwards revealed as Hull.] The attack was on a heavy scale and many houses were damaged.

Fires Soon Out

"There were a number of fires, but they were soon brought under control and all were extinguished by daybreak. Casualties are not expected to be unduly heavy.

"In their attack on the N.E., many of the enemy bombers flew over the East, South-East and Southern England, including the London area. No attack developed in these areas, though bombs were dropped at a number of points. Damage was not heavy at any of these points, nor were casualties numerous."

In Hull a theatre and a dance hall were struck. People were trapped, and two were killed, when a row of small houses was destroyed. After some hours rescuers were able to communicate with people still under the debris, and refreshments were supplied to them.

Refugees Killed

Five women and three men were killed when a heavy bomb demolished four houses in a London district. Two German refugees—Mrs. Benedict, aged 31, and her mother, Mrs. Oettinger, aged 52—were killed just as they returned home from a cinema.

Next door Mr. and Mrs. Randall were getting ready for bed. Their three children, aged 18, ten and five, were already asleep upstairs. The father and mother were killed. The children all escaped with minor injuries.

In the third house, Mr. and Mrs. Gerrard saved themselves by getting under a billiard table. Their son Jack, aged 24, a Home Guard, was killed. In the fourth house Mrs. Richards, Miss Line and M. Jeune, a Frenchman, were killed.

WORST LONDON BLITZ OF YEAR

Night Fighters Battle With Waves of Bombers

By Daily Mail Raid Reporters

EARLY this morning, waves of Nazi bombers roaring over London were pounding the capital with tens of thousands of fire bombs, mixed with heavy high explosives, in the most savage assault this year.

Eden Flies to See the Turks

By Daily Mail Balkans Correspondent

HURRIED military and diplomatic conferences and new defence measures reported in Daily Mail indicate that is rapidly

After several hours of incessant attack, during which the ground defences hurled their mightiest barrage into the sky, the raid had reached proportions rivalling those of the autumn Blitz.

Four hospitals were hit, one seriously, many houses and shops were wrecked, and it is feared that casualties are heavy.

One bomber is known to have been shot down by A.A. guns. As well as the thunder and crack of guns, Londoners heard at times the drone of fighters, the chatter of machine-guns.

APPEAL TO U.S.

'Lend Our Navy Your Yards'

From Daily Mail Correspondent

Washington, Wednesday.

COLONEL FRANK KNOX, United States Navy Secretary, revealed to-day that Britain had asked for the use of the United States Navy yards.

The request was for repair work on some vessels, and was under consideration.

Colonel Knox indicated that it was not a large job.

The Navy had some facilities which the British might use, he told reporters, adding: "We always do have such facilities.

'PACT TO PART AS FRIENDS'

An RAF Super Fighter for Atlantic Battle

By NOEL MONKS, Daily Mail Air Correspondent

LONG-RANGE fighter aircraft so advanced in design that they will revolutionise air warfare are being built secretly for Britain in the United States.

Details are closely guarded, but I understand that the new fighter will be more heavily armed than any now in existence; its range will far exceed that of the Messerschmitt 110, and its speed will be startling.

R.A.F. BEST —MOSCOW

TRIBUTE to the R.A.F. was paid by Moscow radio in a home broadcast last night.

The British, said the announcer, have made evident during the period March 13 to 18 that they have lost no time

It provides the complete answer to Germany's ocean-raiding long-range Condor bombers.

The design is the combined work of the leading British and United States experts. It includes the best features of the Hurricane, Spitfire, Blenheim, and existing United States types. High performance at great altitudes has not been overlooked.

Above left: *'Another Nazi picked out a Surrey Convent School...shattered woodwork lay around as nuns checked damage.'* Daily Mail, 21st March 1941.

Left: *'Convent schoolgirls collected books hurled from ruined classrooms. Footnote: Berlin says the main aim was the harbours and docks.'* Daily Mail, 21st March 1941.

Above right: *'A warden clears up outside a shattered home, in one hand he holds a schoolgirl's hat. Trailing across the broken wall is a dance frock. High in the wreckage suitcases are heaped. Yesterday's picture in London.'*

Plymouth Blitzed

20th March, Thursday

On this day, the King and Queen visited Plymouth to boost the morale of the local population as the city had already experienced nearly 200 bombing raids. Hosted by the Lady Mayoress, Viscountess Astor, the party was entertained with music and dancing on the Hoe. That evening, not long after the royal visitors departed, the Luftwaffe returned to make a devastating bombardment which inaugurated a new level of destruction to the city and its Devonport docks. Attacks took place over two consecutive nights and continued in April, becoming known as the 'Plymouth Blitz'. This night, 125 aircraft attacked from early evening and over a four-hour period dropped 159 tonnes of HE and almost 32,000 IBs, which were well-aimed to give concentrated fire and destruction leaving the city centre more or less a burnt-out ruin.

A secondary raid on the capital by 32 aircraft targeted the docks but in thick mist the bombs were dispersed over a wide area, doing little damage.

21st March, Friday

A doppelganger raid on Plymouth and Devonport consolidated the devastation on the port: an even greater force and heavier bomb load took advantage of the previous night's reconnaissance and still-burning fires to bomb the city accurately. At the end of these two nights the heart of the city was destroyed: the Guildhall and municipal offices were no more and many schools, churches and hospitals damaged or destroyed. More than 300 had been killed and thousands made homeless.

22-28th March, Saturday-Friday

For an astonishing seven nights in a row, Luftwaffe bombing was suspended due to bad weather. Daylight operations took place whenever there was a break in the weather; these were characteristic hit-and-run raids that occurred with little warning and could happen at any time in any place. Usually casualties were few and damage was small but sometimes the attrition peaked with a major incident such as the death of 29 in Poole on 27th March.

Right above: *'When two houses were completely demolished in Plymouth the fireplace and mirrors still stood up to it without breaking, and as this amazing picture shows all the pictures and plates hanging on the wall and china ornaments are still standing on the mantelpieces and even the clock is still going.'*

Right below: Fires still smouldering in Plymouth are hosed by firemen.'

Opposite above: *'The Agony of Plymouth. A view of the damage after the raids in the George Street area.'*

Opposite below: The scene in Russell Street Plymouth in the morning following a night of bombing. There would be no respite in the night to come.

FIRE BOMBS ON TWO LONDON SCHOOLS

Boys Help to Put Out Roof Blaze: "Blitz" on Plymouth

LONDON and Plymouth were the main targets of German raiders last night.

London's raid was short. It was not comparable in intensity with that of Wednesday night and ended well before midnight.

In Plymouth three churches, a cinema, an hotel, stores, business premises and many houses were destroyed or damaged. There were many fires, but they never got out of hand.

"On Smaller Scale"

Here is the Air Ministry and Ministry of Home Security communique:

"Enemy activity last night was on a much smaller scale than of late, and was divided between a town in the South-West of England (later announced to be Plymouth) and London.

"In the former the attack, though not of long duration, succeeded in starting a number of fires.

"These were mainly in business premises, and some of them were serious, but all were being brought

CANTEEN PLEA

TROOPS ASKED "DON'T BUY FOR FRIENDS"

A notice will shortly be displayed in every N.A.A.F.I. canteen appealing to troops not to buy canteen goods except for their own use.

The notice stresses that almost all articles on sale in regimental institutes are now rationed or restricted according to the strength of the unit. By buying goods to send home the soldier tends to create a shortage for himself and his comrades.

FILM KRIEG

Goebbels' Horror Picture

Parachute Mines Descend on Hull

29th March, Saturday

A slight improvement in the weather around Luftwaffe bases in North West France enabled some missions to be flown. Although London had a further night of calm, Bristol and Avonmouth were the targets of minor raids by 20 and 16 bombers respectively; although numerous IBs were dropped, any fires were quickly controlled and damage was not considered significant, though in Avonmouth 11 people were killed.

30th March, Sunday

Little daylight activity by the Luftwaffe in continuing poor weather; over 40 aircraft that set out to raid by night failed to find targets of any importance.

31st March, Monday

Weather conditions continued to hamper Luftwaffe operations but the traditional month-end attack was dutifully mounted on East Coast targets, concentrated on Hull with scattered attacks elsewhere, notably Great Yarmouth. 47 aircraft attacked Hull, dropping 39 tonnes of HE, including 32 of the heavier parachute mines, along with nearly 23,000 IBs. The bombs fell widely over the city and docks area killing around 50 people and damaging over 500 houses and public buildings.

Great Yarmouth provided a secondary target for 24 aircraft that dropped 29 tonnes of HE (including four parachute mines) and 8,000 IBs on the wharves and docks.

Isolated raids took place as far afield as Barrow in Furness, Swansea and Portsmouth.

Right above: '"Here at this moment I have great news for you": Mr. Churchill's characteristic stance when he told Conservative Party leaders of the Slav revolution yesterday.'
On 27th March a military coup deposed the ruling regency government of Yugoslavia because it signed an appeasement treaty with Germany. The heir apparent, Prince Peter, was given the powers of king. This prompted a crushing Nazi invasion the following month, thereby accelerating the invasion of Greece and the opening of the German Eastern Front – all of which Churchill calculated would relieve pressure on Britain.

Right centre: 'Workers clearing damage and debris from Law Courts in the Strand.'

Right below: 'London Inn Damaged in Recent Nazi Raid. 'Jack Straw's Castle', the famous Inn well known to visitors to Hampstead Heath, was damaged in a recent Nazi raid. The Inn is situated at the highest point in London – 500 feet higher than the Cross on St. Paul's Cathedral. Many of the old time prize fights took place at this rendezvous. The picture shows the damaged Inn.'

Opposite above: Plymouth Guildhall after the bombing on the night of 21st March.

Opposite below: The Mayflower Church, Southwark, destroyed by bombs.

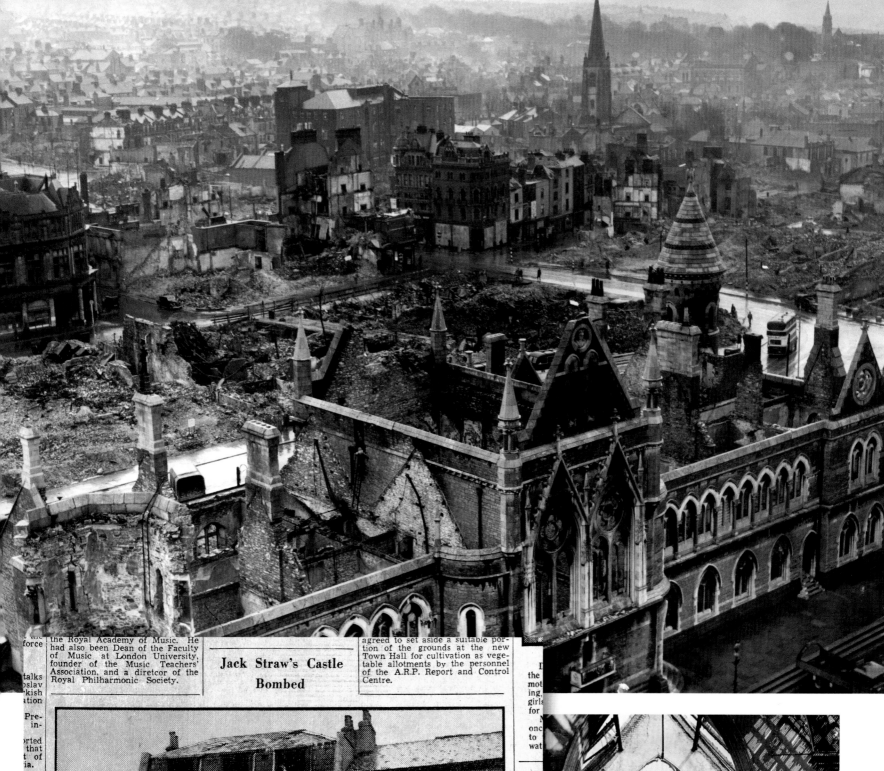

the Royal Academy of Music. He had also been Dean of the Faculty of Music at London University, founder of the Music Teachers' Association, and a diretcor of the Royal Philharmonic Society.

Jack Straw's Castle Bombed

agreed to set aside a suitable portion of the grounds at the new Town Hall for cultivation as vegetable allotments by the personnel of the A.R.P. Report and Control Centre.

A famous London inn which was damaged in a recent air raid is Jack Straw's Castle, at the edge of Hampstead Heath. in London—500 feet higher than St. Paul's Cathedral. Here is a picture taken after the raid. The inn is at the highest point

GERMANY ANNOYED
"Handcuffed" Prisoners

NEW RUMANIA GOVT.
More Civilians Likely

THE NORMANDIE
Sabotage Reports Denied

Above: London's largest crater again at Bank in the City. This picture, taken on 1st April, shows that the temporary bridge had been removed in preparation for proper repairs.

Left: This picture of damage at Blackfriars caused by a bomb in September 1940 was not released for publication until April 1941.

1st, 2nd April, Tuesday, Wednesday

April got off to a quiet start with two nights free from Luftwaffe bombing, however there was some daytime activity, with only one significant incident, on Tuesday, when Seaford was bombed.

3rd April, Thursday

Little in the way of daytime activity but improved weather enabled Luftwaffe night operations to be reinstated and Bristol and Avonmouth were again bombed: 27 aircraft dropped 29 tonnes of HE and 1,100 IBs on Bristol while the 49 raiders attacking Avonmouth unloaded 50 tonnes of HE and nearly 8,000 IBs. Both targets were damaged but the attacks did not have sufficient concentration to have a lasting effect. Elsewhere bombs fell in isolated incidents at other south coast towns such as Portsmouth and Southampton as well as Hull, Slough and Cardiff. Several RAF airfields also came under attack.

4th April, Friday

A busy day over shipping lanes and coastal areas for the Luftwaffe, laying mines but avoiding confrontation with RAF fighters. At night Avonmouth and the Bristol area received their doppelganger attacks: 83 aircraft dropped 80 tonnes of HE and nearly 20,000 IBs in a heavier raid than the previous night. Despite good conditions, including moonlight, bombs were spread over a larger area and though they caused damage, fires were eventually brought under control and the docks were able to recover quickly.

Another minor raid on Great Yarmouth by 18 aircraft but carrying mainly heavy bombs and nearly 10,000 IBs to achieve maximum damage.

5th April, Saturday

As the bad weather returned all Luftwaffe bomber operations by night were cancelled. Even in good weather there had been no daylight attacks on the capital for several weeks and the Germans restricted their daytime activities mainly to attacks on coastal shipping, which meant their planes did not trip the coastal radar warning station alerts and could operate with greater success and minimal losses.

6th April, Sunday

In poor weather only a few Luftwaffe missions were flown by day or night. London was untouched, giving the capital its seventeenth consecutive night of relative peace.

Far Left: 'German bombs find their targets again. This Daily Mail picture shows a nurse salvaging in the wreckage of a London hospital for the aged and infirm, which was bombed on Monday night.' Daily Mail, 9th April 1941.

Left: 'Café de Paris Hit By Bomb During Nazi Raid on Capital. A number of people were trapped and some killed when an enemy bomb fell on the famous Café de Paris restaurant during an enemy raid on the Capital. Girls in dance frocks were rescued from the debris.'

Moonlight Sonata Reprise: Clydeside, Coventry

7th April, Monday

After another quiet day, Operation Moonlight Sonata continued at night with a spectacular attack that focused on Clydeside and Glasgow while virtually covering the country with either air raid alerts or actual bombing raids. The operation involved a force of over 500 aircraft – a mix of bombers and night fighters.

The focus on Clydeside should have taken nearly 300 aircraft to this important shipbuilding and industrial area but only 179 aircraft reached their designated targets in Scotland. 109 bombed alternative targets, numbers of them hooking up with colleagues bombing Liverpool or Bristol. Successfully navigating to Glasgow even with help from the moon and directional beams was not easy and involved crossing substantial areas of Britain; inevitably targets of opportunity were plentiful and some 20 other places were bombed, including London, which received parachute mines and heavy bombs.

Clydeside received 204 tonnes of HE and 26,000 IBs; taking a closer look at these statistics reveals the might of the weapons being used – a total of 39 parachute mines, only 7 of them the lighter version, and 7 SC1000 fell on Dumbarton alone and this was just one part of the attack; the Rolls Royce factory at Hillington was designated to receive its share – 72 tonnes of HE, of which a staggering 14 were parachute mines and 13 were SC1000.

The bomb load on Liverpool was 65 tonnes of HE and over 13,000 IBs; on Bristol it was 32 tonnes of HE and over 6,000 IBs; Great Yarmouth over 3,000 IBs. Considering the breadth of this operation the reported deaths of 130 seem incredibly light. Much damage was done and included specific industrial targets such as John Brown's shipyard in Clydeside and Short Brothers aircraft works in Rochester. This night's work by the Luftwaffe brought terror on a previously unknown strategic scale. The country's defences were still poor but were looking up – five bombers were brought down by AI-equipped night fighters. In a new development, rocket defences at Cardiff reported the first kill during the night. This was the first of the Z-Batteries and the new rocket technology would soon become an important weapon for ground-to-air defence and aerial bombardment. Many of the batteries had been built but the rockets themselves were not yet widely available.

Right above: **Coventry's wrecked shopping centre was left a smouldering ruin after Luftwaffe raids in November 1940. Heavy damage was again inflicted on the night of Tuesday 8th April.**

Right below: **A shopping arcade in Birmingham shattered by bombs.**

Opposite below: *'The Coventry Blitz. There were scenes of devastation following the two heavy night raids on Coventry last Tuesday. The pictures taken give some idea of the damage caused by the indiscriminate bombing. This one shows a destroyed school, with boys sorting among the debris.'*

38 Shot Down in 4 Nights

By NOEL MONKS, Daily Mail Air Correspondent

NIGHT fighters of the R.A.F. and A.A. gunners are out to break their records for bringing down night raiders.

Having shot down 38 Nazi bombers in four nights this week, making 42 since April 1, they were last evening within one of their record total of 43 for March. And last night was the night of the full moon.

Heavy Night Raid on West Town

By Daily Mail Raid Reporters

GERMAN bombers concentrated their forces last night in a two-phase attack on a West of England town.

Waves of raiders flew over, and the attack quickly developed on a major scale.

Thousands of incendiaries and many H.E.s were dropped.

As the raiders roared over in moonlight, guns in all parts of the town sent up a heavy barrage— fiercer at times than ever before.

There was a lull after an intense bombardment and then planes came over t...

R.A...

Brit...
sweeps...
and th...

A s...
which ...
towed ...
attacke...
schmit...
them ...
fight ...
fighter ...
ours w...

An ...

"It ...
bombe...
gunfire...
ten de...
enemy...

This week has proved conclusively that the moon is no longer an exclusively "bomber's moon."

With the rapid improvement in our A.A. defences and "other devices" there are reasons for hoping that ultimately moonlight raiding will be made almost as costly to the enemy as daylight attacks.

It must be admitted, however, that the German night defences are also making good use of the moonlight, but some of our bombers are proving too good for their night fighters and are actually shooting them down.

There are no cases on record where Nazi bombers have shot down R.A.F. night fighters.

With both sides improving their defences against night attacks, bombing at night is becoming more and more a matter of grim determination on the part of the pilots.

More for Berlin

In this the R.A.F. are head and shoulders over the Luftwaffe. We...

8th April, Tuesday

Relatively clear conditions led to many daytime sorties by the Luftwaffe around coastal areas but numerous reconnaissance raids intruded inland, no doubt gathering evidence of the previous night for assessment.

By night another massed force of over 360 aircraft set out, this time with the primary target of Coventry: 237 dropped their bombs on the city releasing 315 tonnes of HE and over 23,000 IBs. Damage was considerable and there were many casualties, including over 280 killed. The city's factories were affected but effective fire-fighting restricted worse damage.

Elsewhere, Portsmouth was the secondary target for a minor attack and many other targets of opportunity were bombed, with Great Yarmouth once again being a victim; other towns on the coast and in the vicinity of Coventry also reported incidents. RAF fighters flew over 250 sorties and claimed six enemy raiders destroyed. As a percentage of the force deployed, this was insignificant but the improvement against previous efforts was highly encouraging to the frustrated leaders of Fighter Command, not to mention their night fighter squadrons who had to stay patient for the very slow supply of their AI-equipped Beaufighters which Sholto Douglas believed would alter the balance of night attacks more in the RAF's favour.

9th April, Wednesday

The Luftwaffe was busy by day but attack proper was reserved for the hours of darkness when Birmingham and Tyneside were the targets for major attacks and Bristol/Avonmouth, Lowestoft, Ipswich and Plymouth were the subjects of secondary raids. The total number of German aircraft involved across the country was over 480.

The raid on Birmingham was carried out by 237 bombers that dropped 285 tonnes of HE and 40,000 IBs over a four-hour period. Fires caused a serious problem owing to water shortages. Destruction was widespread across the city from the centre to the factory areas and suburbs, where many homes and commercial properties were damaged or destroyed; the damage to infrastructure delayed or temporarily halted much of the city's industry.

In the early hours of Thursday morning the attack on Tyneside gained momentum but although 116 aircraft were involved, bombing was over a widespread area causing damage from Newcastle to Tynemouth and the coastal towns north and south of the Tyne, stretching south as far as Hull and Lowestoft. Some targets of military importance were hit but generally the attack was very dispersed.

To demonstrate that the Luftwaffe had failed to disable Britain's attacking capability, on this night RAF Bomber Command raided Berlin, damaging the State Opera House, a symbol close to the cultural and geographical heart of the Nazi Third Reich. No doubt giving Hitler cause for thought this raid would have repercussions later in the month. The Luftwaffe had their own concerns, for on this night RAF night fighters claimed 13 bombers shot down and more damaged: things were changing in the night skies.

Luftwaffe's Easter Message

10th April, Thursday

Birmingham's doppelganger arrived with predictable force, but with reduced intensity. Portsmouth and Nottingham were secondary targets but a large number of bombers that failed to find their designated targets and attached themselves to other raiders led to escalated raids on Southampton, Portsmouth and Yarmouth, while targets of opportunity resulted in bombs falling widely across the country.

Birmingham suffered fire damage but the destruction was considered less severe than the previous night; nonetheless 350 died in the two raids. Many of the bombers failing to find Birmingham located Coventry and delivered their bombs, causing much damage including to the main post office; the death toll in beleaguered Coventry was 126.

11th April, Friday

Easter Weekend arrived and the moon was full; London had not received a major attack since 19th March. As the people of the capital observed the pounding of provincial and coastal cities they must have wondered what was going on. The devastation of New Year's Eve and the insidious threats delivered by Lord Haw-Haw might well have led them to suspect that something very unpleasant was in store for the capital – possibly this weekend.

On Good Friday Winston Churchill travelled by special train to Bristol with his wife Clementine and their daughter in the company of Australian Prime Minister Robert Menzies and US Ambassador John Winant. Churchill was the Chancellor of Bristol University and he was due to confer honorary doctorates on the two men in a ceremony during Saturday. Fortunately the party spent the night in their sleeper compartments with the train in a safe siding, for during the night, Bristol and Avonmouth yet again suffered a major attack. In two distinct phases, very specific raids by over 200 bombers loaded with a total of 200 tonnes of HE and around 35,000 IBs took place on Bristol, Avonmouth and Portishead causing considerable damage. In addition to extensive destruction in Bristol's centre, the area's docks were damaged by major fires. One notable casualty was the city's tram system which was disabled on this night, never to run again. 140 people breathed their last.

As for the great degree ceremony: on arriving at Bristol, Churchill was taken on a tour of the blitzed city then joined the graduation party in the presence of an audience that included many who had not slept all night while fire-watching or on ARP duty. Honours were duly conferred and in the afternoon the Prime Minister's train journey continued to Swansea.

The attack on the secondary target of Portsmouth was relatively minor and other lesser targets also fell victim to off-course bombers.

12-14th April, Saturday-Monday

Uncertain weather conditions kept Luftwaffe operations to a minimum during the remainder of the Easter weekend and there were no major raids, although several minor raids led to separate incidents in which between 10 and 20 people died. No bombs fell on London at all.

Right: *'"We Will Give It To Them Back"' Words of the Premier, spoken when he met civil defenders still working on battered homes in Bristol on Saturday night after the previous night's savage raid. Mr. Churchill was accompanied by Mr. Winant, United States Ambassador, and Mr. Menzies, Australia's Premier. Later he conferred honorary degrees on them as Chancellor of Bristol University, and said: "When I go about the country I see the damage...but I also see the spirit of an unconquerable people." Parts of the city were still smouldering as the ceremony took place. The death toll for the raid, which lasted several hours, is still rising, but casualties might easily have been higher.'*

Below: Fire-fighters at work on a blaze in Pimlico on the night of 16th April.

Opposite top: In the major raid of 16th April St Paul's was hit again – here is a close-up of the huge hole the bomb tore in the North Transept floor.

Opposite centre: *'Leaping flames and billowing smoke rise over the London rooftops. This was the height of Wednesday night's raid, recorded by staff cameraman W.R. Turner from a rooftop while high-explosive bombs crashed into the Thames.'*

Opposite bottom: Nurses salvaging in a wrecked hospital.

15th April, Tuesday

Belfast suffered a major attack; a minor attack on 7th April had alerted the authorities to the city's vulnerability but previous wisdom held that Belfast's distance from European bases and the need to cross the coastal defences no fewer than six times would deter the Luftwaffe. This false doctrine was fully exposed when 180 German bombers rendezvoused over the little-protected city to drop 203 tonnes of HE and almost 30,000 IBs. An astonishing 76 parachute mines were released, the great majority being of the heavier type.

Clear and well-lit conditions permitted accurate sighting on the three strategic targets of the city's docks, the Harland and Wolff shipyards and the Short & Harland aircraft works – all of which were hit with some success. Worst of all was the horrifying death toll of around 700 – an indication of how ill-prepared the city was, being poorly provided with shelters and defences which were the right of the strategic ports in the rest of Britain.

But Belfast was not the only bombing target that night – other raiders were sent to Tyneside and Portland while stragglers that didn't make it bombed alternative targets with 51 aircraft bombing Liverpool. Secondary targets didn't necessarily mean light raids: Tyneside collected 29 parachute mines on this night.

16th April, Wednesday

London's many weeks of relative peace were shattered by the heaviest air attack on Britain to date. Some 890 tons of HE and more than 150,000 IBs were dropped in a raid on the capital carried out by 685 bombers that lasted for about nine and a half hours. Many crews flew multiple sorties to give a conveyor belt bombardment.

Damage was severe over a wide area of London. Many fires were started – 8 major, 41 serious and 2,200 smaller. There were the inevitable interruptions to road, rail and utilities. Many landmark buildings such as St Paul's Cathedral, the Houses of Parliament, the Law Courts and many churches were damaged to varying degrees.

Casualty figures of 1,180 dead and 2,230 badly injured were the highest for any single night's bombing and reflected the severity of the attack in which, for all the devastation caused by the Luftwaffe, German losses could be counted on one hand. This was surely as bad as it could get and the people of London gritted their teeth waiting for Churchill to keep his promise to give it back to the Nazis.

17th April, Thursday

Daylight incidents were few and the target for tonight's raid was Portsmouth once more. As a naval port, the city was important to the Battle of the Atlantic and the force mustered by the Luftwaffe to neutralise it was immense – almost 250 bombers dropped 346 tonnes of HE and 46,000 IBs. In among the HE was a horrendous total of nearly 200 parachute mines, mostly of the heavier type, and 36 SC1000. The ordnance was aimed at fortified and otherwise defended naval targets and although damage was widespread in the Hampshire hinterland the civilian casualties were relatively few. Many fires burned in the naval dockyards.

Hitler's Birthday Raid

18th April, Friday

Overcast skies with low cloud and rain kept Luftwaffe activity to a minimum by day and night, giving the recently pounded cities some chance to recuperate.

19th April, Saturday

However, there was to be no lasting lull: another massive blow was dealt against London – this time the attack was by over 700 aircraft that dropped more than 1,000 tonnes of HE during the raid mounted by Göring in 'celebration' of Hitler's fifty-second birthday. The mounting size of the bombers' payload and the huge number of heavy bombs deployed defies belief: on this night over 250 parachute mines were released, most of them the heavier type; four of the heaviest SC2500s; 10 SC1800s and 271 SC1000. Added to the cocktail were over 150,000 IBs.

Damage and casualties (1,200 deaths) were severe, but the impact of this heavy attack was somewhat limited in its first phase by poor visibility. The intended concentration point, eastward along the river from Tower Bridge to Woolwich, was difficult to achieve and bombing was scattered over a wide area; the second phase was more concentrated causing significant damage to the docks and the East End generally. The scale of this attack was Armageddon-like but London was a very large target and took the terrible blows with grim determination. It would be London's heaviest raid of the War but the residents of the city didn't know that and had to deal with the fear that worse might come.

The press generally focused on Britain's aggressiveness towards Germany and the international aspect of the war. So the Yugoslavian capitulation three days earlier – the outcome of the Nazis brutal intervention in the Balkans – was of more headline interest than the backyard damage going on in England. And context was important at this time: when the rage of the Blitz could hardly have made sense to the population of Britain. Context helped make sense of it all – the opening up of another front in the Balkans forced Germany's hand to turn on its temporary ally Russia and to conquer – something Hitler thought he could do 'on the side' while dealing with Britain. In fact Hitler's seasoned generals had no wish whatsoever to carry out this catastrophic stratagem but the Führer was not to be denied. The compromise, in face of the failed invasion and subjugation of Britain, was to administer a ruinous bombardment to leave it impotent until the moment of Hitler's choosing when the Blitzkrieg would finish the task. Hitler clung to this view in some form or other until early 1944 by which time the Allies had unshakeable confidence that the Nazis would be overthrown.

20th April, Sunday

The Luftwaffe appeared busy during the day but mounted no serious raids; by night very few bombers operated and no significant missions were flown.

NIGHT LONDON WILL NOT FORGET—NOR FORGIVE

ROOFTOP VIEW OF THE RAID

Raid Rescue Squads Dig All Day Long

By Daily Mail Raid Reporters

THROUGH streets covered with hosepipes and running with water, past shells of buildings with smoke and steam pouring from gaping windows, London's workers picked their way to shop and office yesterday.

All day long, after the heaviest and most vicious bombing the capital has yet endured, the firemen were at work and rescue squads sought among wreckage for victims who might still be alive.

"Casualties were heavy and considerable damage was done," said the Ministry communiqué. "It was the greatest air raid of all time," chanted Berlin's Press and radio.

Six raiding bombers were brought down in the night. Daylight revealed to London this catalogue of material damage: Eight hospitals, block of flats, several churches, a number of hotels, schools, big stores, public houses, a theatre, a music hall, two cinemas, a club, and many shops—all hit by the raiders.

The catalogue of human suffering is harder to estimate. But the Canadian Red Cross alone distributed yesterday 8,000 articles of clothing to 1,000 homeless people.

They gave away more than 1,500 blankets and large quantities of food—soup, stew, hash, cheese, and jam.

This work began within ten minutes of the call for help being received.

* * *

IT is hard, almost impossible . . .

workers' flats, neatly arranged around a courtyard, and in the centre was a shelter.

With the freakishness of fate, that was where the bomb fell. The flats hemmed in the blast. Many people were killed in their little homes.

As I write this the search among the ruins of the shelter still goes on.

* * *

ANOTHER bomb missed a surface shelter, but the blast brought a building down, and it crashed on the shelter.

All night the rescue workers delved here and brought out a boy of 13 who was injured but alive.

And it was his courage that the rescuers praised: "He was plucky," they told me. "He could hear us and he kept us at it."

Strange sights there were: Tea and cakes being handed . . .

Captured during Wednesday night's terror bombing of London.

GERMAN AIRMAN

SEE, he is young. I had such hopes of him, my son.
And he was mine. The love I gave he won
By being gentle, understanding, kind.
And now I find
Those eyes that smiled are masked and bleak with hate.
He has no father, mother, save the State,
No God but Steel.
No mind to treasure and no heart to feel
The warmth of friendship and the pain of tears,
With love shut out as we would shut out fears,
To Death indentured and to Murder bound . . .

By Daily Mail Reporter

BOMB GAME —SIX DIE

A BOY found a small British practice bomb in the country on Good Friday.

He threw it down quarries, but failed to explode it. So he took it back to Cheltenham where he lived.

Yesterday he and other children were hitting the bomb with a hammer—they were playing Raiders. It exploded. Six were killed and two injured.

The explosion brought crowds out. The first to reach the scene, a piece of waste ground, were Mrs. Burford and Mrs. Chitty, mothers of two of the children killed.

The dead children are: Kenneth Burford, aged 10; Percy Mitchell, 14; Marion Easdon, 10; Trevor Welling, 6; John Chitty, 7; and Beryl Lewis, 8. The children injured are: Bernard Lewis, 6; and Pauline Chitty, 11.

Children Asked to Fire-Watch

Complaints that senior children had been asked to do fire watching at schools, and that some teachers feared victimisation if they did not do it, were made yesterday at the National Union of Women Teachers' conference at York.

Miss A. A. Kenyon, trustee of the union, moving a resolution demanding that school fire watching should be incorporated in the general scheme, said that teachers were being drawn in to fire watch "by the back stairs." Miss F. M. Brooks . . .

39 Cricket Matches for Lord's

By CHARLES GRAVES

DESPITE the Blitz, the English cricket season will make an official appearance this year on May 3 at Lord's, when the London Fire Service will play Reading University to the tunes of the London Fire Service's own band.

In all, 39 cricket matches are scheduled for Lord's. Admission to all of these will be a minimum of 6d. compared with last season, when in many cases there was no admission fee at all.

There will be six two-days matches, far the most important of which will be the R.A.F. versus the rest of the world (all receipts going to the R.A.F. Benevolent Fund).

Professionals' Future

There is no county cricket this year, and it is doubtful whether county cricket will ever be the same again.

Sir Pelham Warner was wondering yesterday whether anyone, unless he is a professional, will have the time and money to be able to play a three-days cricket match again.

He was also wondering what money cricket professionals will be able to command in peace time. Sir Pelham is well aware that in Australia cricket matches are one-day affairs except for inter-State . . .

Left: This picture of clearing up in Piccadilly after the raid of 16th April was embargoed under the '28-day rule' – 'not for publication before the daily paper on Friday May 16th.'

Above: 'London's Recent Air Bombardment. The bust of Dr. Joseph Parker, the famous nonconformist preacher, still stands amid the ruins of the famous City Temple, burnt out after a recent air raid. This was the only Free Church in the City, and many of Britain's Prime Ministers had spoken from its pulpit.'

Opposite above: The damage in the City Temple – the only Free Church in the City.

Opposite below: 'Firespotting in His Bombed Church. The Vicar of a bombed church was killed by enemy action while on duty firespotting on the porch of his church, during one of the worst Nazi raids yet on the London area. His wife, who was with him, was injured. The picture shows the porch of the bombed church where the Vicar was standing when he was killed by enemy action.'

The Agony of Plymouth

21st April, Monday

The Luftwaffe returned to the task of destroying Plymouth which it had begun with the ferocious twin attacks in March. Plymouth was an easy and quick night-time excursion across the Channel and with early morning fog forecast, the bombers had to get back to their bases before fog obscured them. In the first of three consecutive night attacks, 120 aircraft racked with 139 tonnes of HE and almost 36,000 IBs raided the naval port and the docks of Devonport. The naval installations were seriously damaged and much destruction took place in the city centre; an estimated 6,000 houses were damaged or destroyed.

Elsewhere the Luftwaffe found resources to drop heavy bombs on Great Yarmouth and Portsmouth. The latter would suffer consecutive attacks of varying intensity over the following two nights.

22nd April, Tuesday

This night's raid on Plymouth was virtually a carbon copy of the previous night, but slightly heavier, reviving fires that had been extinguished. By now the Luftwaffe was bombing ruins.

Again Portsmouth suffered a second minor attack in a row but the bombs were heavy enough and nine people died here while 20 perished in Southsea.

23rd April, Wednesday

In the third consecutive attack on Plymouth the Luftwaffe flew in for the kill. A slightly smaller force than on the previous nights was guided to its targets by fires still blazing from the night before. The reporting of the Plymouth Blitz by the press and the BBC played down the damage to Britain's most important naval port. This incensed the city's Lady Mayoress, Viscountess Astor, who berated the officials whom she considered had no feeling or respect for the city's pain. Sadly, there would be more to come. From a modern perspective, the pulverising of Plymouth by the Luftwaffe seems to make little sense: in addition to the wholesale destruction, 400 civilians had died and 256 injured in the three night attacks. However a sideways look at Bomber Command perhaps provides an answer, for RAF planes were nightly attacking the German naval bases of Bremen, Kiel and Wilhelmshaven as part of the Battle of the Atlantic strategy. The concentration of force by the British bombers came nowhere near that of the Luftwaffe and perhaps Plymouth was a Nazi gibe saying, this is the way it's done.

24th April, Thursday

Portsmouth was once more the target for the night but in many cases the load of heavy bombs failed to hit the docks and mistakenly fell on the Isle of Wight.

E OF ATHENS

BATTLE OF ATLANTIC DECISIVE

'War May Spread but End is Certain'—Churchill

ONE of the greatest audiences that have ever listened to one man heard last night's speech by the Prime Minister, who gave a graphic review of the war and in particular of the events of the past month.

Some of the most enthusiastic listeners in Britain's millions were Plymouth people who, bombed out of their homes, are temporarily housed in rest centres.

The United States put aside all other things and interests to-day to listen to Mr. Churchill. Great lines of cars blocked the highways as their drivers stopped and switched on their radios.

Broadcasting officials estimated that more Americans were listening during Mr. Churchill's half-hour than at any other time except when the Presidential election results were announced.

Immediate reaction was this: Britain is looking more and more to America for succour, and America will not fail her.

The speech did a great deal of good here in lifting and bolstering morale, which has been sagging as a result of the Balkan reverse

The impression was that "this is the sort of fighting ally to have."

The Prime Minister gave two settled convictions—that the war must be won in the West—in this island and on the Atlantic—and that it must end in complete triumph for the democracies.

He spoke with deep gravity of the fight to keep Britain's sea life-lines open, and declared that owing to President Roosevelt's decision to extend the United States patrols

Two Down in Night Raids

German bombers were over several areas in Britain last night, and it is believed that two of them were shot down.

Two hospitals were hit by bombs in a coast town in the south of England. One was demolished and it is feared that there have been a number of casualties.

At both hospitals efforts were being made early to-day to rescue imprisoned patients.

Up to early morning there was no London Alert.

Several people were killed—a family of five among them—when a bomb fell on an hotel in East Anglia on Saturday night. It is suggested that car lights in the hotel car park attracted the raider.

VOLCANO BOMBS

THE great German port of Hamburg and the naval base of Bremerhaven had their first taste of our new "beautiful bomb" on Saturday night.

Here is how pilots described the effect of these most-powerful-ever explosives:

Hamburg.—"A huge heaving mass like a volcanic eruption, which rose and settled down into a great red glow fully half a mile in diameter.

"We were ten miles off, but even from that distance it was terrific," said another pilot.

Bremerhaven.—"After it had

U.S. MINERS SAY NO

From Daily Mail Correspondent
New York, Sunday.—Efforts of the U.S. Mediation Board to settle the coalmines work stoppage collapsed to-night. Mr. W. H. Davis, board chairman, said southern operators rejected

Opposite above: 'The Agony of Plymouth. Thousands, nay millions, of sailors have known this as home. Here was the mighty pile of the Royal Sailors' Rest, founded by Dame Agnes Weston. Now, standing in Fore Street, the Needle of Devonport Column can be seen across the littering bricks.'

Above: 'The Agony of Plymouth. Looking across the debris of George Street to the ruined Baptist Chapel and roofless Guildhall.'

Top: 'The Navy Lends a Hand – After Third Successive 'Blitz' On Plymouth. Sailors helping in clearing debris from the streets of Plymouth, after it had been bombed by Nazi planes for the third night in succession recently.'

Opposite below: Dante's Inferno. A Scene in Dante's Road, London, after the previous Thursday's raid. This picture shows a squad clearing away debris.

177

25th April, Friday

While London had a further night of calm the Luftwaffe turned their attentions to Sunderland with 57 aircraft dropping 80 tonnes of HE and nearly 10,000 IBs. The target was the docks and works of the town but it seems that few bombs fell accurately. In the payload were 64 parachute mines, and a significant number of these drifted on the wind to the north shore of the Tyne causing many deaths and widespread destruction from Newcastle to Wallsend.

26th April, Saturday

Liverpool and Merseyside were the destination for the Luftwaffe bombers this night. By another coincidence (or not perhaps), Winston Churchill visited the city the day before in the company of Averell Harriman and James Forrestal, envoys sent by US President Roosevelt. Displaying confidence in the defences of the Western Approaches was important to the recently enacted Lend-Lease programme.

92 aircraft attacked the city with a load of 113 tonnes of HE and over 15,000 IBs; 65 parachute mines were in the mix. In the period of the new moon visibility was poor and despite parachute flares, bombing was dispersed.

27th April, Sunday

Winston Churchill returned to London after a week's tour of the bombed provincial cities to broadcast to the nation. He praised the spirit of every man, woman and child in Britain and gave his impressions of this trip: 'What a triumph the life of these battered cities is over the worst which fire and bombs can do. What a vindication of the civilised and decent way of living we have been trying to work for and work towards in our island.'

Attacks continued on Portsmouth which had been a constant secondary target in recent nights. This time it was a heavy raid by only 38 aircraft that dropped 69 tonnes of HE and 7,000 IBs. In the HE were 41 parachute mines, mostly the heavier version. The attack caused serious damage and a large number of casualties – 85 civilians reported dead.

28, 29th April, Monday, Tuesday

Plymouth-Devonport suffered two major raids on consecutive nights – the Luftwaffe's parting shot. The two main shopping centres and nearly every civic building were destroyed, along with 26 schools, 8 cinemas and 41 churches. In total, 3,754 houses were destroyed with a further 18,398 seriously damaged. During 59 separate bombing raids 1,172 civilians were killed and 4,448 injured. Morale too, despite Churchill's Sunday broadcast, was shaky since Plymouth had been exposed to the most psychologically damaging form of aerial bombardment – namely, concentrated heavy raids for several nights followed by a lull before more nights of heavy raids. Terror and uncertainty was inevitable.

30th April, Wednesday

Poor weather kept the Luftwaffe at bay: Britain, in its corner, like a battered but determined boxer, drew breath and awaited the next bloody bout.

Top: 'St. George's Day Service Amid the Ruins. In celebration of St. George's Day a service was held amid the ruins of the Church of St. Andrew-by-the-Wardrobe, Queen Victoria Street, London. The fine old Church, which was rebuilt after the Great Fire of 1666, was badly damaged during one of the Nazi attacks on the London area. The picture shows the Rev. John R. Sankey conducting the service in the ruined church, with the Union Jack still flying amid the damage.'

Above left: 'This family, made homeless when a bomb damaged their Westminster home earlier this month, are moving to a new billet in a £100-a-week Park-Lane luxury flat.'

Above right: Inspecting damage to St George's Roman Catholic Cathedral, Southwark, on St George's Day.

Merseyside May Week Blitz

1-7th May, Thursday – Wednesday

The first seven nights in May saw Merseyside in receipt of similar treatment experienced by Plymouth in March and April, but in Liverpool's case it was seven consecutive nights of sustained attack interspersed with two concentrated major raids. It became known by the somewhat festive-sounding title of 'Merseyside's May Week'. Damage from the 860 tonnes of HE and 106,000 incendiaries dropped during the seven nights was severe: casualties amounted to 1,900 killed and 1,450 seriously injured and as many as 70,000 people were made homeless.

The Luftwaffe's unremitting onslaught pushed the civilian population close to breaking point and rumours circulated that the people had demonstrated for a truce with Germany resulting in martial law being instated. While this would hardly be surprising under the circumstances, the port complex bore their blitz with fortitude and examples of outstanding bravery by the defence organisations who were stretched to the limit.

The worst raid of the week on the night of 2/3rd brought 298 aircraft over the city to deliver 363 tonnes of HE and 50,000 IBs; fires raged everywhere and the fire-fighters struggled to contain them. The docks were badly hit and a number of ships damaged and destroyed, including the *Malakand* loaded with 1,000 tonnes of ammunition; it exploded spectacularly, destroying the dock and damaging the surrounding wharves. The same night an ammunition train in a siding at Clubmoor was set alight. A 34-year-old goods guard, George Roberts, was later awarded the George Medal in recognition of the leading part which he played in this heroic life-saving action: all along the train wagons were exploding, but he and other men calmly uncoupled the rear section before the flames spread to it then shunted it out of danger.

The pattern of German strategic bombing considerably disturbed the Ministry of Home Security in at least two ways: first they questioned whether the Nazi policy was to destroy Britain's major cities one by one; second they wondered at the might of the Nazi war machine to inflict concentrated devastation night after night on a main target while conducting other major raids across Britain. Yet Military Intelligence indicated furthermore that Hitler was simultaneously preparing a massive attack on Russia. That Britain could continue to function under such pressure is a testimony to Churchill's unwavering leadership and the courage of the population.

Right: **The burned-out interior of St Nicholas Church, Liverpool, which was hit by a number of incendiary bombs in a raid on 20th December 1940.**

Hull Raids Leave 440 Dead and 30,000 Homeless

4th May, Sunday

Nearly 500 German aircraft took to the skies this night with 204 attacking Belfast to drop 237 tonnes of HE and over 95,000 IBs. Observers saw the city from the air as one enormous conflagration that caused considerable damage, including the Harland & Short works. An estimated 150 people died.

Elsewhere, raids continued on Merseyside; Barrow in Furness was also attacked while scattered raids took place across the country.

5th May, Monday

On Monday, by night, the Luftwaffe operated similar numbers to Sunday's attacks, this time directing raids to Clydeside, Tyneside, Plymouth and Hull. The shipyards of Greenock were badly hit but the Clydeside attack was spread over three centres, all of which suffered considerable damage.

Elsewhere the raids continued a high level of attrition with the latest load of firebombs causing serious problems in Merseyside where the water infrastructure was out of action.

6th May, Tuesday

Glasgow and Clydeside received a doppelganger while secondary raids followed the pattern of Monday night. The casualty total for the two Clydeside raids was 306 dead.

On this night the RAF was able to claim 12 enemy planes shot down with another 12 either probable kills or damaged.

7th May, Wednesday

Over 360 Luftwaffe aircraft were engaged in night attacks; while 166 gave the Liverpool blitz its parting shot of May Week; 72 others mounted a major raid on Hull. Merseyside's share was 232 tonnes of HE and 30,000 IBs while Hull received 110 tonnes of HE and a mere 10,000 IBs. As for the terrorising parachute mines, Liverpool took 26 against Hull's 66. The coup de grâce on Merseyside was very damaging and left dock handling capacity reduced to 25 per cent, 66,000 houses damaged or destroyed and 11 out of 12 Rest Centres out of action.

Hull suffered considerable damage to public buildings, commercial property and homes but damage to the docks was reported not to be severe. As the fires died down under the hoses, 10,000 found themselves homeless.

Elsewhere, bombs fell on Manchester, Barrow in Furness and Bristol.

8th May, Thursday

True to form, the Luftwaffe delivered a doppelganger raid on Hull although apparently not intended because the primary target was Sheffield. The heaviest raid of the night turned out to be Hull after poor weather conditions over Sheffield led to a last minute diversion by 120 aircraft that dropped 167 tonnes of HE and almost 20,000 IBs. Damage to Hull was heavy, particularly in the eastern area of the city, and after the two nights over 440 were left dead and 30,000 homeless. Damage to the railway system interfered with the working of the docks but the water supply had not been cut.

Nottingham was bombed by 95 aircraft, seven of which proceeded onwards to Derby to drop the remainder of their load on the Rolls Royce works, along with 16 other bombers for which it was a primary target. In good bombing conditions, the Luftwaffe delivered 137 tonnes of HE and nearly 7,000 IBs on Nottingham; most of the resulting damage was reported to be to residential and commercial property, though the target was an arms factory. Casualties were heavy because of hits on two shelters: including deaths in outlying suburbs, almost 200 were killed.

34 aircraft claimed to have bombed Sheffield in poor visibility and although casualties were reported, damage was not detailed. Elsewhere in the country bombs fell over a wide area from Barrow in the North West to Chelmsford in the South East.

9th May, Friday

No single main target for the Luftwaffe this night but a focus on the airfield bases of Bomber Command. Nearly 100 aircraft ranged over Britain seeking specific targets and often dropping their bombs at a very low level.

Main picture: This is Liverpool after demolition squads cleared up the damage of the Christmas Blitz. 'May Week' saw even greater devastation.

Far left: 'The road to business was not easy. But the girls picked their way through the debris with a laugh and a smile. These Daily Mail pictures show the spirit of the City after 'reprisals'.'
Daily Mail, 13th May 1941

Left: Manchester burns, but this scene could have been witnessed in any of Britain's major cities during the Blitz. Fire crews faced an unequal struggle but fought their tireless foe with determination.

NO. 14,053   ONE PENNY   FOR KING AND EMPIRE   MONDAY, MAY 12, 1941

ABBEY AND PARLIAMENT BOMBED

Debating Chamber Wrecked: Big Ben Damaged

THE Houses of Parliament, with Big Ben and Westminster Hall, and Westminster Abbey and the British Museum, were among the buildings damaged by bombs in what the German High Command yesterday claimed to be a "reprisal raid on military targets in London."

Big Ben, with its face scarred and blackened, having been hit by a high explosive, continued to show the time, though the apparatus which broadcasts the chimes to the world was for a time out of order.

The Debating Chamber of the Commons—the cradle of democracy—was wrecked, and it is feared that it cannot be used again until it is rebuilt. The Speaker's Chair and the Government front benches are now merely charred wood.

High-explosive bombs and incendiaries fell on the Houses of Parliament, and soon flames were seen licking round Big Ben's Tower. They spread shortly afterwards to the Abbey.

One explosive fell into the centre of the Chamber, and in a short time

HE DID HIS JOB— DID YOU?

3 DOWN IN RAIDS LAST EVENING

Coast Attacks

AN Air Ministry communiqué issued this morning said that three Nazi raiders were de-

IRAQ FRONT CABLE

British Force Push Towards Baghdad

From Daily Mail Special Correspondent

IN IRAQ, Thursday (Delayed).

BRONZED troopers man the parapet a few yards away as I begin this despatch from the first post in Iraq to be recaptured from Raschid Ali's rebel forces.

Standing at loopholes in the dun stone walls the men keenly scan the distance under their yellow, flowing headdress. Out of sight, to the east, a screen of our men are pushing out in the direction of Habbaniyah and Baghdad.

Stony, red-brown sands stretch in every direction, featureless except for the line of deeper red marking the trench in which runs the Haifa-Iraq pipeline, dead straight from horizon to horizon.

A line of white steel telegraph poles runs alongside the pipeline.

This message is going back to the cable terminal in an R.A.F. fighter which brought me here with two other correspondents.

The machine is scarred with bullet holes from ground fire during a brilliant raid on the rebels out-

Blitz Idlers Injured in Street

By Daily Mail Reporter

Idle sightseers—some of the thousands who thronged round the bombed buildings in London last night and interfered with the work of A.R.P. workers—were given a sharp lesson.

The pavement suddenly collapsed

BENGHAZI SHELLED AGAIN

HEAVY blows by the Navy and R.A.F. against the Germans in Libya were reported early this morning.

British warships made a second attack on Benghazi late on Saturday night, according to the official German News Agency.

An R.A.F. Middle East communiqué issued at 2 a.m. announced extensive damage to enemy aircraft on the aerodromes at Catania and Comiso (Sicily).

The attack in mid-afternoon came as a complete surprise, and was highly successful. At Catania three groups of H.E. 111's and one cluster of Junkers 88's were attacked. Troops running from mess to shelter were machine-gunned.

At Comiso the attack was even more successful and about 30 officers running into the mess were machine-gunned.

At least six heavy aircraft were left blazing in one group and others in another group were set on fire.

During Saturday night heavy bombers attacked Tripoli harbour. Direct hits were scored on the Spanish Mole and power station and harbour.

An Admiralty communiqué issued on Thursday announced that Benghazi was bombarded on Thursday morning. Ships in the harbour were hit and two supply ships of 3,000 tons and 6,000 tons intercepted and sunk.

Bombers' Moon
Over London

10th May, Saturday

After a considerable lull, the Luftwaffe returned to attack London at the peak of the full moon or, as it became known during the Blitz, the 'bombers' moon'; the River Thames was also at its lowest tidal level, amounting to perfect conditions for the bombers which were able to concentrate on the target area around the docks and the East End. During an eight-hour raid, beginning at 23.15 hours, more than 700 tonnes of HE and nearly 90,000 IBs were dropped into that concentration point by more than 500 Luftwaffe aircraft, flying over 570 sorties – requiring some to fly two or more sorties in order to deliver the tonnage set for this attack.

Fire-fighters were faced with an awesome task: there were 9 conflagrations together with 20 major and about 2,200 other fires in an area covering around 700 acres. In many cases, water supplies ran out and all the fire-fighters could do was helplessly watch flames consume the buildings they had struggled to save.

Casualties from this raid were the largest for any night of the Blitz: 1,436 people died and 1,792 were seriously injured. Damage was severe, mostly from fire, although high explosive bombs including 77 parachute mines wrought fearful destruction. More than 5,000 houses were destroyed making around 12,000 people homeless. Many public buildings suffered damage by fire or HE or both, including the Houses of Parliament, the Law Courts, the Guildhall, Westminster Abbey, Mansion House, the Royal College of Surgeons and the British Museum (where a quarter of a million books were destroyed).

The next morning smoke shrouded the sun and in the streets of London the fire-fighters continued their relentless task. It was not until 21st May that some of the most serious fires were under control and the hoses could finally cease. Transport and utilities suffered severe dislocation. Most railway stations were blocked for weeks. A third of London's roads were impassable on 11th May and 155,000 families were without gas, water or electricity.

Although Londoners didn't know it at the time and certainly would not dare to hope, this would be the last major raid of the Night Blitz on London. Isolated attacks continued but the capital would know an uncomfortable calm until January 1943 when the 'Little Blitz' once more brought destruction from the skies until March of the same year; another period of relative calm then ensued until flying bomb attacks began their vengeful rain in June 1944.

Left top & bottom: *'Aftermath of Saturday's Blitz. Girls who have been blitzed out of their offices, waiting for instructions. City clerks and typists turned up as usual on Monday morning. Many of them found that for the time being they had been blitzed out of their offices, but they took the news with the same good humour that they have shown on former occasions.'* Daily Mail, 13th May 1941

Left centre: A London messenger puzzling out the new addresses of blitzed firms.

Opposite: *'Last Night's Fire Blitz on London. Damage done to the Old Bailey.'*

Houses of Parliament Wrecked by Bomb

Opposite above: *'Westminster Hall Hit During Air Raid. The burning roof of Westminster Hall during an air raid in the Second World War. The interior, with its arches and beams of oak, was the finest of its kind in the world.'*

Opposite below left: *'...a London street scene after a Blitz: battered motor cars, shattered masonry litter the street. It was the most savage raid London has endured. Firemen fought the flames: Home Guards, demolition workers, rescue squads played their part. The Germans called it a 'reprisals' raid. They can call it what they will. London, still slow to organise her defences, will go on fighting the night horror. For London, though it can burn, can never yield.'* Daily Mail, 12th May 1941

Opposite below right: *'Parliament Bombed in Full Moon Blitz. Hitler's Saturday night full moon raiders set the Debating Chamber of the House of Commons on fire. After flames had ravaged the Chamber, a delayed action bomb exploded inside and sent a wall crashing. Several other bombs hit the Parliament buildings. Our picture shows the Members Division Lobby completely burnt out.'*

Left: The destruction caused to the House of Commons meant that it eventually had to be demolished and completely rebuilt: this picture shows men at work in the bomb-wrecked Speaker's Gallery; seen through an archway.

Below: *'Blitz Releases. A view of St. James's Palace which was damaged during the recent blitz. Bombs fell on the south wing of Friary Court.'*

Abbey Suffers in Savage Raid

Above: *'This dramatic picture taken after a raid on London in May 1941 and just released by the censor shows firemen at work on the burning buildings in Holborn.'* Caption is dated 9th February 1942

Opposite above right: *'The King and Queen paid a visit yesterday to Westminster Abbey, where they were crowned four years ago. It was a sad pilgrimage, for the Abbey suffered badly in Saturday night's savage raid. In this picture they are seen standing on the exact spot in front of the High Altar where they received their crowns.'*

Opposite above left: *'Westminster Abbey, Blitzed. Debris strewn in front of the High Altar from the bomb which pierced the Lantern. Clearing up work is in progress.'*

Opposite below left: *'Westminster Abbey Bombed. Debris piled up in front of the remains of the pulpit. The Verger, on the right, inspects the damage, while workmen start to clear up. The canopy is lying on the ground in front of the pulpit.'*

Opposite below right: *'Westminster Upper School Destroyed by Fire Bombs. It is now revealed that among the other places destroyed during last Saturday night's heavy raid on London was the Upper School, Westminster, which was formerly the old Monks dormitory where the ancient ceremony of tossing the pancake was held. This picture shows the wrecked interior of the Upper School showing the Rose Window at the South Side of Westminster Abbey.'*

Hess Lands in Britain

Two other events are worth noting for 10th May: on this day, Herbert Morrison announced the forming of the National Fire Service – ironically coming at the time when the critical need had more or less passed. The NFS would have its headquarters under the Rotunda in Horseferry Rd, Westminster.

The other event was more secret and strange: Deputy Reichsführer Rudolf Hess, flying a night fighter and using a fake identity, attempted to land in Scotland in a highly secret mission to meet with the British government to discuss a peace settlement. Unable to find the pre-arranged landing strip he was forced to bail out, breaking his ankle. Seeking out the contact he hoped would help him in his mission, Douglas Duke of Hamilton, Hess was taken into custody and held for a short time in the Tower of London.

Hess' motivation was complex and his interrogators' reports seemed inconclusive; some say his mission took place with Hitler's knowledge though the Führer's reported behaviour conflicts with this. In any event, Hess became an extraordinary symbol of Nazi War Crimes, the only Nazi of his senior rank to survive the Nuremberg War Tribunal, but doomed to a life in Spandau Prison where he eventually became its sole prisoner, a political pawn of the Cold War.

NO. 14,054   ONE PENNY   FOR KING AND EMPIRE   TUESDAY, MAY 13, 1941

VARNENE

HESS FLEES TO BRITAIN

Nazi No. 3 Bales Out Over Glasgow, Injured

EMPTY GUNS

THE following statement was issued from 10, Downing-street just before midnight :—"Rudolf Hess, the Deputy Führer of Germany and Party leader of the National Socialist Party, has landed in Scotland in these circumstances :

"On the night of Saturday the 10th an Me. 110 was reported by our patrols to have crossed the coast of Scotland and be flying in the direction of Glasgow. Since an Me. 110 would not have the fuel to return to Germany this report was at first disbelieved.

"Later on an Me. 110 crashed near Glasgow with its guns unloaded. Shortly afterwards a German officer who had baled out was found with his parachute in the neighbourhood suffering from a broken ankle.

"He was taken to a hospital in Glasgow, where he at first gave his name as Horn but later on declared he was Rudolf Hess."

BROUGHT PICTURE PROOF

"He brought with him various photographs of himself at different ages, apparently in order to establish his identity. These photographs were deemed to be photographs of Hess by several people who knew him personally.

"Accordingly, an officer of the Foreign Office who was closely acquainted with Hess before the

Rudolf Hess
Hitler trusted him

2 a.m. PICTURE OF HESS'S CRASHED Me.

HESS AS I KNEW HIM

Flight A Staggering Blow to Hitler

By G. WARD PRICE

THAT Hess, third man in Germany and the most trusted member of Hitler's staff, should deliberately forsake the Führer and fly to Scotland is the most fantastically improbable thing that could have happened —yet it has.

It will have incalculable effects in Germany. The Nazis have already begun to spread the tale that Hess is mad. His sanity is a matter which will soon be verified.

It is useless to conjecture what his motives for this dramatic desertion may be.

Some desperate quarrel may have occurred in the innermost ring of the Nazi leaders.

Hess, remembering the fate of Röhm, whose position was equally powerful, but who was shot by Hitler's orders in 1934, has possibly made up his mind to seek safety in flight, even to the enemy.

Or it may prove that Hess, who has always been more of an idealist than the other Nazi chiefs and never used his power to enrich himself, is just sick of the suffering which the criminal ambitions of his associates has brought upon the world.

Party Manager

If he were either insane or disgusted with his Führer's black record, Hess has disguised it well up to very recently.

On the occasion of Hitler's 52nd birthday last month, Hess was one of those who addressed him at the celebrations on board his special train in the Balkans in terms of unlimited admiration.

How can the shattering fact of Hess's deliberate surrender to the enemy be concealed from, or explained to, the German people?

Here is the great manager of the Nazi Party, the Führer's personal deputy, the second in succession to

'MUST WE FIDDLE'— U.S. ASKED

From DON IDDON,
Daily Mail Correspondent
New York, Monday.

THE grimmest despatches ever to come out of London filled the front pages of America's newspapers to-day, chilling and even frightening some of the readers.

Ben Robertson, of the newspaper P.M., sent the most moving despatch.

"We have sent our last cables to far away America about sorrow and spiritual faith and courage," he said.

"Last night we moved into the valley of the shadow in London, and from now on our news will grow graver than it has ever been, and grimmer and more tragic."

U.S. Must Choose

"We've cabled time and again in anguish that England is burning and that America must choose between idling and fighting

CENSUS OF STORAGE BEGINS

SO that vital goods—munitions, equipment, food and valuable raw materials—may be dispersed as widely as possible, the Government need 14,000,000 square feet more storage space.

To find the extra storehouses a census is to be taken of all premises in Britain with a floor area of 3,000ft. or more which have been used for storage in the past three years.

An Order issued last night requires information to be given by June 2.

Sir Cecil Weir, Controller-General of Factory and Storage Premises, and Mr. P. A. Warter, Controller of Storage, have the job of finding the extra space.

"The Government are dispersing stocks as widely as possible." An official of the Control of Factory and Storage Premises said.

"In peace time most commodities are stored in warehouses at the ports or in other vulnerable areas. It is manifestly undesirable that our stocks should be concentrated in such areas.

"The main effort of the control will be directed towards finding a large number of premises to accommodate not only the goods dispersed from vulnerable areas, but also those now being produced in increasing volume by our factories and those of the Empire and the United States."

HEAVY RAID ON MALTA

From Our Own Correspondent
Malta, Monday.—Official communique here stated early last night enemy aircraft raided in three waves. Ground defences, searchlights active. Bombs, wide area caused considerable damage to civilian property. Few civilians killed, some seriously injured. Four Messer-

188

Above left: *'The 'House of Music' Destroyed. The charred remains of Queen's Hall, the 'House of Music' from where many promenade concerts were broadcast over the radio. The Hall was bombed and utterly destroyed in a recent raid.'*

Above right: *'Elizabethan Dining Hall Damaged in Recent Air Raid. The scene in the Temple.'*

Left: *'Historic Temple Fired by Nazi Vandalism. A view of Sergeants Inn from Fleet Street.'*

Opposite right: *'Fetter Lane after the raid. The object in the left-hand foreground is a fire-fighter's hose.'*

Opposite left: *'Famous buildings damaged in recent raid. The damaged buildings of Brick Court, in the Temple.'*

11th May, Sunday

Today and for several days afterwards Londoners waited in fear of the expected follow-up attack. It didn't come. Instead a force of over 500 Luftwaffe aircraft divided its attention between a minor raid on the Billingham chemical plant near Middlesbrough (19 bombers) while in clear moonlight the majority of the raiders (241) sought the airfield bases of Bomber Command scattered across the country. At least 30 civilian deaths resulted in Teesside and Pembroke alone.

12-15th May, Monday-Thursday

During these four nights Luftwaffe operations over Britain were only minimal with isolated bombing raids to keep their presence felt. By day, fighter sweeps and patrols took place over shipping lanes.

16th May, Friday

The last major attack of the Night Blitz targeted Birmingham – an epilogue delivered by 111 aircraft that dropped 160 tonnes of HE (including 27 parachute mines) and 2,000 IBs. Most of the attackers mistakenly attacked nearby Nuneaton where 83 people were killed. A fair amount of industrial damage was done by those bombs that found Birmingham where over 30 died in the attack. Elsewhere bombs fell on other Midlands towns and as far afield as Aberdeenshire and Plymouth.

Left above: *'Famous buildings damaged in recent raid. The damaged buildings of the well known Pump Court, in the Temple.'*

Left below: *'Damage to the Temple Hall and (right) the well known cloisters.'*

Opposite left: Devastation in Jermyn Street, SW1, after Saturday's raid.

Opposite right: *'First Pictures of Recent Raid on the Temple. A view of the chaos taken from the cloisters looking towards Tanfield Court, The Temple.'*

CLEARING UP THE CITY

THE picture below was taken just as a City building was collapsing after being blown up by dynamite. These extreme measures have to be taken by the demolition men when a building, blasted by heavy bombing, has become unsafe.

Hitler Plans Drive On Four Fronts

From CEDRIC SALTER, Daily Mail Special Correspondent

ISTANBUL, Wednesday.

HITLER'S plans for the summer campaign are rapidly nearing completion. They can be grouped under four heads. First, the air blitz on England, which is already in progress. Second, passage through France and Spain to attack Gibraltar.

Third, occupation of Syria as a preliminary to a drive through Palestine towards Suez.

Fourth, pressure on Russia to undertake a policy of aggrandisement in Asia with a view to placing further strain on the Empire's defences.

Points three and four are being watched with the greatest anxiety in Ankara.

'Demoralised'

Travellers arriving from Syria have repeatedly told me that the French Army there is completely demoralised. Their natural discouragement at the defeat of France has been exploited by Axis agents.

Some of them might go de Gaullist if given the opportunity. But most of them, disillusioned and confused as to where their loyalty really lies, will accept Vichy's orders, even to the point of allowing free passage to German troops and—still more important—to the handing over of arms and equipment already in the country.

This would solve Germany's main transport problem.

French Arms

To get a substantial force of men to Syria in troop-carrying planes would not be very difficult. To send them the necessary heavy equipment would present too many opportunities for their destruction by the British Fleet.

The plan is, therefore, that the French heavy equipment already in Syria will be handed over to German and Italian forces as they arrive by plane from Greece and the Dodecanese Islands.

This equipment is, I understand, fully sufficient for 16 divisions, nearly a quarter of a million men.

EDEN, UKES Meet as Before in

Luftwaffe Prepare to Attack Russia

17-27th May, Saturday-Tuesday

Luftwaffe activity continued at a much reduced level after the Birmingham raid but there were still daily sweeps over the coastal areas and shipping, followed by scattered bomb attacks across the country by night. On virtually every night casualties continued. For consumption by the nation, the Ministry of Home Security attributed the Luftwaffe's reduced aggression to the weather but Military Intelligence was aware from its listening and from Enigma decryptions that the true reason was the transfer of Luftwaffe units from Western Europe to bases further east in the build up of German forces, especially the strategic bombing units, in preparation for the invasion attack on Russia in the normal Nazi Blitzkrieg style.

28th May, Wednesday

An aggressive night force of 80 bombers made its presence felt over Merseyside, Northern Ireland and the East Coast. Bombs fell as far apart as Hull and Herne Bay; Folkestone received parachute mines that resulted in a death toll of 11.

Right above: *'The Only Man in London Who Takes It Lying Down. Damage surrounding the tomb of Oliver Goldsmith, celebrated biographer of Dr. Samuel Johnson, in Inner Temple, caused during a recent raid.'*

Right below: Amid the bomb rubble, office workers enjoy a bowl of soup provided by the American Food Convoys.

Above: *'London After a Recent Blitz. An unusual view of the well known St Clement Danes Church, Strand, which has now been gutted.'*

Right top: The bronze bust of Sir William Owen, a conservator of the Museum in the nineteenth century, lies amid the twentieth-century rubble of the Royal College of Surgeons.

Right centre: *'Raid Damage At Royal College of Surgeons. A life-like statue of John Hunter, founder of the College, was bricked up against air raids. As shown the pathological and oldest room was destroyed, leaving the statue intact.'*

Right below: More damage at the Royal College of Surgeons – in this case the 'Skullery pantry' holding skulls of all ages, shapes and sizes was damaged by fire in the raid.

Street at the Heart of the City

Queen Victoria Street was an important thoroughfare into the heart of the City close by the Thames near to St Paul's Cathedral and presented the press with symbols for London in the Blitz. The wide road showed a rapid return to normal but the dreadful damage to St Nicholas Cole Abbey told its own story – the blackened walls and toppled spire lowering over the ruins of the Street. The destroyed Salvation Army HQ was a counterpoint to the very active relief work done by the church throughout the War.

Left: *'Air Raid Damage in London. Damaged church of St. Nicholas Cole Abbey, Queen Victoria Street.'*

Above: A picture taken in late May of Queen Victoria Street shows that despite the scars of many bombings life in the street was carrying on as usual.

Opposite above: The burnt-out remains of the Salvation Army headquarters. The fires on 10th May were so severe and overwhelming that in some cases there were not enough fire-fighters free to attend to a fire and in others, like the situation at the Salvation Army building, there was no water available with which to attack it.

Opposite below: *'Air Raid Damage in London. The church of St. Nicholas Cole Abbey after being burned out in a recent raid. This was the first church completed by Wren after the Great Fire of 1666.'*

29-30th May, Thursday-Friday

Following Thursday night's minor activity, Friday saw 90 Luftwaffe aircraft set out to bomb targets in the Merseyside and Bristol Channel area, where 20 civilians were killed. Elements of the raiders mistakenly bombed Dublin, killing 40 in the undefended neutral city. There was a degree of irony in this for the lights of Dublin – which didn't need to operate a blackout – had on occasion helped Luftwaffe raiders get their bearings for attacks on the cities of North West England.

31st May, Saturday

On the last night of the month, raiding activity similar to Friday took place, resulting in the deaths of ten people. Having been 'trained' by the Luftwaffe to expect serious punishment at the end of the month, the relative peace of these days and nights signalled an important change to the citizens of beleaguered Britain.

An Uneasy Calm

1st June, Saturday

Following the monstrous attack on 10th May an uncomfortable calm had descended on London. Things were less certain over the rest of the country and when the night attacks erupted yet again over Merseyside and Manchester on 1st June over 30 people were killed; the worst incident was a direct hit on a Salford hospital that killed 14 nurses. The same night, the Luftwaffe ranged over the North and Midlands.

7th June, Friday

As the Luftwaffe turned their attention toward the invasion of Stalin's Russia, the raids on Britain and London in particular subsided. However, the odd bombing raid kept the citizens of the capital on their toes: in the early hours, a parachute mine landed in Brentford, West London, causing significant damage. This was a continuing demonstration of the Luftwaffe's versatility – of both their aircraft and weaponry. The crews that were assigned to aerial minelaying could be the same as those that could drop similar versions of the parachute mines on land-based targets. Many of the bombing incidents on coastal towns were the result of drifting mines falling on land instead of the sea. In other cases, parachute mines dropped on land could give the raiders a significant result.

This page: Fires rage in Manchester city centre's Deansgate (Top). Published in the *Daily Mail* to illustrate the destruction of Saturday's raids, the newspaper was forced by the 28-day rule to use a picture from the night of the heavy raid on 8th May even though the blazing building to the left was its own northern HQ. Pictures of the damage to Northcliffe House, the *Daily Mail*'s Manchester office (above left & right), were more recent but would not be published until later in June.

SCOUT DIES IN GAS RESCUE

A TWELVE-YEARS-OLD Boy Scout died when making an heroic attempt to save a seven-years-old girl who was trapped in a hole in Newcastle on Saturday night.

He was Ernest Smith, son of an electrician. The girl was Irene Page, daughter of a coal merchant. Two members of the A.F.S., John Tulip, aged 35, and George Wanless, 37, also lost their lives.

All four died, it is believed, from the effects of sewer gas.

The girl was playing at the rear of some empty houses when she fell down a hole. Mr. Edwin Corbett, a neighbour, was attracted to the spot by the screams of children. When he got there he found the boy Smith with a playmate. Corbett sent the other boy for help and obtained a rope.

Smith volunteered to go into the hole, and Corbett tied a rope round him and lowered him in.

Smith fainted, and at this point Tulip, who was an uncle of the girl, and Wanless arrived.

Tulip was then lowered into the hole and succeeded in getting out Smith.

He was returning for the girl when he, too, collapsed, and Wanless, who went to his assistance, was also overcome.

All Were Dead

A rescue party of police officers and A.F.S. men arrived and brought the two men and the girl to the surface.

Artificial respiration was applied and all were removed to hospital, but they were dead on arrival there.

Mr. Corbett said: " Smith would not have lost his life if another man had been on the spot. I did not suspect there was any gas in the hole.

" I wanted to go down myself, but, of course, Smith was not strong enough to support me, and I had to accept his offer."

HOMES READY FOR 40,000

People who have shut up town houses for the duration and gone to the country may have to hand over their keys to blitzed homeless families.

A Ministry of Health official told a *Daily Mail* reporter yesterday that in the London area 20,000 houses and buildings have been requisitioned and about half—enough for nearly 40,000 people—are ready for occupation by the bombed out

"If," he added, " more homes are needed, we shall certainly use unoccupied furnished houses. People who lock up their homes must be

St. Clement Danes Church

NOTICE

This Church is dangerous, pending repairs, on account of falling pieces of brick and stone. The public are warned to keep away from the walls—those who enter, do so at their own risk, and must keep within the roped enclosure.

MORNING PRAYER & SERMON
are held on Sunday Mornings at 11 a.m. in The Parish House, Portugal Street, near by.

History of the Church—Postcards etc., can be obtained from the Verger, 8, Clements Inn Passage.

THE SECRETARY OF THE PAROCHIAL CHURCH COUNCIL.

Above & far left: *'Service in Wrecked Cathedral. Looking into the ruins of St. George's Cathedral, Southwark, where a service was held before a temporary altar.'*
Sunday services in roofless bombed churches became a commonplace statement of faith and determination for Britain's civilian population.

Left: This notice outside St Clement Danes Church showed the determination of the Parish churches to continue their normal functions as far as possible.

Far right: The Queen came to inspect the damage to St Paul's in the summer of 1941. The photographs of her are dated 12th June.

Right: *Public View of St. Paul's Damage. Whitsun sightseers in the Cathedral.*

Below: *'Queen Sees St. Paul's Damage. The Queen, pictured today, examining the damage in St. Paul's Cathedral. Her Majesty is seen here peering up at the great hole through the roof of the crypt where the bomb penetrated.'*

Barbarossa Relieves Pressure on Britain

22nd June, Sunday

On the day after the summer solstice a combined German/Axis force of over 4 million soldiers surged into western Russia across an 1,800 mile front – Operation Barbarossa was to become Hitler's crowning folly. Churchill noted it as one of the great turning points of the War to date and promised that the Nazi aggression on Russia would be met with intensified RAF bombing. Thanks to success in defending Atlantic shipping against the U-Boat threat, RAF Bomber Command was once more in a position to attack targets on mainland Europe.

Below: *'The Roof of the Guildhall. Workmen building a temporary roof over the Great Hall in the Guildhall.'*

Right: The medieval walls of the Guildhall survived the Fire of London but the wooden roof, that was not as old as the walls, burned, the debris falling into the building.

Daily Mail

LATE WAR NEWS SPECIAL

ITS PIQUANT ITS DELICIOUS — H·P SAUCE

NO. 14,089   ONE PENNY   FOR KING AND EMPIRE   MONDAY, JUNE 23, 1941

GERMANS THRUSTING AT LENINGRAD

'Our Armies Deep in Russian Territory'—Berlin

GERMAN armies were last night reported to be making three main attacks in their great offensive against Russia along a front of 1,500 miles : from Finland towards Leningrad ; from East Prussia towards Moscow ; and from Rumania towards the Ukraine.

These distances are great. A hundred miles of difficult country lie between the Finnish frontier and Leningrad. Moscow is 600 miles from East Prussia. The Ukraine is almost immediately menaced, but the territory stretches 600 miles into Russia.

A fourth thrust is being made in Poland. Berlin radio claimed last night that German troops had crossed the Bug River, which flows in an arc round Warsaw. Long columns were said to have penetrated deep into Russian territory.

Berlin correspondents of Swiss newspapers said the Germans were using several thousand tanks to drive an opening in the Russian front and were expecting "tremendous results."

The attack towards Leningrad is being made by German and Finnish divisions across the Karelian Isthmus—the battleground between the Soviet and Finland only 18 months ago.

EAST PRUSSIA RAIDED

Finnish sources admitted that Soviet aircraft had started fires at several points in Finnish territory. No details of the land fighting were available, but this is one zone where the Russians cannot afford to give ground easily. Leningrad, at the head of the Gulf of Finland and centre of a great military district, is the second city of Russia. Nearby is Kronstadt, home of Russia's Baltic Fleet.

The second German drive — 'from East Prussia — is being made across the former Baltic States of Lithuania, Latvia, and Estonia. This attack appears to have Moscow as its ultimate objective. Moscow would also be threatened from the north if Leningrad should fall.

Reports reaching Stockholm, said a revolt which had broken out in Estonia was being successfully dealt with by Red troops. Some of the rebels

Arrows indicate the direction of the German thrusts into Russia.

. **LARGE MAP SHOWING THE FIGHTING — BACK PAGE.**

U.S. Foresee Three-Nation Move Against Hitler

From DON IDDON   NEW YORK, Sunday.

CLOSE economic co-operation between the United States, Britain, and Russia is expected following the

CRIPPS TO GO BACK

But No Formal Alliance

By WILSON BROADBENT, Daily Mail Diplomatic Correspondent

SIR STAFFORD CRIPPS will fly back to Russia as soon as possible to resume his ambassadorship, if a quick and comparatively safe route can be planned for him.

The British Government wish Sir Stafford to establish fresh contact with the Soviet Government now she is at war with Germany. Sir Stafford's mission will be highly hazardous but important. It is, however, probable that the British Government will not at the moment conclude a formal alliance with the Soviet Government.

Close Contact

Sir Stafford's object in returning to Russia will be to maintain the closest possible contact with the Russian Government, so that the British Government can be fully informed of all developments.

When M. Maisky, the Soviet Ambassador called at the Foreign Office yesterday, at the request of Mr. Anthony Eden, he inquired what Britain's attitude would be, and whether there would be any slackening of our war effort, now that Germany and Russia were at war.

Mr. Eden is understood to have replied that Britain would now increase her efforts rather than slacken them.

Attack First

M. Maisky told Mr. Eden that at no time had Hitler given them any warning of his change of policy, nor made any demands, nor suggested any negotiations.

The Germans had actually launched their attack 2½ hours before the declaration of war was announced by Goebbels to the German people.

In Soviet circles in London yesterday, confidence was expressed that the Red Army would give a good account of itself. It was asserted that Hitler has for the first time come up against a mechanised army numerically as strong as his own.

In British quarters, where the development in Russo-German relations had been closely anticipated,

30 Yesterday!

R.A.F. FIGHTERS and bombers, continuing their sweeps over the French coast yesterday, shot down 30 Me 109's for the loss of only two fighters. Enemy losses in two days total 62 planes.

RAF BRUSH ASIDE THE NEW Me.s

By NOEL MONKS, Daily Mail Air Correspondent

WHILE Hitler's eyes were turned to the East and his armies were marching on Russia, R.A.F. bombers continued yesterday to hammer at his bases in the West. An Air Ministry statement at midnight revealed that 30 Me. 109's were shot down and destroyed—29 by Hurricane and Spitfire pilots and one by a Blenheim bomber—when the R.A.F. continued their offensive sweeps over the northern coast of France.

Our losses were two fighters. The pilot of one was saved.

Bombers accompanying the fighters attacked the marshalling yard at Hazebrouck, which handles the Channel ports traffic.

"The operation," said the Air Ministry News Service, "was carried out to schedule, and the Messerschmitts were brushed aside."

In two days offensive sweeps over the Channel, 88 Me. 109's have been destroyed, 28 being shot down on Saturday, when we lost five aircraft. In addition, four night bombers were destroyed.

Bombers Say Thanks

The fighter pilots have received the thanks of the bomber group and from Sir Archibald Sinclair, Air Minister. That from the bomber pilots said :

"All Blenheim pilots wish to express appreciation of the excellent support provided by the fighter escort."

Sir Archibald Sinclair's message sent to Air Marshal W. F. Douglas, C.-in-C. Fighter Command, said :

"Congratulations on the striking success of your squadrons in recent fighting over France. It shows not only that they retain their ascendancy over German Air Force, but that they can overcome all the disadvantages of fighting over the

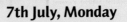

SOVIET ENVOY SEES EDEN

BRITAIN WILL AID THE SOVIET

Churchill Pledge of Fiercer Day-and-Night Bombing

THE Prime Minister, broadcasting last night to the Empire and the world, announced that Britain will give aid to Russia. Technical and economic assistance, he revealed, had already been offered to the Soviet.

And our bombing of Germany, he declared, would continue with ever-increasing weight by day and by night, " so that the Germans may taste and gulp some of the weight of misery which they have showered on mankind."

The Democracies, said the Premier, were determined on the doom of Hitler. The attack on Russia would cause no division of views, no weakening of purpose.

" Invasion of Russia is no more than a prelude to the attempted invasion of Britain," he said ; " he hopes to achieve victory in both before winter.

" Russia's danger, therefore, is our danger. Let us redouble our exertions and strike with united strength while life and power remain."

The speech, translated into Russian, was broadcast to the East almost immediately afterwards.

Fourth Turning-point

Mr. Churchill said :

We have reached one of the climacterics of the war. In the first of these intense turning-points a year ago, France fell prostrate under the German hammer and we had to face the storm alone.

The second was when the R.A.F. beat the Hun raiders out of the daylight air, and thus warded off the Nazi invasion of our island while we were still ill-armed and ill-prepared.

The third turning point was when the President and Congress of the United States passed the Lease-and-Lend enactment devoting nearly two thousand million sterling to help us defend our liberties and their own.

These were the three climacterics. The fourth is now upon us. At four o'clock this morning Hitler attacked and invaded Russia. All his usual formalities of perfidy

BACK Page, Column THREE

LATEST

GERMANS HELD BY RUSSIANS

Moscow, Monday, 4.15 a.m.—First Russian war communiqué states that, during first day fighting on whole front, from Baltic to Black Sea, troops German army have been held by the Russians.—Reuter.

Helsinki, Monday.—Air raid alarm was sounded early this morning.—B.U.P.

N.E. TOWN BOMBED

German raiders dropped high explosive bombs and incendiaries on a north-east town early this morning. A number of casualties have been reported. Raiders Passed sounded in London later this morning.

Left: *'Blackfriars. Damage to a railway bridge in a recent blitz.'*

Opposite above & below left: External damage to Northcliffe House is cleaned up while broken glass and fallen plaster is cleared from the offices.

7th July, Monday

A sharp raid on Southampton killed 26.

14th, 17th July, Monday, Thursday

Heavy raids focused on Hull: 28 killed on the 14th; heavy damage to residential property resulted in 129 deaths on the 17th.

27th July, Sunday

Minor attacks in the Greater London area included unlucky hits on three shelters in Poplar that contributed to the high total of 85 dead.

Opposite below right: *'Yet Another Church Destroyed by Nazis. The Rural Dean Preb. G. Hardy, looking at the remains of his own church, St. Peter's, Plymouth, which was destroyed in a recent blitz on Plymouth.'*

Gordon's
Stands Supreme

NO. 14,135   ONE PENNY   FOR KING AND EMPIRE   FRIDAY, AUGUST 15, 1941

HP *sauce*

HOW THEY MET: FULL STORY
U.S. War Fleet Stood Guard on 4-Day Talks

HE TOLD WORLD

MR. ATTLEE, Lord Privy Seal and deputy Prime Minister (above), made the first dramatic announcement of the meeting in his world broadcast. Now the great eight-point Charter of Freedom is being broadcast to every country in the world—by our own radio, by Russia's powerful stations, and by the mighty broadcasting network of the United States. Night and day the B.B.C.'s powerful transmitters are sending out this new message of hope. By Sunday Mr. Attlee's words will have been repeated 300 times.

Rome Radio Put Over Full Story

World Comment

ROME radio broadcast a full report of the Churchill-Roosevelt declaration last night, but without comment. Berlin dismissed it as "propaganda bluff."

Neutral countries gave long Press reports and showed favourable reaction in the declaration.

JOINT MESSAGE TO STALIN SOON

WASHINGTON, Thursday.—*Mr. Cordell Hull, Secretary of State, hinted to-night that, following the ocean conference, a joint message from Mr. Churchill and Mr. Roosevelt will be sent to Stalin assuring all possible help against the Germans.—A.P.*

From WALTER FARR   Boston, Massachusetts, Thursday.

MR. WINSTON CHURCHILL and President Franklin D. Roosevelt, the two great leaders of the democracies, are to-night both on their way back to their capitals after the most momentous conference of the war, held somewhere in the Western Atlantic.

The conference, I understand, was conducted on an American warship south of Greenland, probably off the Newfoundland coast. It extended over four days.

President Roosevelt, now on his yacht, the Potomac, is expected to arrive at Boston within a few hours. A special train, waiting with steam up, will take him on to Washington immediately.

Lord Beaverbrook, British Minister of Supply, who took part in the ocean conference, arrived to-day in Washington in a United States Army bomber. He went straight to the British Embassy.

General George Marshall, United States Chief of Staff, who was also at the conference, flew in the bomber with Lord Beaverbrook.

Mr. Sumner Welles, United States Assistant Secretary of State; Mr. Averell Harriman, Lease-Lend Defence Expediter; and Sir Alexander Cadogan, Permanent Under-Secretary at the British Foreign Office, it is now known, were also present at the talks at sea.

Officials who are waiting here to greet President Roosevelt when he lands told me that both the President and Mr. Churchill will make broadcast speeches within the next few days.

Red Army Retires
Germans Make Big Ukraine Claims

Berlin radio went off the air soon after dark last night—usual sign of nearby or overhead activity by British or Russian bombers.

From RALPH HEWINS
STOCKHOLM, Thursday.

FIERCE fighting along the whole front from the White Sea to the Black Sea, was reported in the Soviet war communiqué, issued late to-night.

In the southern sector, where the Germans claim sweeping successes, the Soviet admits the evacuation of Kirovograd and Pervomaisk (on the River Bug), 90 miles north-west of Nikolaiev.

The evacuation of Kirovograd, which lies 120 miles north of the Black Sea port of Nikolaiev, suggests that the German Army has made a 95-miles thrust to the east from Uman.

Before the Soviet communiqué was issued, German claims to have encircled a major Soviet-Ukraine army were flatly denied by M. Lozovsky, Soviet Information Chief.

The German Propaganda Min-

'THEY LAUGHED AND JOKED'

OFFICIAL photographs of the conference are not yet released, but the composite picture below gives you a good "preview." The official shots, cables Walter Farr, will show from the way the President and Mr. Churchill are laughing and joking together that the two men liked each other. As soon as they met they began an eager conversation, and for more than an hour they talked alone.

Roosevelt Feared an Attack on Premier
By PAUL BEWSHER

THIS is the inner story of the Great Secret—and why American papers discussed it for a week while the British Press maintained absolute silence.

Mr. Attlee's dramatic announcement of the Churchill-Roosevelt meeting surprised a very large number of people in Britain—but the 140,000,000 inhabitants of the United States had been reading about it, discussing it, since Tuesday last week.

Quotations from these reports had been cabled all over the world—were in the possession of Hitler and the Nazi Higher Command—were reprinted in many countries. But still the British papers remained silent.

There are no two ways about it.

Joint Plan for War Production Agreed

By WILSON BROADBENT, Daily Mail Diplomatic Correspondent

THE basis of a comprehensive war production plan which will ensure Britain's military, naval, and air strategy 100 per cent. efficiency has been agreed on by President Roosevelt and Mr. Winston Churchill. This will be one of the immediate results of their secret meeting "at sea," dramatically revealed to the world yesterday.

There will be other and later developments in the diplomatic field, as well as new measures for ensuring Britain's complete victory in the Battle of the Atlantic.

But for the time being, America's rôle will remain that of the "arsenal of Democracy."

The creation of a joint organisation of British and American experts to co-ordinate production and supply in the United States with the requirements of Britain and of Soviet Russia will be announced shortly.

The headquarters of this organisation will be in Washington, with a counterpart in London, and probably another in Moscow.

Lord Beaverbrook, Minister of Supply, who joined in the conferences with President Roosevelt, arrived last night in Washington for further discussions with American officials.

Apart from this decision, the joint declaration issued by the two statesmen is vitally important for its statement of intentions.

President Roosevelt has committed the United States to collaborate with Britain and her Allies in the organisation of peace when victory is won.

This should not be interpreted as

BACK PAGE—Col. SIX

LATEST

NIGHT RAIDERS NEAR E. ANGLIA

German aircraft were reported during the night near East Anglian coast and later farther inland in the North.

ROOSEVELT-CHURCHILL TALKS

Washington, Thursday.—White House disclosed to-night that those present at Roosevelt-Churchill conference included General George C. Marshall, U.S. Chief of Staff; Admiral Stark, Chief of Naval Operations; Mr. Harry Hopkins, Lease-Lend Administrator; Mr. Averell Harriman, Lease-Lend Expediter; and Admiral Ernest King, commanding U.S. Atlantic Fleet.—Reuter.

Luck of Lord Beaverbrook

MONTREAL, Thursday.

'HAPPIEST MAN'

WAR SAVINGS CAMPAIGN

9th August, Saturday

Churchill and Roosevelt discuss the Atlantic Charter – shaping the post-war future. They met secretly on USS *Augusta* in Ship Harbour Newfoundland. Churchill sailed covertly from Scapa Flow on HMS *Prince of Wales*; a joint declaration was issued on the 14th.

16th August, Saturday

Luftwaffe records viewed after the War indicated that 203 bombers remained on the Western Front of which only 84 were serviceable: this extraordinarily small force explains the numbers of Luftwaffe aircraft attacking at this time – very rarely would there be more than 50 aircraft in the air on any mission.

Opposite: An air raid on Hull in July 1941 caused extensive damage in New Bridge Road, a residential district.

Above: *'From the ruins of a bombed house step the King and Queen, passing through the heap of rubble that was once a front garden. This* Daily Mail *picture shows their surprise inspection of air-raid damage in a Hull suburb yesterday.'*

The King and Queen visited Humberside on 6th August to boost the morale of the city which had now become one of the most frequently bombed cities in Britain.

Left: King George VI and Queen Elizabeth pictured in the doorway of a public air raid shelter when they visited Rotherhithe on 1st August, four days after the heavy raid on the 27th that killed over 80 Londoners.

Reminders of the Night Blitz

Top: View from Aldermanbury looking towards Cripplegate with the ruined tower of St Giles visible right of centre.

Above: The interior of the Wren-built church of St Bride's in Fleet Street was gutted by fire.

Left: *'Front of King's Old Home, Damaged in London Raid. The frontage of 145 Piccadilly, the home for 11 years of the King and Queen when they were the Duke and Duchess of York, collapsed, showering tons of masonry across the road. The house was damaged in the early days of the London air attacks. The picture shows a large gap where the front of the house collapsed.'*

1st September, Monday
A small force of 12 aircraft caused serious damage to Tyneside in a night raid.

7th September, Sunday
On a National Day of prayer, bombs killed 20, mainly in coastal towns of South East England including Ramsgate and Dover.

30th September, Tuesday
In a return to traditional Luftwaffe tactics, 80 aircraft made a month end raid across the country, killing 41 in North Shields.

Above left: **The King inspects Buckingham Palace's Home Guard:** this Sergeant had been a servant in the Royal Household for 48 years.

Above right: *'Famous London Church Bombed. One of the bells of St. James's Church, Piccadilly, which was hit during a London air raid, has now been taken down from the belfry for safety.'*

Left: *'Air Raid Damage in the Temple. All that is left of beautiful old Brick Court.'*

The Miracle of St Paul's

Above: **At the end of September 1941 the *Daily Mail* took a series of photographs which were published later in the year under the title 'The Miracle of St Paul's' showing the devastation to all the areas surrounding the cathedral. This view, looking along Cannon Street, would have been impossible prior to the Night Blitz as many high buildings screened St Paul's from sight.**

Opposite above: *'Buildings that had been severely damaged by fire and made dangerous have been partially demolished. Whole streets have disappeared, but life in the war-scarred City streets carries on as usual. In this picture on the left was the Headquarters of the Salvation Army, which was destroyed. There can also be seen the shell of the well known City Church of St. Nicholas Cole Abbey, which was the first City church rebuilt by Wren after the Great Fire of London.'*

Above: 'This picture shows an unusual view of St. Paul's looking through the west windows of the burned out church of Dick Whittington fame, St Mary-le-Bow, Cheapside, famous for its bells.'

Right: 'The Miracle of St. Paul's. A series of Daily Mail pictures taken from all angles which shows how near St. Paul's Cathedral has been to destruction. This picture taken from a Thames-side building south of the cathedral. On the extreme left was the H.Q. of the Salvation Army. Traffic and pedestrians can be seen going through Queen Victoria Street of which a portion is in ruins.'

Britain No Longer Battles Alone

Above: 'A picture taken from the steeple of St. Mary-le-Bow, Cheapside, showing St. Paul's towering above the wrecked and demolished buildings. In this picture can be seen (left) the Tower of the Church of St. Nicholas Cole Abbey, the first of the City churches to be rebuilt by Wren after the Great Fire of London. Also in the centre of picture slightly to the left of St. Paul's is St. Augustine-with-St. Faith, Watling Street. Both these churches were burned out.'

Opposite page: Mr. George Hicks M.P. for Woolwich East watching the salvage of metal from the blitzed chamber of the House of Commons. A bricklayer by trade, he was General Secretary of the Amalgamated Union of Building Trade Workers from 1921 to 1941. In the company of other colleagues and workmen he is able to keep a professional builder's eye on the demolition of the wrecked House.

October - December

When the Night Blitz ended, Britons fell into a sort of limbo: they couldn't relax as warnings were issued that a worse Blitz could be just around the corner. They also knew that although there was relatively little bombing activity, compared with the intensive nine months of the Night Blitz, a life-threatening raid could erupt at any time. This was often the case in the the coastal towns of Britain which bore the brunt of Luftwaffe aggression. Reporting of the resultant damage was restricted and as a consequence most of the newspaper columns were devoted to the number of Nazi planes shot down, the progress of the war in Europe and developments in the Pacific, since the attack on the US Fleet in Pearl Harbor on 7th December which brought with it the subsequent entry of the USA into the War. Another of Churchill's 'climacterics' of the War which would ultimately bring about the downfall of Hitler's Third Reich.

At this stage of the war, often the press coverage given to the Blitz bombardment was almost retrospective nostalgia, as if to remind the nation that it hadn't just been a terrifying nightmare.

However now that America was an active ally in the War, the whole picture had changed and the year ahead held new promise.

Blitz Ripper

10th January, Saturday
Merseyside's final bombing raid of the Second World War sees houses in Upper Stanhope Street demolished; number 102 had been the home of Adolf Hitler's half brother Alois Hitler.

13th January, Tuesday
A Dornier Do217 bombed north Lowestoft killing 70, giving East Anglia its worst raid of the War.

9th February, Monday
Evelyn Hamilton, the first of four known murder victims of the so-called Blitz Ripper was found in Montagu Place, West End: Frederick Cummins was found guilty of the crimes, convicted in April and hanged in June.

Left: The bombed ruins of St Michael's Church in Great Yarmouth, a few miles north of Lowestoft, attest to the frequency of Luftwaffe bombing of East Anglia: the seaside town on the Norfolk coast was attacked repeatedly, especially in 1941 when it was raided on 167 occasions, destroying much of the ancient town.

Below: *"Ruins in the City of London, after the recent snow-fall."* The capital was shrouded in snow in mid-February.

Above: 'London Raid Memories. When bombs fell in a London suburb during the days of the big raids, one of them made this big crater in a street, breaking mains, twisting tramlines and partly engulfing a bus. This picture was released by the Censor for the first time today.' The date of release was 23rd January.

Left above: The Agony of Plymouth. Looking across the debris of George Street to the ruined Baptist Chapel and roofless Guildhall.' The Daily Mail revisted the devastation of Plymouth when it published this picture on 14th January. In the vacuum left by the ending of the Night Blitz, newspapers revived the memories of the devastation of Plymouth and London.

Left below: 'Lambeth Palace, the home of the Archbishops of Canterbury for 800 years, has been badly damaged during air raids on London, during which it has been hit five times. Now the great rambling building contains little more accommodation than a cottage. The chapel is entirely ruined and roofless and many historic treasures have perished. In April, when the new Archbishop of Canterbury takes over Lambeth Palace as his London home, he will find little more than a ruin. This picture shows the ruined Juxon's Great Hall in Lambeth Palace. The books which lined this Hall are covered in debris – some are charred and spoiled by water. It is in this Great Hall that the Lambeth conference used to be held.' The picture dates from 26th January.

Top: Bombs bursting on cliff defences near Dover.

Left: 'Last Night's Air Raid Damage At Dover.' 'Bomb damage again – the result of the German attack on Dover on Monday night. Thirteen people are known to have been killed and a number were injured.'

Above: 'Last Night's Air Raid Damage At Dover. Officials outside the shelter under a building in which a number of people were trapped.'

5th March, Thursday

Solo raids by Luftwaffe fighter-bombers or their medium bombers such as the Ju88 were a regular occurrence from 1940 but a new tactic gradually became formally adopted: one of the first Jagdbombenangriff, abbreviated form '*Jabo*', took place on 5th March when low flying Bf109s attacked Freshwater Bay, Isle of Wight, with bombs killing three elderly people. This was just the beginning.

23rd March, Monday

Dover was no stranger to attack, both from Luftwaffe fighter bombers and from the long-range guns sited on the French coast. The relatively minor attack on Dover caused more death and destruction than usual, capturing the interest of the national newspapers.

28th March, Saturday

The historic Baltic port of Lübeck was bombed by RAF Bomber Command, destroying the majority of the mediaeval city. The German reprisal action launched the so-called '*Baedeker raids*' – taking the name of the famous tourist guides – that attacked the morale of Britain's civilian population by devastating some of its finest cultural legacy. The direct order for the campaign came from Hitler on 14th April: 14 major raids on Britain's most treasured historic cities followed.

31st March, Tuesday

At the end of March 1942, a specialist fighter bomber unit was created in the Luftwaffe: 10.(Jabo)/JG 26. Equipped with the very latest Fw 190 along with its sister unit 10.(Jabo)/JG 2 this force operated from June onwards against channel shipping and port towns on the south-eastern coasts of England, though in reality they had actually been active from November 1941 and had been very effective in their coastal raiding. Operating in small numbers at high speed and very low altitude, these lightning hit-and-run raids were virtually impossible for the RAF fighters to repel or counter.

Above and far left: '*Last Night's Air Raid Damage at Dover. Demolition squad at work in ruined garage.*'

Left: '*The Miracle of St. Paul's. A series of Daily Mail pictures taken from all angles show how near the cathedral has been to destruction. Picture shows the scene looking across to St. Paul's from the west door of the well-known church of St. Mary-le-Bow, Cheapside.*'
Taken in Autumn 1941 these pictures were repeatedly published to revive the spirits of the readership. According to the archive, this re-appeared in the *Daily Mail* on 28th March.

Baedeker Guides Nazi Bombing

3rd April, Friday

The unpredictable Luftwaffe raids on Britain's coastal towns continued: the residents of Weymouth woke up on Good Friday to find 20 of their fellow citizens dead. Through the month, German attacks continued with new intensity, by day and night, using the Jabo raiding style.

11th April, Saturday

Bomber Command had been trying unsuccessfully to repeat the success of the Lübeck raid of March that shocked Germany to the core, but navigational failures and losses made those subsequent efforts ineffectual. However on this night, raiding Essen, the RAF dropped its first 8,000 pound bomb, which, along with its 4,000 pound little brother, became known fondly as a 'cookie'. Churchill was finally giving Germany a response to the dread parachute mine!

23rd April, Thursday

Exeter was attacked at night by 45 aircraft in the first raid of the retaliatory offensive by the Luftwaffe that became known as the Baedeker Raids, but most of the aircraft failed to find their targets because of cloud cover. 200 houses were damaged though casualties were relatively light with 13 killed. The results would have been very different if the 175 tonnes of HE intended for the city had found its target. The same night the RAF bombed Rostock. The bulk of the Luftwaffe bomber force involved in the Baedeker campaign comprised Dornier Do 217E-4s mostly from KG2 'Holzhammer' based in NL3 Gruppen, but the bomber force had been significantly reinforced by units from Sicily and the Eastern Front.

24th April, Friday

In good moonlight 60 bombers attacked Exeter again with double sorties flown by some crews. Bombing was heavier and much more accurate, killing 80 and severely damaging the city. Bomber Command returned to repeat its bombing efforts on Rostock, this time with considerable success.

25th April, Saturday

The lightly defended Georgian city of Bath was the Luftwaffe's next choice but many bombs fell outside the city: only 92 tonnes finding their target – a substantial load for the relatively small city – resulting in significant damage in the old part of town. Bath's famous Assembly Rooms were gutted by fire. Many Luftwaffe bombers strayed over Bristol where they were greeted by that city's more robust AA defences.

Above left: *'Good Friday Workers. A demolition workman in the City today [Good Friday] swings his pickaxe with his usual vigour.'*

Above right: *'Air Raid Damage, Exeter. A woman with children walking past one of the badly damaged streets. A German pilot last night gloated over raid victims in a broadcast.'*

Right: *'Two women pick their way through debris in a badly battered street in Exeter after the last 'Baedeker' raid on the city. Exeter, though shaken, carries on.'*

Above: 'One of Bath's crescents damaged after a recent enemy raid.'

Left: 'Bath Raid. Thick grey dust covered the houses and roadway after the havoc caused in an attack on Bath by a Nazi raider.'

Georgian Bath

26th April, Sunday

The inevitable second raid on Bath was not so heavy as the first but fires, driven by wind and unquenched because of a water shortage, led to much greater damage than on the previous night. The casualty figure for the two nights of raiding came to 401 killed and more than 800 injured.

In Germany, Hitler made an impassioned speech to the nation, promising to take out Britain's cities one by one in reprisal for Lübeck and Rostock: he had referred to the RAF attacks on the Baltic ports as *Terrorangriffe* (terror attacks) and this was now his agenda for Britain's cultural heritage.

The German press took up the idea of the Baedeker guide as an index for destruction and the Luftwaffe set about making *Terrorangriffe* a reality with its best efforts directed at some of the finest historical cities in Great Britain and their irreplaceable buildings.

Soon after the raids, the King and Queen visited the city in support of the shocked populace.

Left: *'Bath Raid. St. Andrew's Church, gutted by fire.'*

Below: *'Bath feared for its lovely streets, which have suffered from Nazi bombs. Here is a damaged house in a Bath thoroughfare.'*

Above left: 'The King and Queen visited the bombed city of Bath, chosen by the Nazis for their recent 'reprisal' raid. The picture shows the King and Queen passing through some of the bomb-damaged areas of the city. On the right is Alderman Aubrey Bateman, the Mayor of Bath.'

Above right: 'The King and Queen passing the famous old Bath Chair during their tour of the blitzed town.'

Left: 'A Bath-chair – named after the city – being salvaged by rescue squad men. The chairs are a common sight at the spa.'

Mediaeval Norwich

27th April, Monday

While a force of German raiders headed to bomb Norwich, for the next Baedeker raid, RAF Bomber Command visited Cologne; using much less ordnance than was the custom of the Luftwaffe, the RAF's success was aided by the tinder of the mediaeval buildings and a lively wind. Back in Britain, the smaller Luftwaffe forces attacking Norwich and the other Baedeker targets carried out multiple sorties and dropped various weights of bombs, not to mention their latest improved IBs with greater concentrated effectiveness. Although most of the participating aircraft in the Baedeker raids were loaded with around 100 tonnes of HE (giving the status of 'heavy' to the raid), sometimes barely half the payload would reach its target – as was the case with Norwich this night, where Home Security estimated the weight of HE falling on the city to be under 60 tonnes. However this was more than enough to cause horrific destruction to these fragile cities, especially when fire took hold.

The casualty toll on this first Baedeker raid on Norwich was 162 killed and around 600 injured. The ancient infrastructure caused many problems for fire-fighters when water mains were damaged or destroyed by HE bombs – a problem that was common to most of the Baedeker targets.

Top: 'Nazis Make Second 'Reprisal' Raid on Bath. The Luftwaffe have made yet another vicious 'reprisal' raid on Bath. Swooping low in the moonlight, a dozen Nazi planes dive-bombed and fired many of Bath's famous buildings for the second time, and sprayed the streets with machine-gun fire. Although the raid was on a smaller scale than the previous one, it is believed that bigger bombs were used. The picture shows the search for victims in the ruins of St. John's Roman Catholic Church, which received a direct hit. One of the priests was killed.'

Above: 'Bath after its two-night blitz. These pictures show some of the damage caused by the German revenge raids. Surface shelters are intact amid the ruins of homes.'

Right: 'A sailor lends a hand in removing belongings from a house badly damaged during the blitz.'

ADVERTISERS' ANNOU

BAEDEKER BOMBERS GO TO NORWICH, FAIL

EFAT

rries

EY SAVED RAF EW FROM SEA

HEN a plane was forced down into the sea off oast of Anglesey Home Stewart Wood (left) rivate Derrick Baynham d the crew. They are d here leaving Bucking-Palace, where they re-the George Medal. They also been awarded the Medal of the Royal al Lifeboat Institution. rt is 17½, lives at Ches-Derrick, whose home is lton-on-Thames, is 18.

ONLY,' CRIPPS

rprise yesterday in Major L. H. Cripps the duration" only.

ts to help in the vital of shipping and to the administration of war effort.

e adds, "if elected I on the cessation of hos-offer Wallasey to choose peace-time M.P.

ghting this election as a -quickly man," he told eeting last night.

e-poll forecasts are that John Pennington (Nat. hold the seat for the t closely challenged by G. L. Reakes, his second opponent.

rful Merseyside Conser-nisations yesterday threw into a final canvassing cially word came from Remember Grantham and nces."

t will be declared to-

ve of the poll in the -election, and probably affect the decision, a raised writes Emrys munition of the

---

A MAN wanted more money to impress his friends, so he turned to murder in London's West End. He found it easy in the black-out, and—

HE SLEW 4 WOMEN FOR £50

RAF Cadet Guilty

By Daily Mail Reporter

GORDON Frederick Cummins, the 28-years-old R.A.F. cadet, was at the Old Bailey yesterday sentenced to death for murdering four women and attempting to murder two others in five days.

Cummins' crime career, which terrorised the West End more than any other murders since those of "Jack the Ripper," began on February 9 and ended in his arrest on February 13.

On February 9 he strangled Miss Evelyn Hamilton in an air raid shelter in Montagu-place, Maryle-bone, W.

On February 10 he strangled and mutilated Mrs. Evelyn Oatley in her flat in Wardour-street, W.

February 11 (Wednesday) there was no murder or attempt. Cum-mins was on all-night guard duty at his billet in St. John's Wood, N.W.

February 12.—Mrs. Margaret Florence Lowe was strangled in her flat in Gosfield-street, W.

February 12.—Mrs. Doris Jouannet was strangled in her flat in Sussex-gardens, W.

February 12.—An attempt to strangle Mrs. Margaret Heywood in St. Alban's-street, Haymarket, and one hour later on the same night a similar attack was made upon Mrs. Mulcahy W. King in Southwick-street, Paddington, W.

'Son of a Peer'

Cummins joined the Royal Air Force in November 1935, and was married within six months.

At one station in Wiltshire Cummins posed as the Hon. Gordon Cummins. He liked to weave mystery about his birth, and pre-tended he was the illegitimate son of a peer.

His arrival in London meant extra expenditure and a need to im-press his newly found friends. So he turned to murder.

His first attempt was successful. Miss Hamilton's handbag contained about £20. But his total haul for his crimes was only about £50.

He found killing simple in the black-out, but he never reckoned with Chief Inspector Greeno, of Scotland Yard, who pinned upon him the shelter murder by particles of sand from the shelter which were found in his respirator.

Cummins' motive was money. It is believed he mutilated his victims to throw the police off his trail by thinking that a maniac was at large.

MORE WAR-TIME REALITY BY THE BBC

By SETON MARGRAVE

THE change in the B.B.C.'s programme policy, initiated by the Directors-General Mr.

THE SPIRIT OF BATH

TWO women, against a back-ground of devastation, typify Bath to-day. Their daily routine is unbroken. One, with her basket, is out shopping; the other is taking her daily walk. The blitz has battered the fine buildings of Bath—but not her spirit.

Jewel Scene In Hotel

A FORMER Polish officer, Adolf Kon, giving evidence at Marl-borough-street yesterday against a man and woman charged with demanding jewellery by menaces, said his face was cut when the man hit him in a Mayfair hotel.

The officer's evidence was against Maureen Pearle Van Pelz, aged 33, of Marylebone, and Manny Bild, 32-years-old tailor, of Maida Vale.

The prosecution said Mr. Kon met Mrs. Van Pelz about 15 months ago, and afterwards gave her £3,500 in various sums and jewellery worth about £2,500.

The jewellery was returned to him after High Court proceedings. A £5,000 blackmail charge brought by Mr. Kon against Mrs. Van Pelz was dismissed at Marl-

---

'3-star Buildings' all Escape

GERMANY'S "three-star" reprisal raid on Norwich—they threatened to bomb British buildings of historic interest indicated by three stars in Baedeker's guidebook—failed in the very object it set out to achieve.

The raid was sharp. There were heavy casualties and widespread damage. But yesterday the citizens of this 1,300-years-old city rejoiced to find its many ancient buildings still unscathed.

These "spite" raids appear to be taxing the Luftwaffe's resources.

The number of raiders on Mon-day night was possibly not more than half that which returned to Bath the previous night, and only a quarter of Saturday's number.

And, according to German-controlled Calais radio, says *Reuter*, three of the bombers which attacked Norwich are missing.

High-explosive and incendiary bombs were showered on the city for well over an hour.

The dead include fire watchers, ambulance personnel, and a Home Guard. In addition to those ad-mitted to hospital, many other less serious casualties were treated at stretcher stations.

Hospital Hit

A number of fires were caused, one fairly large one by the earliest raider. Most of the bombs fell on residential areas, especially the homes of working-class people.

Very many of these houses were damaged. Rescue parties worked for hours to liberate the people in the wreckage.

A hospital, from which most of the patients were moved to shelter in time, had one wing destroyed by direct hits. Only two patients are known to have been killed, but others are missing.

Some churches, a chapel, day schools, and a mission hall were among buildings damaged.

The Germans yesterday continued their threats to bomb historic buildings.

'Making a List'

The military spokesman of the Wilhelmstrasse announced, accord-ing to the Berlin correspondent of the Bâle *National Zeitung*, that German art historians are making a list of British castles, Tudor man-sions, country houses, and sanatoria "suitable for reprisal raids."

This is speciously justified by the German Foreign Office in these words:

"Britain possesses many old cul-tural monuments of which she is proud, just as Germany is proud of the old Hanseatic towns of Lubeck and Rostock. Should the British continue their wanton and sys-tematic destruction of our cultural treasures we shall pay them back in the same coin by attacking simi-lar objectives."

Not a word that Lubeck was a great supply port for Germany's armies on the northern Russian front, or that Rostock is a vitally important air and submarine-manu-facturing centre.

The Germans are getting rattled.

Woman, 43, 'Wed' Youth of 18

A 43-years-old woman who was stated to have gone through a form

---

TEETOTAL, SHE DIED OF 'HOOCH'

By Daily Mail Reporter

DOCTORS were fighting yester-day to save the lives of seven men who are believed to have swallowed the "hooch," or indus-trial spirit, which since the week-end has killed three women and seven men in Glasgow.

The spirit has been identified as methanol, a form of wood alcohol imported from America.

One man, believed to be a sea-man, collapsed like a log while having a meal in a fish and chip restaurant.

Another, Thomas Peebles, of Dal-muir, warned by the state of his companions, walked into a hospital and told them he had taken some of the spirit and is now seriously ill. His mother died a few hours earlier.

150 Galls. Missing

One of the most tragic victims was a woman who was a teetotaller all her life. She was Mrs. Isobella McCargo, who complained on Satur-day night to her husband that she had a pain in her side. He gave her some of the spirit, and 48 hours later she died in hospital.

Police have warned all other per-sons who have the spirit in their possession either to destroy it or to report to a doctor at once.

"About 150 gallons of the spirit is missing," a C.I.D. officer told me —"almost sufficient to kill half the population of Glasgow, but it is thought that a great deal of this may have leaked from a cask."

All the dead people, and those who are ill, were associated with docks and dockers.

Send Paper: Keep Pins and Clips

Big business houses which have started a new waste-paper drive for the £10,000 competition beginning on May 3 and lasting three months are advised to remove all pins and clips from documents before giving them up.

The pins and clips are a menace to the pulping mills, and one mill spends £30,000 a year repairing damage they cause to its machinery. Covers of ledgers and files can be saved for future use.

LET

219

Ancient York

28th April, Tuesday

The ancient city of York was bombed in a short sharp raid by around 40 Luftwaffe bombers who were unopposed in dropping their 84 tonnes of HE mixed with incendiaries that caused intense fires in the mediaeval centre around the Minster. The Guildhall, almost as ancient as London's, was burnt out, the railway station severely damaged and much destruction caused to residential suburbs. 74 civilians were killed.

29th April, Wednesday

The Luftwaffe returned to Norwich again, this time with a less intensive raid, dropping 49 tonnes of HE; 69 were killed in the attack. The two raids caused considerable damage to homes and commercial buildings; 20 factories were badly hit.

Bombing activity was reduced for the next couple of nights.

Left: 'Norwich Air Raid. Picture taken at Norwich after an enemy air raid shows a worker searching among the debris. The Anderson shelters stood up to the bombing.'

THURSDAY, The Daily Mail, APRIL 30, 1942. ADVERTI

HISTORY-RAIDERS HIT YORK

the partnership most
person? A judge
riod was the seventh
pture had passed."

GE A TEST

ng £5,000 damages
urt yesterday, com-
arriage would have
vention of the co-
is rather a critical
the seventh year.
rapture had passed,
settled down into a

In Sports
ill Test
C Cadets

all Air Correspondent
,000 A.T.C. cadets in
Britain are to be put
eries of physical fitness
them agility, strength,
and dexterity.

have been told to
running tracks on
ments, or even on
hes of road. The ath-
rds which the boys will
reach vary according

nder 16 years, for in-
climb a rope 10ft.,
6min, 20sec., walk 5
20min., swim at least
be able to throw and
with accuracy.

it is hoped, will be
100yds, in as little as
gh 13sec. will gain a
tests will be cor-
more difficult for
The 100yds. in the
ampionships was won

of the A.T.C. Mr
yesterday that
expert

The King at 'Ops'

THE King saw pilots take off from a fighter station for a sweep yesterday and listened in to operations.

Convent Smashed: Bombed-out Women Machine-gunned

From Daily Mail Reporter   York, Wednesday.

THE walls of York still stand to-day, in spite of the wanton Nazi attack early this morning on its ancient treasures. But a famous 15th-century building was destroyed, a convent bombed and five nuns killed, and aged women in one of its almshouses were machine-gunned as they scrambled out of the ruins of their home.

Parts of these grey stone walls are now blackened by the flames of incendiary bombs, but the gates of York still stand high, like the spirit of its people, who, after nearly two hours of intense bombing and machine-gunning, were clearing up to-day.

York was the third historic place to bear the full venom of German attacks. Twenty raiders came over. Five were destroyed.

Ten aged widows in an almshouse were machine-gunned as they tried to find shelter. The roofs and windows of their home had been blown out and the old oak doors forced from their hinges.

Mrs. J. Cunnee, wife of the care-taker, told me: " Our home is part of the old chapel, with walls two feet thick. As we helped some of the old ladies across the gardens to the shelter here one German plane dived and we heard machine-gun bullets rattling through the apple trees.

" There was no panic among the old people. We stood in the shelter of the hall. To-day we have found machine-gun bullets in the garden and some have sliced branches from the trees."

Mrs. Sutcliffe, aged 91, oldest of the widows, told A.R.P. officials when they asked her to move from her damaged home: " I am not going to move for Hitler." And the old ladies are staying on.

The Agony of Bath

Warning for Others

By OLIVE MELVILLE BROWN

BRITAIN'S three-star towns, hitherto clothed in the sem-blance of safety, are now em-braced in Hitler's circle of danger.

Bath was the first—Bath, with its cure for physical ills and its mild-mannered gentility, awoke to war four days ago.

This city, which I saw for the first time a few days ago with a cloud of stone-dust over its broken beauty, had lived for two and a half years under the illusion that it was free from German bombs.

The awakening came on Saturday night. On Sunday night it became reality. On Monday I drove into Bath from Bristol. Fire tenders were still crowding in ahead of us.

★

THE attitude of Bath to bombing, which, I think, is shared by many other towns in this country, is exemplified by an incident which happened there last week.

A member of the W.V.S. had travelled from London to demon-strate and speak about a new type of blitz stove made from

THE King talks to a pilot who has just landed after yester-day's sweeps. The tousle-haired airman still wears his Mae West.

NUNS KILLED

Three nuns were killed and two more are missing in the ruins of one wing of a convent. Two died as they ran from the shelter of cellars to try to help one of the nuns trapped under fallen masonry.

The Mother Superior told me: " The sisters and 18 girl boarders, aged from eight to 16, went to shelter in the cellars. One bomb

FIT FOR THE QUEEN

THE Queen tastes one of the 150 dishes at a food display in London yesterday.

Palace to Use Their Recipes

By Daily Mail Reporter

DISHES from the recipes of Hailsham, Sussex, house-wives are to be served up at Buckingham Palace.

The Queen gave the instruction yesterday when she saw—and tasted —the dishes at an exhibition of war cooking at the Dorchester Hotel, organised by the W.V.S. and Sussex education authority.

" I shall find the recipes useful," she said.

Above left: A church in York after a Baedeker raid. Damage was severe in these provincial towns and cities as they had fewer air defences than other, more likely, targets.

Above right: York's 15th-century Guildhall in flames

Left: 'York Blitz. Wrecked buildings in York after last night's raid.'

Exeter's Centre Razed

3rd May, Sunday

The April Baedeker raids that followed Bath were less severe than on the 23rd April but May's bombing returned to the heavy scale in a devastating night attack on Exeter that wiped out the city's mediaeval centre, leaving ancient buildings gutted or razed to the ground, with the Cathedral also hit. As well as the mediaeval buildings, important infrastructure was severely damaged: the railway station, library, post office, hospital and telephone exchange. 163 were killed and 131 injured. The attacking force of 30 bombers suffered losses of 4 aircraft – all confirmed kills by Beaufighters.

4th May, Monday

Cowes, perhaps not with the same history as Exeter but a noted leisure and shipbuilding centre, was the next target for a heavy raid with over 200 tonnes of bombs being dropped on the small harbour town by 50 raiders, a number of them flying double sorties to give an attack in two waves. 66 people died in the raid.

Main Picture: *'Air Raid Damage at Exeter. Some of the damage surrounding the cathedral in Exeter. Fortunately, except for broken windows, the cathedral has escaped damage.'*

Below: *'We Told the Queen. The Queen asks an Exeter boy about his experiences during the recent German Baedeker raids on the city. The King and Queen have made an extensive tour of the West Country, during which they visited Exeter to see the damaged areas. The King inspected the naval dockyard at Devonport, and parades of naval personnel and marines at Plymouth.'*

Canterbury Cathedral Escapes Destruction

8th May, Friday

The Baedeker raids were having an effect on the cities involved but at a cost to the attacking force which was experiencing unsustainable losses. The 40 aircraft assigned to raid Norwich this night were all that could be mustered and they were laden with over 100 tonnes of HE. However Norwich was better prepared, with barrage balloons added to the AA defence of 3.7 inch heavy guns. Furthermore, Air Intelligence had been tracking the attack: the navigation beams were jammed and a Starfish site lit up as the raid began. The resulting confusion led to the wide dispersal of the heavy bomb-load across East Anglia relieving the city of any serious damage.

19th, 24th May, Tuesday, Sunday

Heavy raiding forces set out for Hull and Poole, respectively, and were generally considered ineffectual.

31st May, Sunday

On the night of 30th May, Bomber Command mustered a force of nearly 1,000 bombers in a show of force to Hitler, originally planning to drop 1,500 tons of HE and IBs on Hamburg; instead, because of weather conditions, Cologne was chosen and widespread damage and casualties were inflicted on the beautiful historic city. In return, Hitler ordered an immediate reprisal on Canterbury, which took place on this night. The city suffered significant damage and it was clear that the Cathedral was the main target. Luckily the Cathedral escaped destruction but its Library was gutted.

Baedeker raids in June were not as shockingly intense as those of the previous two months; in fact they had little effect and were interspersed with considerable hit-and-run raiding.

Left above: *'Raid Damage at Canterbury. The Cathedral Library which was damaged during a recent raid on Canterbury. Soldiers are seen removing debris in the foreground.'*

Left: *'Canterbury Raid. Bomb damage.'*

Opposite above: *'Raid Damage at Canterbury. This was a covered arcade known as The Shambles, which ran from High Street to Burgate Street, Canterbury. It was a happy hunting ground for bargainers, and was severely damaged during a recent raid on the cathedral city.'*

Opposite below: *'Canterbury As Target For Nazi Raiders' 'Reprisal'. Following the R.A.F.'s great night attack on Cologne, Nazi planes made a sharp attack on Canterbury. Shops and a residential area were damaged and there were some casualties. The photo shows troops and demolition workers searching amid the damaged houses. Women householders can be seen in the background salvaging in their second floor room, now completely exposed.'*

Submarine

and Sank

From **LARRY ALLEN**, A.P.

L IEUTENANT STEPHEN his depot ship at Alexand Malta convoy battle as seen by

NO-HAT GIRLS IN CHURCH

FAMOUS LIBRARY IN RUINS

1st June, Monday
Ipswich was the target of an ineffectual attack.

2nd June, Tuesday
Canterbury was raided again this night, then for a third time on the 6th but with less effect on either occasion than on the 31st May attack.

3rd June, Wednesday
Heavy attack on Poole by 75 aircraft caused serious damage but few casualties.

21st June, Sunday
Southampton was hit.

27th, 28th June, Saturday, Sunday
Two serious night attacks on Weston super Mare aided by bright moonlight, with combined casualties of 102 killed and 400 injured.

29th June, Monday
The last raid of the month was on Peterborough.

Baedeker Raids Lose Momentum

While the Baedeker raids wrought havoc on Britain's mediaeval treasures, London did its best to clear up but there were sombre reminders of what the capital had been through. One was the UXB that exploded without warning in Southwark on 6th June, having been dropped on 10th May 1941. The HE bomb was probably an SC1000 or SC1800 and it obliterated Gurney Street causing significant casualties.

Other reminders were more purposeful as newspapers reminded the civilian population of what the country had suffered in the Night Blitz.

As for the Baedeker raids, the shock and awe of the earlier attacks had subsided and in July and August their impact fizzled out, though not without some significant return to form – as with the three consecutive night attacks on Birmingham, 27-29th July. August's raids failed to have more impact than the hit-and-run style of attack that prevailed before the Baedeker campaign was instated. 1,637 civilians were killed and 1,760 injured during the raids on the five main cities attacked, and over 50,000 houses were destroyed.

Both sides learned from the tactics deployed in these months of raiding. History shows that whatever the Luftwaffe had learned, would not save it or Germany from the devastation that would be visited on the Third Reich, which peaked from 1943 onwards, when Allied strategic bombing would make the Night Blitz look like a rehearsal. However, the highly flexible deployment of Luftwaffe forces in the Western Europe theatre would stand them in good stead for future attack: Britain would discover this in the 'Baby Blitz', as it was known at the receiving end – or Operation Steinbock to the Luftwaffe.

4th July, Saturday
General Dwight D Eisenhower, 'Ike', opened the American Red Cross 'Washington Club' in London West End's Curzon St. He had recently arrived in the capital to take up his post of Commander-in-Chief SHAEF (Supreme Headquarters Allied Expeditionary Force).

Right: 'Many Killed and Injured in London Explosion. The scene at Gurney Street, New Kent Road, S.E., where many people were killed and injured when a block of tenement houses blew up. The cause of the explosion has not been given.'

Opposite left: 'Two Years Ago Today First Bombs on Central London. On August 24th, 1940, Central London was bombed for the first time in the present war. Incendiaries were dropped, which caused big fires in the City. An historic and dramatic photograph (hitherto unpublished) taken on this memorable night showing firemen gallantly fighting the fires.'

Opposite centre: 'A Ward of Cordwainer Club Service was held in the ruins of St. Mary-le-Bow Church, for the first time since the Church was blitzed. The dome of St. Paul's Cathedral can be seen through the hollows where the windows used to be, making a new view of St. Paul's Cathedral.'

Opposite right: 'Air Raid Damage at Cambridge. Damage to the University Union Society's buildings at Cambridge during a recent air raid. This picture shows an exterior view of the Union building.'

1st August, Saturday
Jabo raids steadily increased from this date, exploiting the air supremacy of the Fw190; however, the RAF's answer to the Luftwaffe's speedy all-rounder, the. Hawker Typhoon, was now in service with three squadrons but its role had not been clearly established until commanders proposed standing intercept patrols against tip-and-run. This role was adopted by five squadrons equipped with Typhoons by the end of September.

19th August, Wednesday
Two disastrous events blighted the optimistic outlook of the summer of 1942. The first, on this day, was the fiasco of the Dieppe Raid which committed over 6,000 troops and more than 250 ships to capturing the Channel port in order to test German defences and destroy as much of them as possible. Barely 2,000 troops returned, the bulk of the casualties and captured being Canadian forces. Earl Mountbatten, who had command of the raid, justified the losses by pointing towards the lessons learned for the future invasion of France. A key objective was also to draw the Luftwaffe into an aerial battle with a superior RAF force: this gambit failed and instead the tactical skills of the Luftwaffe sank many of the attacking fleet.

25th August, Tuesday
The second disaster was the tragic death of the King's younger brother, the Duke of Kent, who was killed when his plane crashed in Scotland en route to Iceland. A popular member of the Royal Family, he took responsibility as Chief Welfare Officer of the Home Command.

WEDNESDAY, AUGUST 26, 1942

THE DUKE OF KENT KILLED

Brother of the King Dead in Service of RAF

FLYING-BOAT CRASH ON WAY TO ICELAND

The Duke Had Many Wartime Escapes

THE Duke of Kent filled every moment of his time after the outbreak of war with a variety of official duties and personal visits to war victims, wounded, and the bombed-out.

Many times he was in danger from bombs, shells, and machine-gun fire.

Only a week ago, while the Duke was staying in a south-coast town, enemy machines raided the area and bombed and gunned the town.

In November 1940 German batteries on the French coast bombarded Dover while he was visiting the town.

Many times during the Battle of Britain he watched R.A.F. fighters smashing the Luftwaffe. In a visit to one air base the Duke missed bombs dropped on the base by four minutes.

The raid was sustained and he took shelter many feet below the chalk cliffs and had lunch there. After lunch he watched a fierce air battle over the Channel.

Two months earlier—in July 1940—Germans raided an area he was visiting as an R.A.F. group captain. Bombs fell close to the house in which he was staying.

His visit to the machine-gunned town was his last reported public appearance.

★

DURING the intensive night air raids on London the Duke visited many shelters, including one in the East End accommodating 7,000 people, and also various Tube shelters. He saw and talked with the shelterers during the raids.

Once a time-bomb exploded within 80 yards of the Duke's car and a shower of debris fell on the car. After it had all come down the Duke got out and talked with people living around, congratulating them on their coolness.

THE Daily Mail announces with deep regret that His Royal Highness the Duke of Kent, youngest surviving brother of the King, was killed in an air crash yesterday. He was on the way to Iceland in the course of his R.A.F. duties when his Sunderland flying-boat crashed in the north of Scotland.

The Duke is the first member of the Royal Family to meet death in a flying accident and the first to die on active service in modern times. All the crew of the flying-boat were killed.

The crash was not due to enemy action. It occurred late in the day, and the news was released by the Air Ministry shortly before midnight. The Duchess of Kent, the King and Queen and other members of the Royal Family were immediately informed.

In view of the need for secrecy regarding the movements of members of the Royal Family in war-time the funeral will probably take place privately.. No announcement has so far been made about Court mourning.

The Duke of Kent, who would have been 40 on December 20, was probably the most air-minded member of the Royal Family and the first to fly the Atlantic. He had flown thousands of miles under war conditions in a plane equipped for battle with enemy aircraft.

For some time he had been making extensive but little publicised air trips in his capacity as Chief Welfare Officer of the Home Command, attached to the staff of the Inspector General of the R.A.F.

There has been no more reliable aircraft in the world than the type in which the Duke was killed.

Such accidents as there have been in the region in which yesterday's crash occurred.

Numerous hills and other steeply rising ground leave pilots with an exceptionally small margin of safety

How Radio Gave News to World

NEWS of the Duke of Kent's death reached the B.B.C. a few minutes before the midnight news was broadcast.

It was given to the world in fewer than 100 simple words without preliminary announcement.

The Duke as Air Commodore

THE Duke of Kent in the uniform of Air Commodore of the Royal Air Force. He made his first flight in October 1929. Seven years later he became Permanent Grand Master of the Guild of Air Pilots and Air Navigators of the British Empire. On that occasion he said: " Mastery of the air can be the greatest blessing or the greatest danger to mankind." Family picture—BACK Page.

Airborne Troops

'Bock Near Stalingrad' —Moscow

'Situation More Complicated'

Daily Mail Special Correspondent
STOCKHOLM, Tuesday.

THE Soviet midnight communiqué revealed that the Battle for Stalingrad has taken a sudden grave turn. Fighting "north-west" of the city is mentioned for the first time.

The situation is described as having become "more complicated."

Tense battles are raging against large enemy tank and infantry forces which have crossed the Don at the bend south-east of Klietskaya.

The Soviet troops are repelling almost incessant attacks. The Germans are suffering heavy losses.

Stalingrad itself is under heavy attack. Soviet A.A. guns and fighters defending the city have shot down 92 German planes in the past two days.

Gigantic Struggle

The Soviet communique adds that battles raged to-day also in the areas of Klietskaya (north-west of Stalingrad, west of the Don), north-east of Kotelnikovo (south-west of Stalingrad), and in the Caucasus areas of Prokhladnaya, and south of Krasnodar.

The gigantic Battle for Stalingrad is overshadowing all other fronts. It is clear that Bock is throwing in everything to squeeze the great steel city.

Although he has made progress north-west of the town after forcing the Don Bend, he has not yet been able to exploit fully the wedge he drove into the Soviet positions to the south-west.

Marshal Timoshenko's forces, counter-attacking in full force, have cut off many of the tanks he drove forward.

In one battle the leading German tanks charged straight into a Soviet minefield and blew up.

The remainder slowed and proceeded more cautiously. The waiting Red Army gunners held their fire and then all the Soviet anti-tank batteries blazed simultaneously.

Dozens of tanks were smashed.

Sea-Air Battle for Solomons

TWO JAP CARRIERS HIT

From **WALTER FARR**, Daily Mail Correspondent
WASHINGTON, Tuesday.

AMERICAN Flying Fortresses and carrier-borne planes are engaged in a great battle against a powerful Japanese fleet of warships and transports bearing down on the three American-held islands in the Solomon group.

It began two days ago, and is increasing in ferocity as enemy aircraft-carriers, cruisers, and at least one battleship approach Tulagi, Guadalcanal, and Malaita, recaptured by American Marines three weeks ago.

So far the battle has been fought between American planes and Japanese warships and planes. There is no news to-night of any Japanese landing, or any indication that the enemy fleet has yet reached the islands.

American planes have scored hits on two carriers and a battleship, set fire to a cruiser and a transport, and damaged other cruisers. No ship has been claimed as sunk, and there has been no clash between surface warships.

The presence of at least one battleship indicates that the Japanese are prepared to risk heavy naval loss to reoccupy Tulagi Harbour. Previously nearly all the fighting in the South-West Pacific has been waged by carriers and cruisers.

This is how the battle developed, according to the latest information available in Washington: On Sunday the Japanese launched a heavy air attack against the airfields on Guadalcanal Island. They lost 21 planes.

During Sunday night enemy destroyers came close to shell shore positions on Guadalcanal, which shelters Tulagi Harbour from the west.

On Monday American planes hit a cruiser and a transport north of Guadalcanal and left both burning fiercely.

These ships appear to have been apart from the main enemy fleet.

BACK PAGE-Col. SIX

LATEST

JAP CONVOY BOMBED

To-day's communiqué from General MacArthur's H.Q. reports that Allied fighters and bombers destroyed Jap gunboat and heavily strafed two transports in attack on convoy off South-East New Guinea.

Allied fighters destroyed 13 Jap fighters on the ground at Buna. Eight tons of bombs were dropped in raid on Rabaul. —A.P.

PLANE MISSING

Washington, Tuesday. — A U.S. Navy plane, with a crew of four and ten passengers, is overdue on the way from Kodiak Island to White Horse, Alaska.—Reuter.

For Energy

227

DUCHESS KNEELS BY DUKE

Alone in Chapel

By Daily Mail Reporter

THE Duchess of Kent knelt in prayer yesterday beside her husband's coffin in the Albert Memorial Chapel at Windsor Castle.

Earlier in the day the coffin had been taken to Windsor Castle from Scotland. The last part of the journey from Euston was made on an R.A.F. tender.

The coffin was covered with the Union Jack and the R.A.F. flag, and on it were two small wreaths, one from the Duchess and her three children and the other from the King and Queen.

N.C.O.s of the R.A.F. formed the bearer party.

As the coffin was removed from the tender and carried into the Albert Memorial Chapel, a guard of honour of the Grenadier Guards presented arms.

The coffin will remain in the Albert Memorial Chapel until the funeral at St. George's Chapel.

When the Duchess arrived she went straight to the chapel and requested that she should be left quite alone.

She placed on the coffin a small bunch of red and white roses, the Duke's favourite flowers, which she picked in the garden at The Coppins, the Iver home of the late Duke.

In Deep Mourning

It was nearly ten minutes before the Duchess, who was in deep mourning, emerged from the chapel. . . . same train that brought

Lightning Day Raid on Bristol

RESCUE workers carry away a victim of the day raid on Bristol yesterday. The wreckage of a home is still smouldering and firemen are pouring water on the débris.

Three 'Double-deckers' Afire After Raid: Passers-by Helpless to Rescue Trapped Crowd

By Daily Mail Reporter

BOMBS from two German aircraft yesterday morning wrecked three double-deck buses in a Bristol thoroughfare and caused heavy casualties. The planes flew in at a great height. Two of the buses, one crowded with passengers, were stationary.

The explosions killed men, women, and children outright. Some were trapped when the buses caught fire.

People who rushed from surrounding streets to the scene of the bombing were helpless.

They could hear the cries of people inside the blazing buses, but could do nothing to save them.

Mr. H. Sheppard, who was 100 yards away when the bombs fell, ran to the spot with two other men.

They found a woman of 25 still alive, trapped by her feet. Behind her, a man was trying vainly to crawl to the door.

Mr. Sheppard, his head bandaged from a burn received during his attempts at rescue, said simply: "We had to leave them both. The heat got so terrific. That was what made it so terrible. People were burning to death and there was nothing we could do."

Escaped

One woman threw her bag to Mr. Sheppard and then jumped from the upper deck of a bus into the arms of people below. She was one of the few who escaped.

Mr. Sheppard told me: "We heard no sound of the plane nor of the bombs, until the explosion. Within a matter of seconds

28th August, Friday

August's bad news was not finished: a lone Luftwaffe Ju86 flew over Bristol at 09.30 and released a single 250kg HE bomb from an estimated height close to 40,000 feet. Falling on a bustling city centre street without warning, it demolished three crowded buses as well as inflicting great injury in the busy Broad Weir. A total of 48 people died. The irony was that the raider was tracked by British radar as it crossed the Channel and as it arrived over Bristol but no RAF fighter at the time could reach the bomber at such altitude. This incident was one of a number that pushed the development of a Spitfire adapted for high altitude, after which such raids ceased.

2nd September, Wednesday

US troops paraded through the City to the ruined Guildhall; American forces were gathering in Britain prior to the planned Operation Torch invasion of North Africa in the first half of November.

29th September, Tuesday

A small Jabo force of five raiders bombed a number of targets in South East England, including a small school in Petworth, Sussex, during study hours. The direct hit killed 31, most of them pupils.

Top: *'Bombs kill boys in school during today's raid on a southern county.'*

Above: *'The Wrecked Class rooms. This is the school in a small Southern England town hit by the bombs of a sneak raider yesterday morning. About 70 boys were at their lessons when the bomb crashed through the roof. Several boys were killed. Others who escaped helped rescue squads to dig beneath the debris. Note the school desk on a heap of debris, apparently undamaged. As the school attendance records were destroyed it is not yet known how many boys were in the class when the bomb fell. Ten boys may still be missing.'*

Above left: *'The twenty-six victims of the bombed village school were buried in a communal grave in Sussex today.'*
Daily Mail Saturday, 3rd October 1942.

Opposite above left: *'Lightning Day Raid on Bristol. Rescue workers carry away a victim of the day raid on Bristol yesterday. The wreckage of the home is still smouldering and firemen are pouring water on the debris.'*

Opposite above right: *'Raid Damage in Bristol. Enemy planes made a sharp attack on Bristol yesterday morning, when one of the bombs destroyed three buses. Passengers and passers-by were amongst the casualties. Fires which broke out were soon brought under control by the N.F.S. The raiders were only over the town for a very short time. This picture shows some of the damage caused by the enemy planes.'*

Operation Torch Draws Fire

31st October, Saturday

Canterbury was attacked during the largest daylight raid mounted by the Luftwaffe since 1940: 60 Fw 190s crossed the coast attacking Deal then 30 continued to make a low-level attack on the city. Equipped with single 500kg bombs, the raiders killed 32 and injured 116 (one Fw 190 was lost). The raiders were over land for about 6 minutes, travelling at high speed. The most effective counter to these attacks were standing patrols by the Hawker Typhoon and the Griffon engined Spitfire Mk XII, both of which had the low altitude speed to intercept the Fw 190. Improvements in the performance of British fighter aircraft and their tactics, aided by accurate radar interception, led to ever higher losses by the Jabo units, made worse by increasingly effective ground-based weapons. In the London raid of 20th January 1943 by 90 Jabos and their escorts, 8 of the aircraft and their pilots were lost, shot down by the RAF.

8th November, Sunday

The launch of Operation Torch pulled back units from the Luftwaffe fighter bomber force from northern France to Provence and this had a major impact on activity, significantly reducing bombing on Britain.

15th November, Sunday

Civil Defence Day: 1,500 Civil Defence personnel from around the country paraded on this national Day of Thanksgiving. The King took the salute from the steps of St Paul's Cathedral, whose bells, along with those of other churches in the country, rang out for the first time since they were silenced for the Battle of Britain, when they were reserved for warning the population of pending invasion. The peal of bells and the knowledge that Hitler's Wehrmacht had suffered its first great defeat in North Africa gave the nation great optimism: the War was no longer marching solely to Hitler's drum.

16th December, Wednesday

December's raiding by the Luftwaffe was much reduced and patchy but today was the worst of the month when in daylight 11 Jabo fighters ravaged coastal settlements in the south of England killing 14 people in low-level attacks with bombs, cannon and machine gun fire.

31st December, Thursday

Total civilian casualties in the bombing raids of 1942 were 3,236 killed and 4,148 wounded: heavy losses but much reduced from the period of the Night Blitz

Left above: 'Built Six Years After Columbus Discovered America – Destroyed By The Nazis In 1942. Columbus discovered the islands off what we now know as America in 1492 – and six years later while he was still making his voyages, this house in Canterbury, now the oldest in the cathedral city, was built. This is how the Nazis left it after a recent raid on the city – wrecked almost beyond repair.'

Left: 'Damage and casualties were caused when an enemy raider made a daylight attack on a Thames estuary town. A shopping centre and offices were damaged by bombs while the streets were swept by machine gun fire. This picture shows Civil Defence workers searching for survivors amid the damaged buildings after the attack.'

Left: Middlesbrough Railway Station after a bombing raid in November 1942.

MONDAY, The Daily Mail.

Blitz Towns Go On Parade

THE KING TAKES SALUTE

By Daily Mail Reporter

CULMINATING point in Britain's Day of Thanksgiving, heralded by the peals of thousands of long-silent bells, was a service at St. Paul's Cathedral yesterday afternoon attended by the King and Queen and 1,500 men and women of the Civil Defence services.

The men and women were drawn from every heavily bombed area, and as each detachment later marched past the King and Queen it bore the name of its town — a "battle roll of the blitz."

The Bells

THIS was a day golden in the hearts of men
When old, wise friends, after long contemplation,
Spoke to us again.

*

THEY had been silent through all tribulation,
Waiting and watchful throughout the nights and the days
To warn a nation.

*

AND now they spoke:
Give praise. Give praise
For faith rewarded, burdens borne,
The night that fades before the dawn.
Give praise!

*

THEY spoke and ceased.
The morning air was still.
The halted tractor crawled
across the hill.

The King, in the uniform of Admiral of the Fleet, took the salute on the steps of St. Paul's. A City Police inspector led the procession of heroes; behind him came the band of the National Fire Service.

First in the procession came Dover, "front-line" town, then London, bus drivers and nurses walking behind the wardens and members of rescue services, and, behind, Coventry, Birmingham, Southampton, Bristol, Merseyside, Sheffield, Manchester, South Wales, Portsmouth, Hull, and Plymouth, and many more.

There, too, were the Baedeker towns — Exeter, Bath, Norwich, York, and, most recently attacked of all, Canterbury.

Medal Ribbons

There were no jingling medals, but hundreds of them wore medal ribbons for gallantry in the blitzes.

The Archbishop of Canterbury preached the sermon at the service.
Dr. Temple said: "We are more
Chr....

Woman Ringer

MRS F. R. DEAL took her place among yesterday's bellringers at St. Paul's Cathedral.—Daily Mail picture.

ROMMEL TRIE

Escaped British Retreat Turned

From EDW
Daily Mail Spec

TOBRU

FROM the middle
Rommel's fl
British officer has b
of the retreat—as th
see it. For a week h
he escaped when
captors.

I met him as he
main road at Gamb
in the desert betwe
He was not at all
because the enemy
only a few hours e

The most remarkab
the Germans was th
defeated and with the
they still do not seem
is probably out of Nort

"They have a child
Rommel, will get them
"The belief was m
officers—the men look

A ROMMEL TU

"I saw Rommel
much the Field-Marsha
were very theatrical

"He came up in
tured British tank, t
effect, rode up and d
manner, apparently
morale.

"A rumour th
deliberately spr

Direct Hit on School

16th January, Saturday
RAF Bomber Command mounted a 200 bomber raid on Berlin – returning after 14 months to bomb in poor weather. Bombing was scattered as a result but the message delivered in 8,000 pound weapons was clear. By coincidence Berlin was poorly defended that night and only one of the 190 Lancasters was lost.

17th January, Sunday
After the losses by attrition to their Western forces, reinforcements came into service and a retaliatory night attack was ordered on London – the first heavy raid on the capital since July 1942. The raids were in two waves of 40 and 50 aircraft, some crews flying double sorties. Damage to London was widespread but generally not serious. The same night a large force of heavy RAF bombers made a repeat raid on Berlin.

20th January, Wednesday
28 low-flying Fw 190s carrying SC500 HE bombs made a surprise daylight raid on London: barrage balloons were down for the safety of RAF local flying and the Jabo force was able to penetrate the capital's defences. Sandhurst Road School in Catford received a direct hit. 38 children and 6 teachers were killed. 33 of the victims were buried in a communal grave – 7,000 attended the memorial service conducted by the Bishop of Southwark.

Left: **Rescue workers frantically search the ruins of Sandhurst Road School for survivors when it was hit in a daylight raid on Wednesday. The air raid warning came too late for teachers and children to take shelter.**

Below: *'Bananas From the Queen. Children injured in the bombed Lewisham school had a surprise visit from the Queen yesterday. Her Majesty took them bananas, brought from Casablanca by Lord Louis Mountbatten for the Princesses. This is Maureen Hills, aged 11, talking to the Queen.'*

Opposite below: *'Roof top raiders bombed an inland South East Town to-day. Picture shows: All that was left of the bombed school after it had received a direct hit.'*
On 24th March at Victoria Road Junior School, in Ashford, Kent, 300 children were saved when they took refuge in the playground shelters. The three-minute raid on the town killed 50 and seriously injured 77.

celling all Army leave and ordering all men to rejoin their units immediately added to the confusion. The reports add that the

Russians during their advance by-passed Hungarian G.H.Q. in Alexiskaya, pressed on 30 miles, and isolated the G.H.Q.

Deepen Drive harkov

INCREASES

yesterday swept on 30 over a wide front to ov, Hitler's great base. a special communiqué,

Wreckage—the Second Enemy

A SHIRT-SLEEVED policeman directs some of the rescue - workers grappling with wreckage at the London school hit by the Luftwaffe in their daylight raid yesterday. Soldiers and firemen, business men and parents helped. The digging went on all night. Daily Mail pictures of the school are in Page THREE and BACK Page. Full story in Page THREE.

124 Victims in Bombed School up to 2 a.m.

34 Known Dead, Many Missing

Night Digging

By Daily Mail Reporter

EARLY this morning hundreds of rescue workers were still digging in the light of flares for trapped children in the wreckage of a London suburban school, bombed in yesterday's daylight raid.

By 2 a.m. the total casualties had risen to 124, including killed, injured, and missing.

Of these, 70 children were rushed to one hospital. Some were dead on arrival. Six died in hospital and a number are seriously ill. Others are recovering and have been evacuated from the hospital.

The number of dead at 2 a.m. was known to be 34. This figure includes the six who died in hospital.

Four teachers are among those killed.

Because all parents whose children were missing did not report to the A.R.P. authorities direct, it cannot be stated for certain how many are still buried in the wreckage.

Three times during the night the

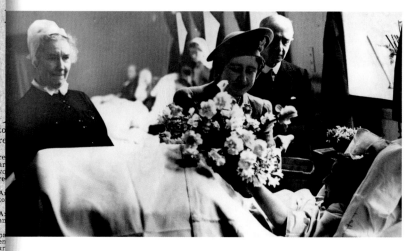

1st March, Monday

The major raid on Berlin by RAF Bomber Command on this date caused more destruction than any other to date. Britain expected a major retaliation bringing about heightened anxiety in the capital. By night the air raid shelters were heavily subscribed.

3rd March, Wednesday

Luftwaffe retribution came this night. Although their forces were so depleted that only 35 aircraft could be mustered for the attack, the result would exceed their expectations, especially when only 10 were able to penetrate the capital's outer defence. When the air raid alert sounded hundreds of people rushed to the Bethnal Green tube station which was routinely sheltering up to 10,000 people; as they filed into the shelter down steep steps, one of the new Z batteries fired a barrage of rockets. People panicked at the unfamiliar sound and surged into the shelter crushing those at the bottom of the stairs. The deep shelter used an incomplete tunnel extension of the Central Line that was only accessible by one main entrance and a distant emergency exit. In one of the worst tragedies of the Blitz, 173 people died in terrible and pointless circumstances. However, much worse now lay in store for the German people as the five-month-long strategic bombing campaign, the Battle of the Ruhr, launched on the 5th March with a massed raid on the industrial city of Essen.

7th March, Sunday

Hitler had much frustration with the progress of the bombing campaign on Britain. During March, 29-year-old bomber veteran, Dietrich Peltz was appointed as the new commander of the Luftwaffe attack force for Britain with the title *Angriffsführer England* and was given the objective of building a strategic bombing force for a major programme in 1944. However Luftwaffe aircraft losses during 1943, thanks to effective night fighters and intensive AA protection, made his task impossible. On this day, SKG10 flew its first operational mission – against Eastbourne: 12 aircraft killed 21 people in a fierce surprise raid.

SHELTER STEPS OF DEATH

Vital Brya

12 Raid Coast Town: 2 Down

Two of a dozen raiders which bombed an English south-east coast town from roof-top height yesterday were shot down into the Channel by R.A.F. fighters. The raiders were believed to have consisted of eight F.W. 190's and four Me 109's.

Bombs caused damage over a wide area in the town and about 12 people were killed.

A woman and her two young children sheltering under the stairs had a remarkable escape. A bomb tore through the front of the house a few feet above their heads and exploded in the garden, but they were unhurt.

Bombs also fell on a bank, a store, an empty garage, and an hotel. Two churches were damaged.

THIS exclusive picture was taken from the top of the tube shelter steps on which 178 people were killed in an appalling accident during Wednesday night's raid on London. Workmen were busy getting the staircase ready for last night's shelterers. Centre rails were put up.

60 Children Died in Shelter Disaster

Left top: *'Londoners are apt to forget that there is an area of England – the south-east coast – where the blitz is ever-present. Though the syrens only wail occasionally in Town these days, they are very frequently heard on the coast where hit-and-run raiders dash in, drop their bombs, and leave death and desolation in their wake. Photograph shows: the scene of devastation in the Main Street of a south-east coast town after a hit-and-run raider had sneaked over in a recent raid. There used to be a furniture store, a bank and a hotel on the right of the picture. Now there is only a pile of rubble with a street lamp standard leaning over at a crazy angle. Rescue workers are already on the spot ready to start operations.'*

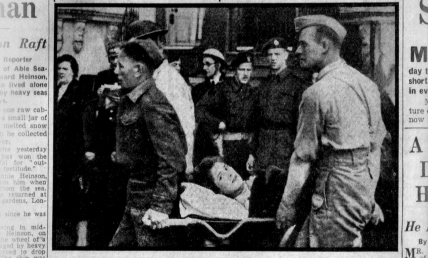

MOTHERS WANT TO

Thirty Millio

CHILDREN BURIED IN S. COAST RAID

RATION
BOOKS
QUEUE

Troops Help in Rescues

From Daily Mail Correspondent

A SOUTH COAST TOWN, Tuesday Night.

TWENTY-FIVE enemy machines, including a dozen Focke-Wulf 190's, with a strong fighter escort, swept over here this afternoon in the most concentrated raid this town has yet had.

They were met by a terrific A.A. barrage, which t three down. A fighter shot down a fourth. The

Top: The raid on Brighton by 22 Jabos of SKG10 on 25th May killed 21, damaging numerous buildings and the railway. The viaduct at Preston Park was put out of action, as this picture dramatically shows. The line was operational again just over four weeks later after speedy repairs to the fallen arch.

Above: Holy Trinity Church, Margate, was destroyed on Tuesday 1st June by Jabo raiders that dropped 14 SC 500 HE bombs on the town killing eight people.

234

Aberdeen Attacked

21st April, Wednesday

98 civilians and 27 servicemen were killed in a night raid on Aberdeen carried out by 30 of Peltz's new fast bomber group. In preparation for the raid the aircraft were moved to a forward base in Norway from where they launched the attack, appearing without warning at Aberdeen after flying across the North Sea as low as 30m above the sea. Around 40 bombs were dropped, each plane carrying a 2,200kg load. As was often the case, the Press was obliged to play down the impact of the raid, as shown in the extract from the *Daily Mail* below.

23rd May, Sunday

In a ferocious Jabo attack on Bournemouth, 22 Focke Wulfs destroyed 59 buildings and damaged 3,442. The attack took place at 13.00 as the busy seaside town was sitting down for Sunday lunch and the hotels were filled with billeted service personnel. The Central Hotel and the Metropole took direct hits. It was at the Metropole that a great number of airforce people died and the figures were kept from public knowledge. 77 civilians and 131 military, including Americans, perished. Luftwaffe losses were relatively high with four aircraft shot down.

30th May, Sunday

A daylight Jabo raid on Torquay in the afternoon killed 40 and injured another 40. Many of the casualties were in church for a children's service. Five of the raiders were shot down: one clipped the steeple of the town's catholic church, flicking his bomb onto St Marychurch across the way, where Sunday school was in progress. 21 children were killed.

Above: *'Raid Damage on a South West Town. Photograph shows: A church destroyed by a direct hit in a recent raid on a South West Town'.*

SCOTS TOWN BOMBED

Roof-top Raid

A heavy barrage met raiders who last night dropped high-explosive and incendiary bombs on a town in the north-east of Scotland.

A tenement building received a direct hit and there were a number of casualties, some of them fatal. Others were trapped beneath buildings, but rescue work continued during the raid.

The raiders came in at roof-top height and machine-gunned streets and houses. A number of bungalows in one part of the town were damaged. Two churches were hit.

CROWDS GUNNED ON BEACHES
20 Children Killed in Church, 15 Missing

From Daily Mail Correspondents

CHILDREN playing on a crowded holiday beach were machine-gunned and a congregation of children were buried in the ruins of a church —20 of them were killed and 15 are missing—when sneak raiders swept in from the sea at lunch-time yesterday to attack a south-west coast town. Later two other seaside towns, both on the East Anglian coast, were raided.

The raiders, all Focke-Wulf fighter-bombers, skimmed the sea to raid the south-west. They met fierce anti-aircraft fire. Four of them were destroyed; two of them by gunfire in the first few seconds, another by gunfire later, and a fourth by a Typhoon fighter. A raider shot down over East Anglia brought the total to five.

One of the enemy planes in the south-west raid crashed in a street in Torquay. The Germans announced last night that they had raided Torquay and that four of their planes were missing.

As the sneak-raiders rose to clear the cliffs they sprayed the beach with machine-gun fire. Men and women flung themselves across their children to protect them from the bullets.

CONVOY ATTACKE OFF PORTUGAL

Lisbon, Sunday. — Germ plane to-day attacked a Bri day's raid on Rennes was g convoy of three merchant escorted by two corvettes the Portuguese coast. One was hit. The crew left the s which drifted, escorted by of the corvettes. The con was sailing in the directio Gibraltar.—Reuter.

LORD CECIL HURT

Viscount Cecil of Chelwood, who is 78, was injured last night when he fell from the platform into the orchestra pit at the Royalty Cinema,

HEAVY DAMAGE AT RENNES

Vichy radio stated last n that the damage done in S day's raid on Rennes was g greater than that caused b attack last March.

Many Dead in East Grinstead

Above: 'Raid on South East Coast Town. The Church that was wrecked when about 12 Focke Wulf fighter bombers, five of which were destroyed by RAF Typhoons, attacked a South East Coast Town.'

13th June, Sunday

A serious night attack on Grimsby and Cleethorpes: in the four days following the attack 365 UXBs had to be cleared; in this raid the Luftwaffe dropped many hundreds of the anti-personnel SD2 butterfly bombs. 2kg in weight, they had a lethal blast radius of 25m but could do damage over a much wider area. Dropped in containers of 23 or more they would burst open and become armed in descent through rotation of the 'wings' of the deployed casing. 225gm of TNT was primed to explode, using various different fuses, often mixed in the container to cause maximum disruption. Once armed the fragmentation bomb was too dangerous to defuse and it had to be exploded in situ. In this episode, damage to property was considerable and 74 people died as well as 110 seriously injured.

Just before this raid, Peltz's fast bomber campaign was scaled down considerably when two thirds of his SKG10 units were withdrawn from his command to counter the anticipated invasion of Italy by Allied Forces, following the success of Operation Torch.

17th June, Thursday

A night raid on London by a single Fw190 caused a spectacular fire at Mount Street sorting office when a single SC500 dropped on the building. 75,000 parcels were lost in the fire and operations moved to Nine Elms for the duration of the war.

28th June, Monday

A huge force of over 600 RAF heavy bombers raided Cologne again, this time killing nearly 4,500, injuring over 10,000, destroying more than 20,000 properties and forcing 230,000 out of their damaged homes. This was Cologne's worst raid of the War, leaving its famous cathedral badly damaged.

9th July, Friday

Ten aircraft, including Dornier and Junkers bombers, used the cover of poor weather to penetrate inland towards London. The worst of the bombing killed 108 in East Grinstead when a cinema took a direct hit after a stick of eight bombs straddled the High Street; they were dropped by a single raider that then strafed the town. Two of the ten raiding aircraft, both Dorniers, were brought down.

29th July, Thursday

Hamburg received the special attention of Churchill and Bomber Harris, chief of Bomber Command, who, together, concocted the heaviest bombing campaign of the war to date for the North Sea port. Operation Gomorrah began on the 24th, initiating eight consecutive days and seven nights of relentless bombing; on this date alone, the worst raid of the Operation, an estimated 40,000 were killed in a freak firestorm and an estimated 800,000 were left homeless. It was now the turn of the Nazis to wonder at the wrath that was descending on them. In fact, in every respect, the Allied bombing campaign was continuing from the point where the Luftwaffe had halted and would achieve even greater and more gruesome success .

Above: 'Soldiers helping to damp down the fire at a SE town after this afternoon's raid.'

Left: 'Heavy casualties are feared as the result of a cinema being hit during a raid on a SE town this afternoon. Picture shows: Rescue work in progress at the bombed cinema.'
The two pictures on this page show the scenes of destruction in East Grinstead High Street after the raid on 9th July.

17th August, Tuesday

The German military machine continued to threaten Britain with new weapons: on this date the Junkers 188 was first deployed against England. It could carry a single 1,000kg bomb externally and 10 50kg bombs racked in its internal bay. In an attack on Lincoln, 9 out of the 88 bombers were downed without a single bomb landing on the city.

Not only were Luftwaffe weapons and aircraft no longer able to match those of their Allied opponents, the Germans were failing in the technology and intelligence battles which had seen Allied Strategic bombing using all the direction-finding technology that the Luftwaffe had pioneered, but with greater effect. Allied Military Intelligence was superior to Germany's and it was this that invariably gave the former a major tactical advantage – to the extent that, on this date, the RAF was able to bomb Peenemünde, Germany's experimental site for the development of its V-weapons. For there was at least one area where Germany's technology was unrivalled – that of the pilotless bomb and the new and highly secret rockets – the vengeance weapons, which Hitler intended to use in finishing off Britain and her Allies. It was estimated that the bombing of Peenemünde set back Germany's V2 programme by two months, enough to make a vital difference in the outcome of the War.

7th November, Sunday

If the Luftwaffe could no longer fill Britain's skies with attacking aircraft, at the end of October they recommenced a consistent and continuous series of small-scale attacks on London and the South East. The consequences could be terrible, as the direct hit on a Putney dance hall proved when 76 were killed and 114 injured.

15th November, Monday

Fighter Command was renamed Air Defence of Great Britain on this date: the ungainly title lasted less than a year.

22nd November, Monday

Today saw the most effective raid on Berlin of the War by the Allies, which killed 2,000 and made 175,000 homeless as a result of firestorms created by IBs. Göring planned revenge on Britain with the new Heinkel HE177 four-engined heavy bomber to be deployed in raids with the code name Steinbock.

Göring issued orders for Operation Steinbock on the 3rd December, bringing together a bomber force under Dietrich Peltz that would launch no fewer than 300 aircraft in the first attack. It was Peltz's intention to commence operations at the end of the full moon – around the 18th December but bad weather put the date back to mid-January. Ultra had already picked up instructions such as those of the 13th December that reduced Luftwaffe strength on the Italian front by two thirds in order to reinforce Peltz's Luftflotte 3, which, as 1944 dawned, would now number nearly 500 aircraft..

31st December, Friday

At the end of the year, the total of civilian casualties from bombing in Britain duing 1943 stood at 2,327 killed and 3,450 seriously wounded. The toll was steadily falling, but the numbers were still enormous.

FEAR BRAND
STOCKINGS

Daily Mail

NO. 14,918   ONE PENNY   FOR KING AND EMPIRE

'New Planes and New Bombs on London'

BUDAPEST radio said last night: "The German aircraft bombing London are of a new type. According to a statement from Berlin, they use also a new type of bomb with a special filling, called the 'K' bomb. It weighs more than 1,000 pounds and has been nicknamed by the German airmen the 'Dicke Emma' (Fat Emma)." The German Overseas News Agency announced the raid shortly after the "All Clear" sounded in London. It said: "On Wednesday evening the sirens again sounded in the British capital and a few minutes later the first rounds of A.A. fire followed." The agency added that attacks are likely "almost every night."

MANY FEARED TRAPPED IN BIG LONDON FLATS

4 Raiders Down Last Night

Daily Mail picture taken early this morning shows one of the blocks of flats almost burned out inside. Many people are feared buried in the ruins.

GERMAN squadrons—first fast fighter bombers dropping flares and incendiaries, and then heavier machines with loads of H.E.—renewed the attack on the London area last night. From the ground the raid did not appear to be as concentrated as on recent nights, but damage and casualties were caused in many areas.

The raiders were met by the usual heavy barrage, which, though sporadic, was as intense as in any of the previous raids. By midnight it was known that four enemy planes had been destroyed.

The attacking formations came in over the south, south-east... over wi... area, and...

In th... class flat... soldiers'... ing, it is...

For attacking... cones. A... one distr... bursting... and divi...

One... block of... in the w...

Early... many, t... rubble. centres... way and... aid of... ing up o... axis.

Shot Down Two Night Raiders

WAVE OF FLAME KILLS 6

War-work Women
By Daily Mail Reporter

BURST of flame which in a second enveloped the shed in which they were working caused the death of six women war workers in a factory on the outskirts of a town in the West Riding of Yorkshire yesterday.

In hospital, suffering from severe burns, are six more women. Five others were allowed to leave hospital last night after treatment.

As girls ran from the blazing shed where one of the factory processes was operated the works fire brigade and other helpers made heroic efforts to force their way into the burning building.

One of the staff put on asbestos clothing, and while other members of the fire party poured water on to the blaze he attempted to get through the flames. Each time he was driven back.

Girls Ran

Names of those who lost their lives were: Mrs. R. Robinson, Mrs. M. Higgins, Mrs. C. Johnson, Miss J. Nied, Miss B. Pickles, and Miss E. Green. They were working together among a series of isolated buildings when a washroom flame lit up the hilltop village in which the factory stands.

William Dawes, night shift miner, who had just come home from work, told me:

"In a second the place was a mass of flames. I made a dive inside the corridor. Girls were running out of the building. I could see them silhouetted against the flames.

"We dragged boxes away from the flames until our hands were scorched."

Luftwaffe Reinforce Bombers in France

New Squadrons

By Daily Mail Air Correspondent

ABOUT 100 German aircraft, it was stated authoritatively last night, probably reached London during Tuesday night's raid. A further force of approximately 70 bombers crossed the coast but failed to reach the capital.

Ten raiders are confirmed destroyed, and this total may be raised to 13 when further likely anti-aircraft claims have been fully investigated.

From statements made by an R.A.F. commentator last night, and from other sources, new facts...

DUTCH BUY BRITISH AIR LINERS

First Order for the 'Tudors'

By COLIN BEDNALL,
Air Correspondent

THE Royal Dutch Air Lines, K.L.M., one of the most enterprising and successful merchant air-services of the world, has decided to buy British aircraft for the first time.

A very valuable order is being placed for a number of the new Tudor 32-ton air liners which, as announced last month, are now being prepared by the Avro Company as successor to the York.

This order is the first foreign acknowledgment of Britain's potential importance to civil aviation. It shows the wisdom of past agitation for Government recognition of its importance.

Foreign orders, plus the requirements of our own air-line operators, will ensure the retention of a healthy aircraft industry in Britain after the war. That is needed not only for peace-time prosperity, but as a safeguard against any future wars.

Led the Rush

K.L.M. have previously employed American aircraft almost exclusively, operating in 1939 a fleet of nearly 70 Douglas air liners of various luxurious and expensive types...

Six London Raiders Destroyed

And Three More Over There

Mosquitoes of the Air Defence of Great Britain went on the offensive last night over enemy territory. There they shot down three enemy planes and left others blazing on the ground.

GERMAN planes early this morning made another fire raid on London. Six were destroyed.

The attack was preceded by attempts to mark out the target areas.

The raiders, however, after dropping their flares, were time and again forced to turn away by the terrific barrage of rocket and high explosive shells.

Few planes succeeded in penetrating the outer barrage, although the raiders attempted to confuse the defences by approaching from the north-east and the Thames Estuary.

A lull followed after some time and more raiders approached the capital from the south, but were beaten back by the barrage.

In one London district a canister of explosive incendiaries caused 12 fires in one street. Industrial premises and a garage with petrol exploding were all engaging the attention of the firemen at the same time.

Evacuated

A large number of people were evacuated from their houses as the fires spread to a big block of tenement dwellings, and to smaller houses.

In a large garage more than 200 taxi-cabs and private cars were removed by soldiers, civilians, and A.R.P. guards, just as petrol began to explode.

In another area an H.E. fell near a publishing firm, killing two men and seriously injuring five. Traffic was diverted over a wide area.

Several 'fire' watchers marooned on the tops of buildings were rescued by firemen.

A Congregational church was destroyed by a fire bomb, and a school in an outer district was hit.

From the time they crossed the coast towards London raiders were challenged by R.A.F. night fighters, who engaged them in fierce combat all the way.

During yesterday long-range American Mustangs shot up airfields from the Paris area to the Pyrenees, 450 miles away.

Coast Guns Open Up on Ships

Big guns on the south coast opened up against enemy shipping across the Strait of Dover at 9.28 last night. About 100 rounds were fired in 40 minutes.

TUESDAY, The Daily Mail, FEBRUARY 22, 1944.

BATTLE OF THE FIRES: BLITZ SILHOUETTES RETURN TO LONDON

THESE scenes of London during Sunday night's fire-blitz—taken by Daily Mail photographer F. E. Rust— recall the nightly spectacles of the heart of the Empire in the brave days of 1941. Steel-helmeted fire-fighters tackled big blazes, with the flames spreading in the night sky, but so efficiently did the N.F.S. and street fire-parties co-operate that the Luftwaffe's second attempt in three nights to set London on fire failed. Incendiaries fell in large numbers.

Five Lean Years—and Here is the Food Britons Will Eat

By Daily Mail Reporter

FIRST BANANAS, 1947

NOT until 1950—first year of world surpluses—will you be able to shop as freely at the grocer's, butcher's, and dairy as you did in 1939. This is the agreed opinion of food experts who last night analysed the prospects for Britain's menu.

"Five lean years" are just beginning—Colonel Llewellin, Food Minister, has given that warning. Yesterday he added: "We are going to be very short of meat and dairy produce for a considerable number of years after this war is won."

It may be rather a gloomy picture, but unfortunately it is a true one."

Experts assured me, however, that we shall not go short of nourishing food, and every year a few more commodities will get less scarce.

There should be more Mediterranean fruit in 1945; 1946 will see more fish. Highlight of 1947, when the experts see as the turning-point in the lean years, will be the first bananas.

Dairy produce will be coming in increasing supplies in 1948. Sweets come off the ration in 1949. Then in 1950 the five-year days of plenty will seal ice-cream.

CALVES IN BIG TEST

Better Beef Plan
By PERCY IZZARD,
Agricultural Correspondent

THERE is a good many calves about the country today whose parents never saw one another.

Artificial insemination is making practical progress. It has passed from the exclusive consideration of scientists to become a subject of keen interest among farmers.

Mr. Hudson, Minister of Agriculture, and last week that it may be some years before definite conclusions are obtained. The purpose of the progeny must prove themselves producers of milk or beef.

As the case may be, as well as of stock that maintains the standard of quality.

So Mr. Hudson, an important part of whose policy is to raise the quality of the nation's herds, is urging farmers to breed better bulls, and small farmers particularly to take advantage of premium bull schemes.

Meanwhile, the experiments continue. The two centres at Cambridge and Reading and the private station at Kimble, Buckinghamshire, are successfully inseminating hundreds of cows yearly.

The thing needs a policy and a plan. It has been suggested that the Milk Marketing Board should be the controlling authority.

In carrying out its work I would think it should go forward a five-years plan involving a national chain of about 60 centres uniformly run.

SUGAR 'GUARANTEE'

This is the bill of fare food experts drew up:

1944.—Cut in the meat ration is...

Three Lemons Each

COMMON LORE

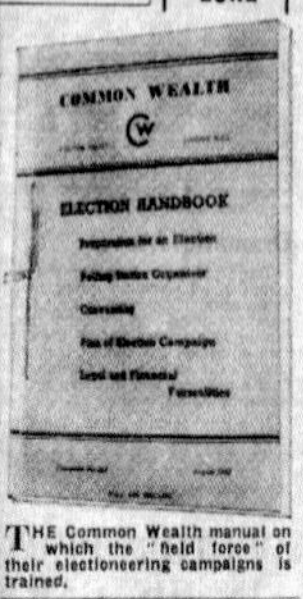

BY OCEAN PLANE TO ELECTION

United Front for Govt. Candidate

By Daily Mail Reporter

BURY ST. EDMUNDS,
Monday Night.

A NEW figure may at any moment make a discorderting appearance in the by-election scene here.

Mr. H. C. Drayton, official prospective National Liberal candidate for this constituency, is flying home from South America—where he had gone on Government business—and may arrive in Britain to-morrow.

Recently he cabled from the Argentine that he was in full agreement with the party truce. Now supporters of Major Keatinge (Con.) are rubbing their hands in glee.

They believe that if Mr. Drayton were to come to Bury St. Edmunds he would immediately give his support to the major—so the discomfiture of Mrs. Corbett Ashby (Ind. Lib.).

Our side, however, says: "Mr. Drayton is practically unknown here, so it would not matter a hoot...

CANDIDATES:
Major E. M. Keatinge (Con.).
Mrs. Corbett Ashby (Ind. Lib.).
Polling day: February 29.

ELECTION HANDBOOK

Faster, says Beveridge

White Paper Chase

SIR WILLIAM BEVERIDGE, welcoming the White Paper on medical services, at Oxford yesterday said: "I should like to see the Government proceed faster and faster, but by Bills instead of White Papers.

"Instead of a crusade the Government has been involved in a White Paper chase," he added.

"It was essential that doctors should not be organised by a Civil Service. He hoped the doctors and the Government were more in agreement upon than than the White Paper indicated."

'LOST' MP: A TOWN COMPLAINS
By Daily Mail Reporter

12 NURSES DARE JUNGLE FRONT

From Daily Mail Special Correspondent
ON THE ARAKAN FRONT, Sunday (delayed).

TWENTY flying ambulances are bringing back the wounded of the Seventh Indian Division, on the far side of the Mayu ridge. Some of these soldiers will find 12 British nurses waiting to tend them—the first women to serve so close to the Arakan front.

They are the only white women within 130 miles of Chittagong.

The first five, Miss D. M. Field of Peterborough, the matron, and Miss O'Sullivan, of Swerne, Killarney; Miss J. M. Burry, of Dundee; Miss M. E. Batstone, of Wellington, Somerset, and Miss F. J. Blaylock, of Carlisle, arrived on Friday night, aching with weariness after bumping over hot, dusty roads.

Early yesterday morning they were at work in casualty clearing stations in the neighbourhood of Bawli Bazaar, a village a few miles north of the Ngakyedauk Pass, over which the wounded will be brought out.

From down the road came the thud of mortar bombs and the crash of shells.

The nurses took no notice. They just carried on.

One At a Time

The matron, Miss Field, has spent seven years nursing in Burma, and marched out with our troops when we withdrew to India. Today, seven miles nearer the front, she is back in the thick of things.

The ambulance planes now bring-ing back the wounded carry only one patient at a time. They began to operate last Monday, and so far, besides six Seventh Division casualties, they have brought back 130 cases from the West African troops area.

Five Down in Fire Blitz

AT least five of the Luftwaffe raiders which attempted on Sunday night—for the second time in three nights—to set London on fire were shot down.

Women and children were killed and, as usual, residential property suffered the most damage. One of the raiders crashed in the back gardens of a London suburb, setting fire to several houses. As it hit the ground a sheet of flame shot nearly 100ft. into the air. The crew are believed to have been burned to death.

When incendiaries penetrated the roof of a convent nuns braved the flames to save their possessions.

An H.E. fell near the entrance of a hospital. None of the 600 patients was hurt, but a doctor, three nurses, and a fireman were injured.

Left R.A.F. Killed in Civil Plane

A WORD RECONDITIONED
Lord Horder at Brighton

Americans Invade New Island

The Baby Blitz

The New Year began quietly with little Luftwaffe activity until the Steinbock raids began towards the end of January. This was the grand revenge offensive ordered by Göring. No doubt the return to heavy raiding on London had an impact on the country, bringing back scenes that had not been seen since the Night Blitz. However, the Luftwaffe forces could neither support the volume of the raids or the loss rate for long and as Allied invasion plans progressed, the window of opportunity for manned bombing raids on Great Britain swung firmly shut. Operation Steinbock raids became known, rather patronisingly, in Britain as the 'Baby Blitz'.

21st January, Friday

The first Steinbock raid targeted London in two bombing waves. The systematic planning of Steinbock under Peltz assigned each area of London to the name of a German city that had been devastated by Allied bombing. The first attack on 'München' focused on Waterloo; 'Hamburg' was the designation of the Westminster area. Although the heaviest attack on the British mainland since that of the end of July 1942 on Birmingham, damage was not significant and many of the bombs fell outside their target area. Peltz's training of his force brought in new tactical ideas and weaponry. In choosing to avoid the full moon, navigation aids became vital to success – especially when Luftwaffe aircrews had to approach their targets circuitously yet with very specific approach runs. Despite carefully planned pathfinder routefinding aids that started in mainland Europe and even provided flares on buoys in the Channel, the pathfinder performance and general navigation of Steinbock gave poor results despite 447 sorties being flown. The total of bombs loaded that night was around 500 tonnes but only 32 actually hit London with 236 falling indiscriminately outside. The loss of 16 bombers in the first night was hardly an auspicious start.

29th January, Saturday

Of 285 sorties only 130 managed to penetrate inland and only 30 of them managed to drop their 36.5 tonnes of bombs on London. The new incendiary bombs weighing just over 2kg were loaded onboard 1,000kg containers that could be carried in the new four-engined He177 heavy bombers – 343 fires were attended by NFS; 59 people died in this attack. During January's raids, the Luftwaffe lost 57 aircraft.

3rd February, Thursday

240 sorties dropped 67 tonnes of HE on London. For the Steinbock raids the Luftwaffe publicised a new explosive mixture for their HE bombs – The England Cocktail. Home Security noted the increased effectiveness of the bombs.

20th February, Sunday

200 sorties flown by night, with the main target 'Hamburg': a stick of bombs fell between Horse Guards Parade and Downing Street, causing damage to the Treasury and killing four. There were heavy casualties throughout London with 216 civilian deaths.

22nd February, Tuesday

The first of three successive nights of bombing on London: the worst incident a direct hit on a block of flats in King's Road, Chelsea, on the 23rd, killing at least 72 and injuring 111. On the third night, the 24th, a timber yard and its creosote store burned furiously and the fire was attended by 50 pumps.

21st March, Tuesday

One of the heaviest of the Steinbock raids: Paddington Station, which had managed to avoid much damage until now, was hit. Ten raiding aircraft were brought down.

18th April, Tuesday

A quiet start to the month until this first major raid, which was to be the last of the Baby Blitz for London as the Luftwaffe focused on the threat of invasion. Ten German aircraft were shot down.

29th May, Monday

Raids on Falmouth and Portsmouth. This night would see the last of any major manned bombing initiative of the War on Britain. Things were looking up for Britain with the dwindling power of the Luftwaffe and the invasion of Europe imminent.

Above: *'The King and Queen talking yesterday to Civil Defence workers and residents of a London street hit in Thursday night's raid.'* On Thursday 24th February, 170 aircraft set out to bomb London; 74 civilians were killed.

Opposite: **The Baby Blitz brought back scenes like this from earlier years, which Londoners had hoped would never return.**

Daily Mail

4 EDITION

NO. 15,006   ONE PENNY   FOR KING AND EMPIRE   WEDNESDAY, JUNE 7, 1944

BEACHHEAD WIDER AND DEEPER

Savage Fighting in Caen Streets : Front Now 100 Miles Across and Troops Still Pour In

THE first historic day of Europe's liberation has gone completely in favour of the Allies. "We have got the first wave of men through the defended beach zone and set for the land battle," said Admiral Ramsay, Naval C.-in-C., last night. "Naval ships landed their cargoes 100 per cent." Our troops and tanks are firmly ashore at many points along 100 miles of the Normandy coast from Cherbourg to Le Havre. They are ten miles inland at Caen; five miles inland at the base of the Cherbourg peninsula. The sea is rough on the beaches but reinforcements are pouring in. German coastal batteries have been mostly silenced. Casualties among both airborne and assault landing troops have been much lower than expected. Losses at sea were "very, very small." Against the 7,500 sorties flown by the Allied Air Forces the Luftwaffe put in only 50.

1,000 'TROOP CARRIERS' IN FIRST AIR BLOW

TWENTY-FOUR hours have sufficed to smash the first fortifications of Hitler's vaunted West Wall. The Allied Navies and Air Forces, operating in unheard-of strength, have put the first wave of General Montgomery's armies safely ashore on the magnificent beaches of Normandy according to plan.

"Impregnable" strongpoints built up over three years by the famous Todt Organisation crumbled in a few hours under 10,000 tons of bombs and shells from 600 warships.

Minesweepers have swept away the mines. Engineers have cleared the underwater "fences."

Berlin Says Caen Air Coup Fails

Beachhead Battle : 3 a.m. Picture

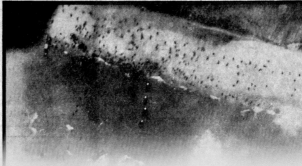

5.27, AND NAVY WENT IN

First Cable from Invasion Fleet

From DESMOND TIGHE, Combined Press Reporter.

ABOARD A BRITISH DESTROYER OFF BERNIÈRES-SUR-MER, Tuesday, dawn.

GUNS are belching flame from more than 600 Allied warships. Thousands of bombers are roaring overhead, fighters are weaving through the clouds as the invasion of Western Europe begins.

Rolling clouds of dense smoke cover the beaches south-east of Le Havre as the full fury of the Allied force is unleashed on the German defences.

It is the most incredible sight I have ever seen.

The First In

We are standing 8,000 yards off the beaches of Bernières-sur-Mer and from the bridge of this little destroyer I can see vast numbers of naval craft of all types. They moved in to attack at 5.27 a.m.

Under the Supreme Command of Admiral Sir Bertram Ramsay, two forces are taking part in the assault —a British and Canadian unit under Rear-Admiral Sir Philip Vian, of Cossack fame, and an American task force under Rear-Admiral Alan G. Kirk, U.S.N.

Portugal Stops Wolfram

D-Day Decision

WASHINGTON, Tuesday.

PORTUGAL agreed, on the eve of the invasion, to stop all shipments of wolfram to Germany and to close down the wolfram mines, it was announced in Washington to-night.

Edward Stettinius, the U.S. Under-Secretary of State, disclosed that the United States, Britain, and Brazil co-operated in persuading Portugal to stop the wolfram trade.

The Portuguese decision was made on June 5.

The announcement said that the Portuguese Government undertook on June 5 to impose a total prohibition of exports of wolfram and also to cease immediately the production of wolfram in Portugal.

The announcement said: "Th

RAID FREE NIGHT FOR BRITAIN

During the hours of darkness there were no reports of enemy

Operation Overlord: D-Day

6th June, Tuesday

In the early hours, airborne forces spearheaded the Allied invasion of Normandy to capture forward objectives prior to the massed landing of troops and equipment on the beachheads designated by Operation Overlord.

In tactical terms, the RAF now dominated the skies, not just over Britain but across northern France, where for weeks they had patrolled, supported by Allied strategic and tactical bombing of Luftwaffe bases, destroying their fighters before they could become airborne.

Opposite: A fraction of the 7,000 vessels participating in the Normandy landings, taken from an RAF plane early in the morning. 160,000 troops were landed on the first day of the invasion.

Right: Even when the beachhead was under friendly control, the final wade from the landing craft to shore demanded strength and nerve.

Below: For weeks before the invasion Allied fighters and bombers had taken possession of the skies over France. Here are wrecked aircraft at an airfield near Paris. Not only had such action secured the invasion forces it had virtually excluded the Luftwaffe from their attacks on Britain.

12th June, Monday

For some time Hitler had been alluding publicly to a secret weapon that would punish his enemies. His senior military officers were aware of the development of rocket bombs that could be launched ceaselessly against Britain, whose Intelligence services were already closely tracking these developments. The first V1 was launched at London one week after the successful Allied landing in Normandy. The official name, Fieseler Fi 103 was subsumed by the Nazis into the more potent 'Vergeltungswaffen' – revenge or retaliation weapons – that included the V2 rocket and the V3 long-range cannon. V for Germany meant Vengeance whereas V to the Allies was simply their sign for ultimate Allied Victory. The range of the V1 was 130 miles from ramp launch or 320 miles in an aerial launch from a Heinkel 111; its warhead contained 850kg of high explosive.

At the campaign's peak, over a hundred V1s a day were fired at south eastern England – 9,251 in total, with 4,261 destroyed in the air. Numbers launched decreased as sites were overrun until October 1944 when the last V1 site in range of Britain was taken by Allied forces. The remaining V1s were aimed at the port of Antwerp and other targets in Belgium, with 2,448 V1s being launched. When the last site was overrun on 29th March 1945, casualties stood at 22,892 (almost all civilians).

The first V1 struck London next to the railway bridge on Grove Road, Mile End: six civilians were killed in the blast, which made 200 homeless. It was just one of four launched this day: three others failed on take off. This same night, to ensure Britain got the high explosive message, long-range guns on the French coast fired 42 shells on Folkestone, damaging over 1,000 properties.

It was already clear that the new bombs falling on London had no respect for place or person and Home Security set in motion a new evacuation. These pictures were taken on the 8th and 10th July.

Above: 'Children Leave London. Thousands of children have been evacuated from Southern England to the Midlands, North of England and Wales. Photo shows: Children waving goodbye at Euston.'

Right: Trying not to look too anxious, hundreds of children line up at a London station to board a special train to take them out of the target area of the flying bombs. For the parents who had seen their children evacuated in 1939 this was a terrible déja vu, making them wonder just how bad the bombardment that lay ahead could be.

'PILOTLESS' ATTACK
Midgets Too Costly in German Material
DAY OF RAIDS THEN 3 NIGHT BLOWS

At least three people were killed and several badly injured by a pilotless plane which crashed on houses in Southern England during the first of three attacks last night following a series of day raids. Houses were wrecked and an adjoining shopping centre was considerably damaged. Later guns engaged planes which appeared of the pilotless type. Normal planes are also thought to have been used.

By COLIN BEDNALL, Daily Mail Air Correspondent

IN their mad quest for both a military novelty and a substitute for the Luftwaffe, it is believed, from the nature of the pilotless planes used against this country, that the Germans have prejudiced other forms of vital war production to produce these weapons.

They are extremely costly devices, and have absorbed many thousands of man-hours, both in their production and in their launching.

It would appear certain that they contain many intricate and elaborate devices.

The red light seen on the flying bombs as they approach their target may have been placed there to enable ground controllers to place them on their course after they become airborne.

It might be feasible for the Germans to employ the radio beam principle, best known under the name of the Lorenzo Beam in peace-time, to direct the flying bombs towards their objective across the Channel.

But in their tremendous respect for gadgets the Germans may also have installed automatic devices.

This being the case, it may take the enemy a little while to prepare for another prolonged attack.

Each individual launching would take some time to prepare, apart from the fact that the enemy would have found it no easier to move up pilotless planes to the coastal areas of France than he has found it to move tanks.

It is believed that the Allied bombing forced him to establish assembly depots beside each launching installation.

The flying bombs have probably arrived in parts, and must therefore be assembled before being put into action.

A point has arisen as to who is responsible for dealing with the German novelty.

It combines characteristics for which both the War Office and the Air Ministry might be concerned, but perhaps its true grading is indicated by the fact that it was the Minister of Home Security who handled the matter in the House of Commons yesterday.

THESE three views of the German pilotless plane—(1) Head-on; (2) Plan; (3) Side view—were issued by the Ministry of Home Security last night. The wing span, it was officially stated, is 16ft., the length of the plane 25ft. 4½in. The section marked x in the third drawing is the propulsion unit.

GERMAN RADIO HAS GLOATING NIGHT
'Vengeance for RAF Has Begun'

THE entire German radio system at short notice last night changed its programme, after announcing several times that a special broadcast would be made by Hans Fritsche, Director-General of the German radio information service.

He ... plane ...

"The ... with d ... ment ... have p ...

"Rep ... clared ... attacks ... mere p ...

"How ... many ... this wo ... man le ... accordi ...

"Suc ... time. ... German ... right m ... product ...

"Rep ... ment of ... will be ... Comma ... make fo ... wait ar ... go on ...

"Tho ... prised ... hit back ...

BBC ANNOUNCE RADIO 'BAFFLE'

MILLIONS of people in Britain, after a day of robot raids on southern England, heard the B...

HITL... ... against ... controll... defendi... said: ...

"We... hearted... Führer... in Wil...

Damage is Small: Morrison

THE Minister of Home Security made this announcement late last night.

"The enemy has begun to use his secret weapon—the pilotless aircraft. The damage it has caused has been relatively small, and the new weapon will not interfere with our war effort and our sure and steady march to victory.

"The enemy's aim is clearly, in view of the difficulty of his military situation, to try to upset our morale and interfere with our work.

"It is essential that there should be the least possible interruption in all work vital to the country's needs at this time, and the Government's counsel is that everyone should get on with his or her job in the ordinary way and only take cover when danger is imminent.

"There is no reason to think that raids by this weapon will be worse than, or indeed as heavy as, the raids with which the people of this country are already familiar and have borne so bravely."

The Pilotless Plane

Fe...
The ... has ... to F...
Day w... in t...

From t... Reuter's Sp... ABOARD H...

THE visit areas in ... lunched ... Montgom... advanced H...

He ... open-air In... six miles fr...

He made ... to France a... Arethusa, w... bombarding ...

He landed ... Courseilles ... stormed ash... in the mor... from Arethus... shells from ... which we ... way in, tore ... head, engag... range of 90 ...

His 'Ma...
The range ... were the bi... seen actuall... this war.

Bo'suns pi... Arethusa ea... ten minutes ... way for F... H.M.S. S... escorted the ... of Spitfires ... viding a cou... the moment... returned hom...

At once, ... of the Elect... ham, the F... Ramsay, Alli... Chief Marsh... Chief of the ... eral Laycock ... Operations, ... many, went ...

With a 'M... jacket over ... stayed on th... over, watchin... craft of ever... from the be...

He had a ... bridge befor... glimpse of th... moment late... was broken ... nouncing to ... on board.

Complete...
The visit ... pletely secret ...

Wearing a ... Admiral of ... drove straigh... Montgomery ... zone.

With an ... American m... with tommy-... passed along ... road through ... Graves-sur-M... were in reser... days ago.

After lunc... open-air inve... grounds. Th... officers and m... General Kell... Canadian Th... ceived the C.O...

Three or fou... cluding many ... mandos and ... watched the r... three sides of...

"Monty" c... and then took ... his three rep... a full-half-hou... maps the who... so far.

'Vive la...
By this tim... spread, and t... towards the ... open ca... r...

Hitler's Vengeance Weapons

15th June, Thursday

144 flying bombs made landfall out of 200 launched, forcing the censor's embargo to be lifted on the reporting of flying bombs but only mentioning 'South of England' for location. Reporting broke on Friday 16th, calling them 'pilotless bombs' – they quickly became commonly known as 'doodlebugs' and 'buzzbombs' – part of the British bravado which attempted to neutralise the deadly threat with humour.

Top left: In a Deep Shelter on 20th July: compared with the spartan and often squalid conditions found in the makeshift shelters during the Night Blitz, the new deep shelters were a home from home with sanitation and even double bunks for married couples. Shelterers brought their own bedding.

Top right: *'They'll sleep safely– 4-year old Sylvia Carter and brother Jack, waiting on the family bedding, outside the first London deep shelter in use.'*

Right centre: Families that stayed in the capital could now use the deep shelters, construction of which began towards the end of the Night Blitz. Stockwell was first in opening to the public. The possible consequences of not using the shelters were plain to see in this photograph.

Right below: This home in southern England was damaged in the first wave of flying bombs.

Guards Chapel Tragedy

18th June, Sunday

Six days after the attacks had begun, 500 V1s had been launched at Britain; at 11.20 one hit the Guards Chapel, Wellington Barracks in the heart of Westminster. The chapel was full for morning service and amid the total destruction of the building, 58 civilians and 63 service personnel died while 68 others were seriously injured. The commanding officer of the Scots Guards was among the dead.

27th June, Tuesday

By the end of the first two weeks of the V1 barrage, 1,600 had been killed and 4,500 seriously injured — a casualty rate as high as the worst month of the Blitz in September 1940: Hitler's vengeful threats appeared to be coming good.

30th June, Friday

48 were killed in the capital when a V1 landed in Aldwych in front of the Air Ministry building at the corner of Kingsway. The pavements were crowded with people taking their lunch break in bright sunshine. The bomb caused terrible carnage among the 200 casualties. Damage to the Ministry would have been worse but a protective wall absorbed much of the blast, being destroyed in the process. Bush House across the street also suffered damage.

Above: The Guards Chapel, completely wrecked; it would eventually be rebuilt in 1963.

Below: 'Morrison Shelter: Mr & Mrs Barnes and Mrs Hesman were in this Morrison Shelter when their house received a direct hit. All three were rescued uninjured. They said they always use the Morrison.'

HERBOURG TRAP

insula

TROOPS JERSEY

'Flying Bomb' Hits Full Church

NIGHT RAF RAID BASES

LURID stories of British Government "orders" for the evacuation of a panicking London are being told by Berlin radio. Goebbels has pulled out all the organ stops —See BACK PAGE.

Coast Guns and RAF Kill Robots

Shot into Sea

From Daily Mail Reporter

SOUTH COAST, Sunday Night.

RESIDENTS of this part of the South Coast have to-day found a new war diversion — watching some of Hitler's sightless robot planes come to grief in the Channel or in the open fields a few miles inland.

From these front line cliffs we have watched them come over to-day, flying from Calais and Boulogne, varying their direction lines in the hope of getting through to Southern England.

Not all these blind robots are allowed to pass. As soon as they come within two miles of the British coast we are at them, either with shells and anti-aircraft guns or with Allied fighters.

The fighters which patrol the Strait are looking on the robots as their rightful prey.

One at a Time

We have watched scores of exciting races in the past few days. The robots fly at a speed which we estimate at not less than 250 miles an hour, but the fighters can, and do, overtake them.

We have watched robots explode harmlessly in mid-air at the end of a

Last night and early this morning R.A.F. bombers were pounding selected targets on the French coast where it is believed pilotless planes have operational bases. Yesterday a small force of Liberators blasted Pas-de-Calais targets.

By Daily Mail Reporter

HITLER continued his attacks on Southern England with his blind flying bombs throughout the week-end. Intermittently during the night and day the robots came over the house-tops, causing casualties and damage.

Many of the bombs made their final plunge on houses, but often there were few casualties, or none at all, mainly because people in the line of flight took the precaution of seeking shelter.

One wrecked a little church, where 150 people were attending morning service, yesterday and killed some of the congregation.

A convent and a hospital were other targets.

Indications are that success is rewarding the combined efforts of fighters and ack-ack gunners to bring down the robots.

The fighters are making every effort to put them down in the sea before they can reach the coast.

General Sir Frederick Pile, G.O.C. A.A. Command, has been watching operations on the coast during the week-end, and visiting the A.A. units engaged on the job.

Not since the Battle of Britain have the anti-aircraft crews had so much action in daylight. A.T.S. girls on the sites have never before been on duty for such long periods of intense activity, but they have vied with the men in keenness.

Some girls were ordered to rest, but they sacrificed part of their sleep to return to the sites when the guns went into action again.

The bomb which hit the church crashed through the roof and exploded as the congregation was singing the first hymn.

It killed a number of wor-

CAVE HQ FOR RUNDSTEDT

Under Chapel

STOCKHOLM, Sunday.—Rundstedt has established secret headquarters deep in the side of a mountain "somewhere in France." Above is a small chapel where French people

FINN MINISTER LEAVES STOCKHOLM

Stockholm, Sunday.—Baron George Gripenberg, Finnish Minister in Stockholm, has gone to Helsinki.—Reuter.

FIVE JAP SHIPS SUNK BY BOMBS

American planes sank five Japanese merchant ships in a

urks Send ack Nazi Warship

ANKARA, Saturday (delayed). 800-tons German naval auxiliary Kassel, similar to warships used during the campaign, has been re-passage through the and has sailed back Black Sea.

is the first act of the new policy on German shipping by Prime Minister Sara-

Kassel was kept in Turkish but was kept surveillance until the Ankara ment formulated its policy

3rd July, Monday

A V1 fell on a block of apartments in fashionable Turks Row Chelsea, at 07.47: the enormous blast blew out the front and back walls of the block, resulting in a death toll of 64 and 50 wounded – all US service personnel who were billeted there. In addition 10 civilians died; this was the highest number of military personnel killed by a V1 in Britain.

6th July, Thursday

Unable to delay any longer, Churchill finally made a full statement to the nation: 2,752 killed by flying bombs and about 8,000 injured; 2,754 flying bombs had been launched against Britain and by mid July 170,000 had left London to find safety in billets outside the Capital. By September the evacuee figure had risen to 300,000, with another 500,000 aided by rail tickets and billeting certificates. In all some estimates indicate that as many as 1.5-2 million Londoners fled during the flying bomb attacks.

9th July, Sunday

Deep shelters that had been held in reserve since their completion in 1942 were now opened – the first at Stockwell, the second 4 days later. Ten shelters each holding up to 8,000 people were planned but only eight had been completed.

Above left: Doodlebug spotters keep watch for inbound flying bombs. There was no advance warning of a V2, which fell out of the sky faster than the speed of sound, after its rocket motor cut out. The tell-tale engine note of the V1 or the flame from its exhaust helped the observers but with the naked eye the fast-moving flying bombs were little more than a dot in the sky. However, it was the spotters job to warn the local people and businesses in their area to take cover.

Above centre and right: Blood-spattered office workers emerge from bombed Aldwych buildings on 30th June. The man in the photo, right, is in stockinged-feet carrying his shoes and his shredded jacket. It was not uncommon for victims of bomb blasts to have their outer garments completely blown off.

elpful **Mothers with You**
ned 5s.

's Swim Cost
m £2 7s.

Loud Speakers Direct Rescues

FLATS WRECKED BY ROBOT

Voices Under 25ft. Debris

By Daily Mail Reporter

LOUD speakers and searchlights aided rescuers last night in looking for victims lying under 20ft. high piles of débris, after a flying bomb had hit a block of flats in Southern England.

Within a few minutes of the hit, Civil Defence workers, including many women, were on the scene. Cranes were used to lift slabs and blocks of masonry.

Faint voices from beneath the wreckage brought rescuers to one mound at least 25ft. high, and within half an hour they had brought out three people alive.

It is feared the death roll is heavy.

The Regional Commissioner watched the rescue work, directed through loud speakers.

Stretcher parties and doctors were standing by, through the night, to help the released victims into ambulances.

Midnight Rescu

Mine Ghost

SILENT the house and dark
    each room,
No hand will touch the bolted
    door,
Who laughs within the bitter
    gloom?
Who prowls the empty floor?

Oh, do not seek that tenant's
    face,
Nor linger desperately near.
A shadow hangs upon this place,
And on the door—" No
    Beer."
               H. R.

The Blind Soldier

Victim of another bomb yesterday was ex-soldier Bill Stevens, who was blinded in this war. He returned from a walk and found that his home, for which he paid £850, was blasted and made uninhabitable.

His wife collapsed when she saw him, but soon recovered and took him round, explaining the damage.

In another district yet another blind man figured in an incident. He warned his neighbours, a mother and child, to take cover in an Anderson shelter.

They escaped the blast which damaged their home.

In another area people who stood in the street estimating that the bomb would fall on waste ground became casualties.

A heavy death roll is feared in one district where a bomb fell as two buses were passing. Rescue workers dug for trapped people, and in an hour three were brought out

France Costs Hitler One Million Men

WHEN the Battle of France began with the June 6 landings there were more than a million armed men in the German armies in France, said Mr. Robert E. Sherwood, Director of the Overseas branch of the U.S. Office of War Information, broadcasting yesterday.

"To-day it is certain," he went on, "that only a very small fraction of these once powerful forces will be able to reach the frontiers of Germany in this war.

"The master plan of Tehran is rapidly unfolding in the West. Reports from neutral Swedish journalists in Berlin indicate that Hitler and Himmler and the German generals are by no means sure that they have seen the last of this master plan.

"They are discussing the possibility of new Allied landings in France, Holland, Belgium, and even in Western Germany itself. However, there is not much that Germany can do about such possible landings except discuss them.

"All she has left in the way of reserves is the Gestapo. And the Gestapo must be kept at home to protect the Nazis from the German people."

THE midnight scene amid smashed masonry of bombed flats in Southern Engla in the floodlights' glare, warde

Return fror Normandy, Killed by Ca

From Daily Mail Correspond

NEW YORK, Monday

IT was good to be back on " Avenue" again, 23-years-Private Virgil T. Peavler and friend, Private Silas E. But were thinking last night as th stood together on Westbu avenue, Long Island.

Only a few weeks before it had been fighting side by side Cherbourg, had been wounded a flown back to the United State

16 ROOMS FOR COUPLE OF 78

Refused to Billet

For refusing to billet a bombed-out mother and her four young children in a 16-roomed house a 78-years-old householder was fined £5 at Cheltenham yesterday.

The chairman of the Bench, Sir Francis Colchester-Wemyss, told the man, Harry Grant Maby, of Charlton Kings, that if he had been able-bodied and younger the Bench would have inflicted the maximum penalty of £50.

The prosecution said there was only Maby and his 78-years-old

at's   Something new has caught his

Attacking the V Bombs

10th July, Monday

It quickly became obvious that AA and the RAF were in conflict: pilots were endangered by the AA barrages and the gunners were impeded by the presence of the fighters in the skies. In a conference to discuss protocols of defence against V1s, strict rules were drawn up and AA guns were moved to the coast for more effective interception. The new standing orders simplified previous conditions governed by status codes *Flabby*, *Fickle* and *Spouse*. The zone of AA operations was called the Gun Belt and the Ministry term for flying bombs was *Diver*. The number of barrage balloons deployed in the target area increased from 500 to 1,750 by the end of July. The first defensive measures took out 24% of the inbound flying bombs, but the improved tactics and the introduction of radar-controlled guns and ordnance with the new proximity fuse led to 80% destruction by the end of September.

Military intelligence was gathered on the flying bomb threat as soon as the first signs were identified. The renowned intelligence guru, RV Jones, led the research and analysed aerial photos that identified the test sites and ultimately the launch sites, which the RAF duly tried to put out of action. Every V bomb that landed was analysed and from the pattern of landing the programming of the guidance system could be calculated. Jones observed that in development-testing the bombs typically fell short of their target. He realised that if disinformation about the location of the bombs that fell could be sent back to the Germans then they would re-programme the guidance systems incorrectly and thereby miss their intended targets.

Jones used this approach, particularly with V2 bombardment, controlling the information sent back via German spies under the control of MI5, so that although the launching batteries thought the bombs were falling on their central London targets, in fact most of the brunt was borne by the suburbs of South London. Newspaper reporting was therefore very sketchy and anything published about V bombs falling on London simply referred to the location as 'the South of England'.

Above left: An RAF Halifax bombs concrete structures identified as launch sites for V1 flying bombs in the Pas de Calais area on 6th July.

Above right: A flying bomb is successfully destroyed in the air after striking the cable of a barrage balloon. Other balloons are visible around the explosion.

Left: *'Captured Flying Bomb Site in France. One of the many flying bomb sites captured during the British advance on the Pas de Calais. The site was destroyed by German engineers before they retreated.'*

The photograph, dated early September, shows the launch ramp aligned on South East England.

Below left: This V1 which failed to explode was displayed in an exhibition in Piccadilly at the end of October.

Below: Canadian troops clearing a captured V1 launch site near Zutphen in the Netherlands inspect a flying bomb that misfired: it was the markings on the ground from the many misfires that betrayed many of the launch sites, as well as the development site at Peenemünde.

Bottom left: Fragments of fallen V1s were carefully harvested for every piece of intelligence. Here is shown the dump where the Ministry stored the wreckage, tended by a female mechanic.

Bottom right: *'A member of the French Resistance and Sgt H A Barnet of Montreal, Canada, examine the interior of a robot bomb which crashed near its launching site in the Pas de Calais area. The ball-like object is a fuel tank.'*

Left: One of the Temple's historic buildings in Temple Place was also damaged after a direct hit on the building next door – the offices of the Cable and Wireless Company.

Below left: A dramatic rescue from the rubble of burning flats at the corner of Boundary Street and Calvert Street in Shoreditch after a flying bomb fell on 22nd August.

Below right: Rescue workers at Old Jewry where a V2 fell, killing one person and injuring about 25 on the 6th October. This coincided with a crisis in public information. Home Security continued to withhold information about the rocket attacks and newspaper reporting was strictly limited. However, on the 6th, the *New York Times* broke the story. But it wasn't until November after Germany made a specific announcement that Churchill was forced to make a statement to the House, admitting that Britain had been under rocket bomb attack for several weeks. Until the formal announcement was made, Home Security tried to divert attention from the rocket attacks by finally making public details of the parachute mines that had been falling since 1940.

Opposite top: The Elizabethan timber-framed Staple Inn, Holborn, was completely destroyed by a flying bomb on the night of 24th August, having been saved from the flames of the first Great Fire of 1666 by diarist John Evelyn.

Opposite Centre: A hospital in the South of England was hit in August killing 2 patients and injuring 3 nurses.

Opposite bottom: Lewisham Hospital hit on 26th July.

SCORES OF ROBOTS FALL TO TEMPESTS AND AA

Lift Coast Ban, Says the South

Visitors Wanted

By Daily Mail Reporter

UNOFFICIAL talks are going on among municipal authorities along the South Coast to see what they can do to have the ban on visitors lifted.

When the talks are over—within a few days—it is expected that the Government department who have the power to lift the ban will be approached in force.

General opinion along the coast is that, now the Second Front is firmly established on the Continent, the necessity for secrecy has passed, and that a continuance of the restrictions is unnecessary and harmful to the areas concerned.

A leading South Coast business man told me last night:

YEARS DON'T COUNT IN WEHRMACHT

'It Would Cheer South'

By Daily Mail Reporter

TOURING the South of England this week-end, I have watched scores of flying bombs destroyed by our Tempest fighters and Ack-Ack gunners. "People inland would be heartened if they could see it," a resident said to me. "This shows you that our fighters can deal with them. They are making a fine job of it."

The people who watch this new Battle of Britain keep their eyes on the waiting Tempests.

Any sudden spurt by these fighters means that doodle-bugs are approaching — and later the watchers hear explosions that tell of another "dead" robot.

I visited an inland village—a place that seemed as tranquil as in the 1938 days when all that the inhabitants worried over was the crops, the weather, the pigs, and the poultry.

Yet 60 minutes before it had been about the noisiest village in England. Its old farm-houses

'Monty' Thanks the Nurses

THE general drops in to thank his girl "lieutenants" for the war they are fighting—and winning. They are Army nursing sisters, at a hospital near Bayeux, trim in their new berets and battle-dress. The Normandy front line is miles away from the town now, but their battle goes on 24 hours a day, tending the sick, healing the wounded.

V2 Bombs Launched

28th August, Monday

In the last major attack of the month, 90 of the 95 flying bombs approaching the coast were destroyed – 65 by guns, 23 by fighters and 2 by barrage balloons. By now RAF fighters had learned some skills in bringing down the flying bombs. The most successful intercepting aircraft being the Hawker Tempest, designed by Sidney Camm who had also designed the Hurricane. The fast and powerful Tempest brought down about one third of all the flying bombs that were destroyed by aircraft.

7th September, Thursday

In early September the Allied advance through northern France to Flanders brought an end to the launching of V1s from their coastal stations and there was a lull in the bombardment of Britain

On this day Duncan Sandys, head of the Crossbow Committee responsible for countering the V weapons, chaired a press conference announcing the neutralising of the V1 threat. This was poor timing because the very next day the first V2 bombs began to fall, just as the headlines proclaimed Sandys' message that the danger was over.

An estimated 2,754 civilians in London were killed and 6,523 injured by the 1,115 V2s that targeted Great Britain; a further 2,917 servicemen and servicewomen were also killed by the V weapons.

The V2 rocket was 46ft long and 5ft maximum diameter; it weighed about 13 tonnes, carrying almost 1 tonne of HE. Its fuel was alcohol and liquid oxygen and the rocket was launched vertically from any hard surface. Unlike the V1, which needed a launch ramp, the V2 was therefore much more mobile, though requiring specialist transport. Not much was known in detail about the V2 until the remains of one that had mistakenly fallen on Sweden on 13th June were secretly acquired by the British government. RV Jones' report included a technical drawing that was proven to be remarkably accurate, except for the guidance system – from the amount of radio equipment on board it was assumed the weapon was radio controlled when in fact its navigation was by its own on-board systems. The rocket could fly at up to 3,600 mph at an altitude of 50-60 miles with a range of up to 225 surface miles. RV Jones painstakingly gathered the evidence for the rocket's existence though many of Churchill's trusted advisors rejected the possibility that a rocket weapon was viable.

17th September, Sunday

Operation Market Garden, the failed airborne attack to capture the bridge over the Rhine at Arnhem, temporarily deprived Germany of its V2 launch sites in the area of The Hague after the battery was forced to move to avoid capture by the advancing Allied forces. This took London out of range very early in the V2 campaign. Accordingly, V2s were targeted on East Anglia, especially Norwich and Ipswich, until the collapse of Market Garden when, once more, V2s were unleashed on Britain's capital in even greater numbers.

6th October, Friday

Information about the V2 had been kept under embargo by the censor though it was known to the military and the ARP in London – but not necessarily outside. The *New York Times* let the cat out of the bag on this day. Although the cause was not elaborated upon, the results of the V2 that fell on Old Jewry were widely reported and to divert public attention, the censor released material via the media on parachute mines that had been embargoed since 1940. This quelled the questions about what were called 'flying gas mains' by some, 'Big Bens' by others.

10th November, Friday

During the month, as V2s began to fall consistently on Britain, V1s were now launched from He111 bombers. As far as effectiveness went, the first 100 V2s killed only 82 people. Churchill finally announced in Parliament that V2s had been landing since September.

25th November, Saturday

The continuing bombardment of Antwerp diverted V2 and V1s away from London but on this day London's worst V2 incident took place at New Cross, South London, destroying a packed Woolworths store, killing 160 and injuring 108. This terrible toll was overshadowed by the V2 that fell on the Rex Cinema in Antwerp in December killing 567 – of which 296 were Allied service personnel. Around 150 V2 bombs fell on Britain during November.

WOMEN AND CHILDREN ADVISED TO LEAVE LONDON

Rocket Bomb Threat is Still With Us, Says Premier

V1 HAS DAMAGED 800,000 HOUSES

Ancient Mace —New Shell

Slaughtered

Tank Successes

The Churchill

London Target

Robot Toll

Beaten Germ Choose 'Goo

By PERCY CATER, Parliame

Home Guard Stood Down

3rd December, Sunday

The Home Guard officially stood down and paraded before the King and Queen through London. The *Daily Mail* reported on 4th December, The King and Queen and two Princesses stood for nearly an hour at the saluting base. The biggest crowds of the war lined the procession route.

That evening there was the 'Home Guard Stand Down Concert', given by the *Daily Mail* with stars such as Tommy Trinder, Elsie and Doris Waters, Vera Lynn, Cicely Courtneidge, Violet Loraine and George Robey.

24th December, Sunday

Around 40 V1s launched from He111s over the North Sea targeted the Manchester area: the worst impact was in Oldham where 30 houses were destroyed and 25 people killed.

26th December, Tuesday

68 were killed and 99 injured in the V2 raid on Islington that destroyed the packed Prince of Wales pub. Over 130 V2s fell in December.

Top left: **Houses were completely obliterated in this V2 blast on 9th October. The scene is one of total desolation.**

Left: **Sniffer dogs work with a rescue squad in the ruins of a hospital in early January 1945.**

Far left: **Bombs in the North. A rescue party searches for bodies. Many homes were damaged in the V bomb attack on Oldham, Lancashire. Here rescue gangs are at work in Abbey Hills Road where a whole terrace was destroyed on Boxing Day.**

Opposite left above: **The night sky is lit up with tracer as AA opens up on an incoming flying bomb which can be seen plunging to earth in flames towards the left of the photograph.**

Opposite left below: **Street shelters stand intact in Islington after a flying bomb attack in September.**

Opposite right: **The night of 6th December, a V2 hit the Red Lion pub on the corner of Duke St and Barrett St close to Selfridges in London's West End. The blast seriously damaged the Base Transportation Office located across the road, which was the HQ controlling all service movements around the UK. The staff included many Americans, seven of whom were reported killed.**

3rd January, Wednesday
In January V2s were falling at the rate of about ten a day but of the 50 or more V1s launched over 3/4th January, only one reached the capital. The last aerial launch V1 attack took place in the early hours of 14th January. But V2 launches reached 220 during the month. On this day a V2 badly damaged the Royal Hospital Chelsea.

28th February, Wednesday
Throughout the month approximately 240 V2s fell on Britain.

3rd March, Saturday
New long-range versions of the V1 began launching from a site in The Hague; the same night 200 German night fighters carried out Operation Gisela, attacking returning Allied bombers as they landed, successfully shooting down 20. Ironically some may have been returning from a disastrous raid on Holland to destroy V2 storage sites near The Hague; 69 tons of HE fell mistakenly on a Dutch town causing 800 civilian deaths. Gisela was the largest attack force since May 1944 and virtually the Luftwaffe's swansong.

This page & opposite: This extraordinary sequence of photographs captures the chaos in the minutes following the devastating explosion of the V2 that fell on Smithfield. In the picture sequence opposite right, traders and other civilians work with police and ARP to release a casualty but it's clear there was nothing that could be done for this unnamed victim.

The images on this page top left show the ironwork forming the roof and facade of the handsome Victorian building twisted beyond recognition and tangled in the rubble causing complications for the heavy rescue squad seen at work with a crane (this page left centre).

Smithfield Market Destroyed

8th March, Thursday

One of the worst V2 incidents of the Blitz was the devastation of Smithfield, London's historic meat and poultry market – an extensive enclosed indoor market at the corner of Farringdon Street and Charterhouse Street where the rocket landed. At 11.10 it was filled with buyers and sellers, while others were queuing outside to get in. The V2 fell out of the sky virtually destroying the crowded building, its blast making a crater that penetrated the railway tunnel and extensive sidings running below; the casualties, commodities and rubble mingled in a horrible melée. The decorative ironwork that formed the intricate facade collapsed in a tangle, making rescue work even more difficult. 110 people died immediately from the blast and many more were seriously injured.

20th March, Tuesday

The final manned airborne raid on Britain by the Luftwaffe. In this last burst of activity, Hull had received a final attack on the 17th, recording the last civilian death from manned bombing.

27th March, Tuesday

As the inhabitants of Hughes Mansions in Stepney were eating breakfast a V2 made a direct hit, demolishing two five-storey blocks of flats, killing 134. This was the highest death toll of any V2 explosion. A reported 225 V2s fell in March and the one that fell on Orpington at 17.00 was the last to fall on Britain. The Blitz on Britain was finally over.

ON the edge of the sky-line, behind the medieval figure that dominates the cathedral dome of | captured Neuss, you see the towers and chimneys of Düsseldorf, a key centre of German war industry. | Between the Allied Forces and this important prize flows the Rhine, seen in the middle distance.

V1s AGAIN: MAY BE LAND-BASED

2 Armies Reach the Baltic

Zhukov Leaps 63 Miles in 4 Days

TWO Russian armies have broken through to the Baltic coast, Orders of the Day from Marshal Stalin announced last night.

Marshal Zhukov, after smashing strong enemy defences east of Stargard, has jumped forward 63 miles in four days to reach the Baltic in the Kolberg area, north-east of Stettin.

Marshal Rokossovsky has captured Köslin, important junction on the Danzig-Stettin railway, 25 miles to the east of Kolberg, and driven on to the coast.

The record number of 60 generals was mentioned in the Order to Zhukov, suggesting that a major force—at least one full army group—had been employed to carry out the lightning break to the sea.

Double Trap

Guderian's armies from Danzig along the coast of North-Eastern Pomerania to Kolberg, are now in a giant double pocket created by the combined Red Army drive.

There are thus two tremendous Red Army wedges across Pomerania to the coast, and the enemy troops in Eastern Pomerania are cut off from those in Western Pomerania.

Zhukov has now completely cleared his northern flank from the possibility of counter-attack, a pre-

Luftwaffe Back Last Night

Piloted planes again crossed the coast of East Anglia last night and were met by a heavy barrage. They dropped flares. A number of small bombs were dropped in one town by a low-flying raider.

By COLIN BEDNALL

V-WEAPONS, including once again flying-bombs, piloted fighter-bombers and medium-range bombers of several different types have all been launched against England recently in a strange, sudden outburst of German offensive activity.

It has even been rumoured that jet-bombers were included in the attack, but this has no confirmation.

It would seem more likely that the enemy is reserving his jet aircraft for work on the Western Front.

The scale of the piloted bomber attack on Saturday night was the heaviest since the introduction of V-weapons last summer.

Going into action against enemy aircraft for the first time this year, defences, including R.A.F. night interceptor fighters, shot down six enemy aircraft — considered a creditable performance in view of their long inactivity.

Day Launches

As some of the flying bombs came across in clear daylight it would be unwise to assume that they were launched from aircraft. The types of bombers which have carried flying bombs in the past are too old and slow to venture over the North Sea in such conditions.

The Germans will now have had time to build flying bombs capable of reaching this country from the Continental coastline still in their hands.

They would probably be larger than the original "Doodle-Bugs." The piloted bombers crossed the

The Princess Joins ATS as Subaltern

PRINCESS ELIZABETH has joined the A.T.S. and is training as an officer-driver. The following official announcement

The last V2 falls on Orpington

Opposite top: A flying bomb wrecked Speakers Corner, Hyde Park on 18th March, blowing an enormous crater in the ground and destroying trees. Note the banner on Marble Arch – and the sandbagged emplacements on top!

Opposite centre: The V2 that hit the Memorial Tabernacle on Tottenham Court Road on 25th March simply blew it apart. Some ironwork is left standing. The brick elevations of the Goodge Street deep shelter to the right are hardly touched.

Opposite below: Devastation in Camberwell in January.

Above right: The last V2 fell on Orpington at 17.00 hours on 27th March 1945. It killed 34-year-old Ivy Millichamp, as she stood in her kitchen: the last person to die in the Blitz.

Left top: A February V2 shattered homes in Walthamstow.

Left centre: A bombing victim gets first aid from rescuers in Westbourne Grove.

Left: A factory in City Road, in London's East End hit by a V1 presents a depressing picture: although the end of the war was genuinely in sight, many must have wondered how the devastation that was everywhere around the country could ever be repaired and normal life resume.

Left: *'The King and Queen, with the two Princesses, yesterday made a victory tour of some of London's most-bombed districts. Here you can see the Queen, talking to the smiling mothers and children of the battered little victory streets.'*

Allied victory in Europe was confirmed on 8th May. The two images here show the contrast between the fire and ferocity of the Blitz and the determination and humour of the people of Britain who hung on to their belief that the nation, its military forces and its leaders would win out in the end.